Urban
Sociology

MARK ABRAHAMSON

Syracuse University

Prentice-Hall, Inc., Englewood Cliffs, New Jersey

Library of Congress Cataloging in Publication Data

ABRAHAMSON, MARK.
  Urban sociology.

  (Prentice-Hall series in sociology)
  Includes bibliographical references and index.
  1. Sociology, Urban. I. Title.
HT151.A26   301.36'3   75-25728
ISBN 0-13-939512-1

Page	Photo Credit
Opposite *1*	Port Charlotte, Florida
5, 244	The City of Winnipeg, Department of Environmental Planning.
11, 116, 219	Central City Association of Los Angeles.
40, 57, 84, 150	Downtown Brooklyn Development Committee.
104, 170	Old Philadelphia Development Corporation.
178, 226	Redevelopment Agency of the City of San Diego.
204	Texas Eastern Transmission Corporation.
240	Downtown Council of Minneapolis.
261	Market Street Development Project. All other photos by Mark Abrahamson.

© 1976 by
Prentice-Hall, Inc., Englewood Cliffs, N.J.

Prentice-Hall Series in Sociology
Neil J. Smelser, Editor

10 9 8 7 6 5 4 3 2 1

Prentice-Hall International, Inc., **London**
Prentice-Hall of Australia, Pty. Ltd., **Sydney**
Prentice-Hall of Canada, Ltd., **Toronto**
Prentice-Hall of India Private Limited, **New Delhi**
Prentice-Hall of Japan, Inc., **Tokyo**
Prentice-Hall of Southeast Asia (Pte.) Ltd., **Singapore**

Contents

iii

Preface

What impresses me most about the field of urban sociology is its history of sometimes subtle, sometimes overt, antagonism between the ecological and nonecological perspectives. The former clearly have done the better job of conceptually delimiting a realm of inquiry and of developing methodological tools relevant to the task. At a more abstract level of analysis, the latter surely have done the better job of relating a rich theoretical tradition in sociology to a wide range of urban phenomena. For me, the saddest commentary on the field has been the tendency of the strengths of the two approaches to remain relatively unjoined. And they have remained unjoined, because proponents of each perspective often simply have overlooked the relevance of the "other camp's" works. (This is the subtle conflict.) However, the two also have remained separate, because various advocates have overtly defined the concepts of the other perspective as irrelevant to urban analysis, or irrelevant to sociology. (This obviously places the antagonism up front.)

Of course, there have been those who viewed the entire conflict as a "myth"; for example, Leo Schnore. However, their statements have had about as much influence as Kingsley Davis's view that functionalism is a myth. In both cases, scholars proposed what could be, but what *could be* was at variance with what people believed to be true. The definitions of reality won out. The first thing I set out to do in this text was to integrate the two approaches in a quiet way. Students are, I think, very uninterested in hearing sociologists air each others' linen. They rarely know enough about conflicting camps to find polemics interesting. Therefore, I have tried to borrow from each perspective where relevant and not call much attention to the fact. I also borrowed from urban economics, geography, political science, and history.

In the past decade or so I have been much impressed with the growing number of truly comparative studies. Their existence has greatly facilitated the writing of a book about cities—not just American cities— and that was the second thing I wished to accomplish. Except for a few chapters devoted explicitly to American phenomena, I have endeavored to write a comparative urban book.

I am very appreciative of the intellectual and interpersonal support I have received from a great number of people while writing this book. To give full vent to my feelings in this regard would result in acknowledgments as lengthy as the book itself. Therefore, very brief expressions of thanks will have to represent enormous feelings of gratitude.

My colleagues in the Sociology Department are a wonderful group of human beings and scholars—always interested in discussing problems and always supportive. They provided a marvelous context within which to work. This is also true of the Maxwell School whose traditions exposed me to a number of urban issues I otherwise would have overlooked.

Janie Ellison typed most of this manuscript—with care and good judgment. She also guarded my door and my appointment calendar and knew how to protect my time pleasantly. If it were not for her help I would *still* be writing this book. Mary Belle-Isle also helped to type and duplicate portions of the manuscript. She, too, was thoughtful and careful, and she always made sure there was coffee! Thanks, Mrs. B.

Ed Stanford, my editor, and everyone else I have dealt with at Prentice-Hall have been uncommonly pleasant and helpful. Even when my lack of progress frustrated me I enjoyed my association with them.

Finally, I want to thank a number of people who read portions of the manuscript and/or listened to my fumbling ideas: Lou Kriesberg, Hal Mizruchi, Bill Pooler, and Manny Stanley.

And to my wife, Mar—thank you for knowing how to live with me while I am writing.

Mark Abrahamson
Syracuse, N.Y.

Trade city problems for a place in the Florida sun in peaceful Port Charlotte.

Follow the sun to Port Charlotte, Florida where the living is relaxed.

Pollution of all kinds. It's reason enough to leave crowded, pushy cities. But finding a better place to live—clean, beautiful, uncrowded —seems harder than it is.

Such advertisements as this one appeal to growing dissatisfactions with city life.

1 Conceptual Approaches to Urbanism

THE QUALITY OF LIFE in cities is a major contemporary concern, one tied to fears that there will soon be no life at all if environmental pollution continues unabated. The patience of urban dwellers has been stretched to the limit by commuting to work at a snail's pace, by the fear of walking outdoors at night, and by the downright bizarre ways some people in cities behave. Because of these problems and others, city life is losing much of its appeal. In an August 1972 survey, Gallup found that only 13 percent of Americans would prefer living in a city. This figure continues to drop, from a high of 22 percent in 1966 and 18 percent in 1970. Of course, many more people would now prefer to live in the suburbs of a city. And more than 50 percent consider a small town or a farm the ideal place to live. Among those who do live in cities, only 20 percent would continue to do so if they could go wherever they wished.[1]

There is no denying that city life in America is losing some of its appeal, but city life has always been associated with massive problems. Congestion and crime are to today's cities what the great plagues were to medieval cities, and many current problems are not unique to our time. In seventeenth-century London, for example, fishermen were protesting that pollution of the Thames was killing the fish; and throughout the city people lit pitch bonfires to try to cleanse the foul air. Even earlier, the fact that urban relationships were becoming too impersonal because of a cash marketplace was decried by Aristotle.

This line of argument must go no further, however, or it will suggest that all cities everywhere are substantially alike. In fact, there are both

[1] Reported by George Gallup, Princeton, New Jersey, December 17, 1972.

similarities and differences, and they are what this book is about. In many respects, the study of cities is simultaneously the study of man. There has been a great historical coexistence between cities and "civilization." Given man's curiosity about himself and his institutions, it is not surprising that cities have been particularly emphasized for serious study. Correspondingly, since people want to be original and creative, it is not surprising that there are almost as many ways of studying cities as there are individuals doing the studies. In sociology, with a little bit of generalizing, they may be categorized into two dominant approaches.

The first is an *ecological* view that has its origins in botany and biology. Developed largely at the University of Chicago during the first decades of the twentieth century, the ecological perspective focuses on the spatial distribution of urban activities and on the processes and forms of urban growth. The second view emphasizes *social, cultural,* and *psychological* dimensions. It focuses on the distinctive orientations of urban man and on the distinctive patterns of human relationships characteristic of urban settings. The historical background of this latter approach is more diffuse, for it is the culmination of diverse contributions from both sociology and anthropology.

There is, unfortunately, historical competition between the two approaches, but considering both simultaneously will increase our total understanding. Further, ecological and sociocultural processes are often mutually reinforcing in their consequences for urban development. The aspects of cities that are stressed in each approach do differ, however. To clarify the origins and emphases of each, they first are presented separately.

THE ECOLOGY OF CITIES

In 1921 Park and Burgess introduced the term *human ecology*. Botanists, biologists, and others had previously used the term *ecology* in studying plant and animal communities. After Darwin, the ecologists viewed each organism and each species in a territory as competitors in a struggle for existence. However, the adaptations made by a species in its survival effort often have consequences that are beneficial to another species, even though that was not the original intent. When cats prey upon field mice, for example, the number of Humblebees increases, because field mice destroy Humblebees' nests. The chain of interconnectedness in an ecological community may be extended still further: the amount of red clover growing in fields is ultimately dependent on the number of cats, because fertilization of this clover is dependent upon Humblebees. The more cats, the fewer mice, the more Humblebees, and the more red clover.[2]

[2] Paraphrased from a classic example presented by Darwin in Robert E. Park, "Human Ecology," *American Journal of Sociology,* 42, 1936.

For ecologists, the interrelations that involve "competitive coopera-tion" among all the species in a territory define an ecological community. One major contribution made by Park and Burgess was to apply this "web of life" perspective to human communities, and to cities in particular.[3] They focused on the city of Chicago, but their data from other American and European cities suggested that there were typical patterns of growth whose principles were everywhere the same. The major principle they de-duced was competition for space.

How cities grow: Concentric zones

In virtually every city, said Burgess, the central shopping and business district has the highest land value. This is where we find the department stores, museums, theaters, city halls, and the great hotels. Almost inevi-tably, he concluded, the economic, cultural, and political life of the city is concentrated in the center.[4] Thus, the downtown area of a city is some-what analogous to the nucleus of a cell.

The geographical and ecological centers of a community are not nec-essarily the same, however. The location of the former must, by definition, be equally distant from all points in the community (and a geographical center could exist only within a perfect circle). The ecological center, which is determined by time and transportation costs rather than by distances, is the point of maximum accessibility from all parts of the metropolitan area.

The fully developed central business district, in turn, has two centers. One is defined by the convergence of communication, and it is a financial or credit center (for example, Wall Street). The second is defined by the convergence of lines of transportation, and it is a retail merchandising cen-ter (for example, Fifth Avenue or Michigan Boulevard). Combined, they form the central business district that is fixed, by transportation and com-munication, at the ecological center of the metropolitan community.[5]

As the metropolitan area grows, various types of businesses and insti-

[3] Park and Burgess collaborated for ten productive years as colleagues at the Univer-sity of Chicago, even though their backgrounds were very different. After a brief career as a newspaper reporter, in which he specialized in stories on political corrup-tion, Robert Park entered graduate school (in sociology) while in his thirties. He re-tained a gruff manner that later frightened many of his students, but not Ernest Burgess. Twenty years Park's junior, Burgess was the son of a minister who lived much of his life with his father and unwed sister. See Robert E. L. Faris, *Chicago Sociology, 1920–1932* (San Francisco: Chandler, 1967).

[4] Ernest W. Burgess, "The Growth of the City," in Robert Park, Ernest Burgess, and R. D. McKenzie (eds.), *The City* (Chicago: University of Chicago Press, 1925).

[5] Whether the transportation-retail center or the communication-finance center should be considered *the* center is open for conjecture. An early discussion of how the center should be defined was presented by Earl S. Johnson, "The Function of the Central Business District in the Metropolitan Community," in *Contemporary Society* (So-cial Science 3), University of Chicago, 1932.

Transportation and communication converge in the central business district, but its congestion has hampered both of them (Manhattan, New York).

tutions become locked into increased competition for the most desirable (accessible) space at the center. Those activities that can benefit most from the central location and are therefore able to afford the high rents will win out and dominate the central district (fashionable retail stores rather than warehouses). A similar struggle for dominance occurs throughout the metropolitan region, and the result is a number of specialized functional areas: rooming house areas, manufacturing areas, and so on.

In sum, competition in a plant community is a struggle for places with access to sunlight; in a human community, the competition is for the greatest accessibility to specialized markets or clients. The plant species or human activity that wins out is the one that is able to make the most efficient use of the valued location.

Cities grow, Burgess proposed, through a process of expansion in which the population flows outward from the center in a form described in the well-known theory of *concentric zones*. Each succeeding zone, or circular area, illustrates urban expansion the way the rings of a tree indicate its continual stages of growth. (Of course, natural barriers, such as lakes or mountains, would sometimes prevent the forming of a complete circle.)

The first zone is the central business district. Encircling this nucleus is a zone of transition that is being "invaded" by small business and factories, but also has many residents living in dilapidated boarding houses and tenements and above retail stores. It is in this second zone that Chinatown, Little Italy, and ghettos are most likely to be found.

The area within the third circle is the zone of workingmens' homes. It is inhabited by second-generation immigrants who have "escaped" the area of deterioration, but want to remain close to the industries that

utilization: single-family residences, light industry, and so on. Then he drew in a social data map indicating nationalities, delinquency rates, and the like. The land-use and social criteria maps were found to be substantially alike; that is, to coincide in differentiating a large number of "natural areas." No matter how the areas were grouped, however, they never resulted in concentric circles. For example, areas with concentrated numbers of foreign-born residents and high rates of delinquency were found to the south and east of New Haven's central business district. To the north and west, though, were industrial areas and the only areas in the city in which native Americans predominated. In other words, it was not possible to find either homogeneous social characteristics or consistent land use within any complete concentric circle.

Another important conclusion of Davie's study was that areas often tended to form along radial streets or thoroughfares. These are the streets that connect the outlying areas of the city with the central business district. Business and commerce tends to be distributed along these radial streets, especially at important intersections. Residential areas of all types also tend to follow the radial streets because of good transportation facilities, and to follow the commercial and business sections. Thus, special areas tend to be strongly influenced by the location of radial streets and highways.

The importance of transportation lines was emphasized by Homer Hoyt in his *sector theory* of urban development. In this modification of concentric zone theory, only the central business district is viewed as a complete circle. A zone of transition with predominantly poor people in dilapidated housing is expected to be located outside the downtown, but not completely surrounding it.[9] Manufacturing and wholesaling expand out from the center of the city, but they do not end outside Park and Burgess's zone two. Rather, they extend the entire length of the metropolitan area, following the transportation arteries—boulevards, rail lines, or the like. Thus, the distribution to land uses and of social characteristics radiates out from the center in a number of sectors.

According to sector theory, cities partially resemble the original concentric zone formulation. Later ecological models, such as *multiple nuclei* theory, bear little resemblance to the concentric zone model. Because they apply primarily to metropolitan areas rather than cities, these models will be considered in Chapter 10, where the focus is on metropolitan areas.

Basic to the ecological perspective of Park and Burgess was an em-

[9] Homer Hoyt, *The Structure and Growth of Residential Neighborhoods in American Cities* (Washington, D.C.: Federal Housing Administration, 1939). For a more recent view, see H. Kirk Dansereau, "Some Implications of Modern Highways for Community Ecology," in George A. Theodorson (ed.), *Studies in Human Ecology* (Evanston, Ill.: Row, Peterson, 1961).

phasis on economic competition.[10] Where an activity would be located was seen to be determined by its ability to produce the greatest profit in a given location. This in turn involved competition for locations between various land uses that would minimize the amount of "obstruction" created by ecological considerations. (Specifically, this meant proximity to related functions, transportation, etc.) The serial nature of territorial succession was considered to be essentially predetermined by economic considerations.

A substantial modification of this emphasis came with later studies of community change. Firey's study of the Beacon Hill area in Boston is particularly illustrative.[11] For about a century after 1800, Beacon Hill had few equals as a fashionable residential area in Boston. It was characterized as stately, elegant, and charming; and many upper class families were able to claim continuous residence on the Hill for many generations. Around 1900, however, a new area called Back Bay was developed. This new site became defined as the most fashionable area, and many of the old families left the Hill.

A familiar process of ecological invasion then occurred: specialty shops moved on to some streets, older mansions became rooming houses, and property values continued to fall—permitting still more invasion. Firey documents the transition by showing a marked decline in the number of Boston's Social Register families living on Beacon Hill. (There was a corresponding increase in Back Bay).

The symbolic quality of the Hill to upper class Bostonians led to a halting and then a reversal of the invasion-succession trend, however. The old families that remained on the Hill banded together. They purchased old houses, modernized the interiors, and sold them to individual families. Beginning around 1915, the percentage of Social Register families on the Hill began to increase, and by the 1940s it was twice its pre-1900 figure. The large apartment-hotels and specialty shops that were then denied locations on the Hill would actually have represented fuller utilization of potential property values than did the restored residences. In addition, other areas of Boston provided equally accessible locations and even better physical conditions. Thus, Firey concludes, there is a noneconomic aspect to land use on Beacon Hill—perhaps even an anti-economic use—that can only be understood in terms of human sentiments and symbols. As areas

[10] Throughout the 1950s and most of the 1960s, sociological theories tended to emphasize the role of consensus in maintaining social order. Conflict was viewed as sporadic and disruptive. The backgrounds of more recent theories of conflict, Janowitz points out, are clearly found in Park and Burgess's view of social organization as an accommodation of conflicts. See Morris Janowitz's introduction to Park and Burgess, *Introduction to the Science of Sociology* (Chicago: University of Chicago Press, 1969).

[11] Walter Firey, "Sentiment and Symbolism as Ecological Variables," *American Sociological Review*, 10, 1945.

come to possess symbolic qualities, in other words, the sentiments involved can substantially alter ecological processes.

Ecology vs. social interaction

The earlier emphasis on economic competition was part of a distinction made by many orthodox ecologists between the variables they were studying and the variables emphasized by other types of sociologists. The distinction was never very clear or very tenable, but it involved the separation of ecological variables such as location and transportation costs from variables relating to social interaction, such as norms and values.[12] The latter category was more or less a dumping ground for many abstract sociological concepts with which ecologists did not wish to deal. The distinction was also invidious: the ecological were viewed as the real forces, and the interaction, normative, and cultural variables as epiphenomena. The symbolic characteristics of a Beacon Hill tended to be disregarded. Sociologists primarily interested in urban norms, values, and institutions in turn viewed the research of ecologists as only peripherally related to the major issues in sociology. Looking back, the polemics offered by each school were profitless. Both extreme positions led to invidious rankings of the other that were without foundation because they exaggerated the separation of the two types of variables.[13]

Although Park and Burgess did make this distinction, it was actually in the work of the ecologists who followed them that sociocultural factors became substantially more subordinated. Park's treatment of moral regions, for example, was directly tied to a conception of the "liberating" qualities of urban norms, a social-cultural force. Cities, he proposed, encourage the expression of unusual, bizarre, or different tastes and interests by providing a place in which the persons who have them can congregate and thereby mutually reinforce one another. "The small community often tolerates eccentricity," Park stated; "the city, on the contrary, rewards it."[14]

Similarly, in the famous concentric zone theory Burgess expressed an appreciation of an interplay between social and ecological forces. Zone two, the zone of transition, for example, was characterized by social disorganization: broken homes, delinquency, crime, and so on. The social disorganization of zone two, one of the hallmarks of that zone, was essentially social-cultural in nature. It is newcomers to a city who predominate in the zone of transition, and there is almost always a "disorganization" of attitudes among newcomers. They are temporarily caught between two

[12] An early statement of the dichotomy was presented by James A. Quinn in "Ecological Versus Social Interaction," *Sociology and Social Research,* 18, 1934.
[13] See, for example, Leo F. Schnore, "The Myth of Human Ecology," *Sociological Inquiry,* 31, 1961.
[14] Robert Park, "The City," *op. cit.,* p. 610.

worlds: the one they left and the one into which they are not yet quite assimilated. The concentric zones were thus based on a conceptualized interplay between ecological location and social-cultural forces.

Throughout this book, variables of all types will be considered, sometimes simultaneously and sometimes separately, depending on the specific issues under consideration. The two viewpoints are being discussed separately here only to clarify their distinctive origins and emphases. When we turn to the nonecological perspective, we find the boundaries of this approach so vague that it is almost impossible to label. Cautiously, however, we may term it interaction and orientation.

INTERACTION AND ORIENTATION: WIRTH

The writings of Louis Wirth are an interesting point at which to begin exploring this perspective.[15] As a graduate student at Chicago, Wirth studied under Park and Burgess. In his dissertation on the ghetto, completed in 1925 and published as a book in 1928, he analyzed the experiences of immigrants in relation to the ecology of cities. He emphasized psychological, social, and cultural aspects of their lives; the ghetto was viewed not only as an ecological phenomenon, but as "a state of mind."[16]

Subsequently, Wirth differentiated three conceptions of urbanism. One was a physical (including ecological) structure; the second was as a social structure and organization; and the last involved the distinguishing attitudes and "personalities" of city dwellers. Critical to Wirth's argument, however, was a view of urbanism as transcending its physical structure. As the "initiating and controlling center of economic, political and cultural life," the influence of cities did not stop at their geographical boundaries.[17] The proportion of people actually living in them was not a true measure of the influence of cities as "molding forces" or as "generators of culture."

The degree of urbanism of any given community was indicated by three characteristics: the size, density, and heterogeneity of its population. The larger, more dense, and heterogeneous a population, the more the community could be expected to display a distinctly urban character. Each indicator was seen as capable of exerting an independent effect on social structure and attitudes. Large size, for example, precludes intimate contacts among everyone in a city. Heterogeneity makes people accustomed to seeing others very different from themselves, and they become tolerant of differences. But it is apparent in Wirth's analysis that the effects of size, density, and heterogeneity are also congruent and cumulative. Combined,

---

[15] While Wirth's was not the pioneering work in the same sense as Park's and Burgess', his papers on urbanism are clearly among the most influential precursors to contemporary sociological views. Particularly notable is "Urbanism as a Way of Life," *American Journal of Sociology,* 44, 1938.

[16] Faris, *op. cit.,* p. 71.

[17] "Urbanism as a Way of Life," *op. cit.,* p. 1.

Downtown shoppers illustrate Wirth's three characteristics of urban places: size, density, and heterogeneity (Los Angeles, California).

they result in an urban man who is sophisticated and rational, but is also fragmented and lonely.

Sophistication and loneliness are clearly relative terms, and the question now is Wirth's referent; that is, urban men are sophisticated or lonely in comparison to whom? He provides no precise answer to this question— nor did others, such as Weber, who were drawing similar contrasts.[18] Wirth compared modern urban life to formerly nomadic peoples, to primitive societies, to country life, and to folk societies. Essentially, he (and his contemporaries) seemed to be arguing either that certain "master trends" culminated in the emergence of contemporary urban life, or else that with respect to the dominant characteristics of modern cities, all other forms of social organization are sufficiently different to be classified together. For the moment, we may accept either alternative and treat primitive, folk, and other societies as equivalent expressions of a "non-urban" category.[19] Among the dominant features of urban life for Wirth are the decline of the family; formality and impersonality; rationality, tolerance, and secularization; and specialization and standardization.

Decline of the family

In cities, many of the educational, recreational, and other functions previously performed within a family context are relegated to other institutions (such as schools and churches). Correspondingly, at a psychological

[18] See, for example, Max Weber, *The City* (New York: Free Press, 1958).
[19] Their combination is confusing though because of the apparent nonhomogeneity of societies included in the category. In terms of social organization, for example, there is a profound difference between primitive and peasant, or folk, societies. See Jack M. Potter et al., *Peasant Society* (Boston: Little, Brown, 1967). (See especially the introduction by George M. Foster). We shall return to this problem in later chapters.

level, urban dwellers' identities are not bound up with their family roles. Because people are geographically more mobile, regular contact between kin is often impossible in extended families. Although some people may happen to be close to their uncles or cousins, such relationships are neither generally expected nor facilitated by an urban social organization.

Part of the basic difference in the importance of kinship is vividly expressed in the following examples:

Nonurban Pattern	Urban Pattern
A young, married Kiowa Indian girl: "Bow Girl came and sat beside her. . . . They were quiet for a long time, because, being sisters, they didn't need to talk with their voices."[20]	A professional thief from Chicago, Denver, San Francisco, etc.: "We don't know where my brother is at. I think he might be dead."[21]

There is ample evidence, however, that part of the decline of the family may be more apparent than real. Focusing upon family name-giving in Chicago, for example, Rossi reports that between the 1920s and 1960s there was no decline in the amount of extended family involvement.[22] Komarovsky's study of a contemporary blue collar community in metropolitan America shows that daily life centers about family and extended family.[23] And in a London suburb, over half the married women continue to live in the same building or the same street as their parents.[24]

In sum, there are substantial indications that family and extended family have not lost their vitality in urban societies. Correspondingly, more recent studies of nonurban societies suggest that their presumably high rates of extended family interaction and the harmony within their kinship systems may both be nostalgic myths. As illustration, consider this traditional proverb from the peasants of Southern Italy: "From your own relatives, go as far as you can."[25] (We shall return to the urban family in Chapter 4.)

Formality and impersonality

In an urban society, people interact for limited and specialized purposes: as teachers and students in a classroom, as buyers and sellers in a store, and so on. Their total contacts are quite extensive, Wirth observed, but the

[20] Alice Marriott, *The Ten Grandmothers* (Norman: University of Oklahoma Press, 1948), p. 64.
[21] Bill Chambliss, *Box Man* (New York: Harper and Row, 1972), p. 1.
[22] Alice S. Rossi, "Naming Children in Middle Class Families," *American Sociological Review,* 4, 1965.
[23] Mirra Komarovsky, *Blue-Collar Marriage* (New York: Random House, 1962).
[24] Michael Young and Peter Willmott, *Family and Kinship in East London* (Baltimore: Penguin, 1957).
[25] Joseph Lopreato, *Peasants No More* (San Francisco: Chandler, 1967), p. 115.

relationships are so impersonal that urbanites do not really come to know each other as "whole persons," nor do they care about the people with whom they typically interact. Thus, they respond to appearances (such as clothing) rather than to individuals as individuals.

Similarly, daily life entails the formal controls of clocks and traffic lights rather than responsiveness to friendship and sentiment. It is particularly among the professions that formal controls (for example, professional codes of ethics) are necessary as substitutes for what once were personal claims. And the advantage, in an urban society, of a large corporation is that it "has no soul."

Nonurban Pattern	**Urban Pattern**
A Crow Indian brave (and his friend) asked to smoke a pipe symbolizing his willingness to die for his friends: "He said . . . 'if you get killed . . . your friends will feel grateful.' I took the pipe and began to smoke. . . . My comrade also smoked the pipe."[26]	A young woman in New York calling her (female) obstetrician after deciding to seek an illegal abortion: "I told her to forget it . . . , 'o.k., dear.' And she hung up. Not even asking how I was. And this was a doctor. A woman. A person."[27]

Again there is more than one side to the argument, however. Studies of contemporary urban slums, for example, indicate a social life characterized by intimate associations on street corners, in retail stores, and so on.[28] And quite another view of friendship in nonurban societies is provided in the story of Sanchez, a Mexican peasant:

> I'm not leaving you anything—said the dying father—but I will give you a piece of advice. Don't get mixed up with friends. It's better to go your life alone.[29]

Rationality, tolerance, and secularization

In part because of the impersonality of relationships, Wirth felt that urban orientations would tend to be utilitarian; that is, people would enter relationships after calculating potential gains rather than for the intrinsic satisfaction of association. (Such satisfactions are presumably precluded by the very nature of segmentary relations.) Similarly, routine exposure to

[26] R. H. Lowie, *The Crow Indians,* New York: Harper, 1935, p. 178.
[27] Anonymous, "I didn't have the baby, I had an abortion," in Charles H. McCaghy et al. (eds.), *In Their Own Behalf* (New York: Appleton-Century-Crofts, 1968), p. 15.
[28] See, for example, Gerald Suttles, *The Social Order of the Slum* (Chicago: University of Chicago Press, 1968).
[29] Oscar Lewis, *Children of Sanchez* (New York: Random House, 1961), p. 6. Formality and impersonality, as urban characteristics, will be a recurring issue in this book.

Wirth proposed that routine exposure to different ways of life produces urbanites who are tolerant of differences (Manhattan, New York).

divergent life styles produces an orientation that is not only rational but relativistic, with a toleration of differences that leads to a secularization of life. Freedom from moral and religious restraints makes the urbanite free to purchase commercially an entire range of recreational "kicks" (prostitutes, drugs, etc.).

The basic ideas of rationality and of tolerance and secularization are illustrated below:

Nonurban Pattern

The Eskimo after a whale hunt: "As the whale is cut up, certain parts of its body are ceremonially handled, and very special rituals are performed to return the whale's spirit to the sea unangered. It is given food, and no disturbing noises are permitted."[30]

The Ashanti of Africa believed that if certain crimes were committed, then: "Hunters would have ceased to kill, children would have ceased to have been born, crops would have refused to bear fruit . . . and all would have been [chaos] in the world."[32]

Urban Pattern

A London prostitute's experience: "Complexions, features, hair, lost their individuality. . . . Not, of course that I stopped showing interest in clients as individuals—merely, I feign this interest now, and the imitation passes as genuine so there is no loss on either side."[31]

How does a professional thief feel about prison: "I didn't exactly like it . . . well, that was the price you had to pay. On the other hand, I could buy new Cadillacs and $200 suits when I had found a fat mark. How often do you do that?"[33]

[30] E. Adamson Hoebel, *Anthropology* (New York: McGraw-Hill, 1966), p. 241.
[31] Anonymous, "Streetwalker," in McCaghy, *op. cit.*, p. 25.
[32] R. S. Rattray, *Ashanti Law and Constitution* (New York: Oxford, 1927), p. 304.
[33] Chambliss, *op. cit.*, preface.

It is exceedingly difficult to measure concepts such as rationality and secularization. It is correspondingly difficult to demonstrate that urban orientations are more rational or secular. A variety of evidence will be presented that does, however, tend to support aspects of Wirth's hypotheses.

Specialization, standardization, and voluntary associations

Wirth argued from an ecological perspective that increases in population density (in plant or human communities) would produce differentiation. Only through increased specialization can greater numbers be supported in a fixed area. Thus, cities are associated with a diversity of occupations. But the tendency for each city to specialize in certain functions leads to still greater degrees of occupational specialization.

Although urbanites are highly diversified, the facilities and services of a city are geared to the "average person." Mass education, the mass media, and so on—because of their mass clienteles—operate as "leveling" influences. Further, individuality is necessarily lost in the representative system by which interests are expressed. To participate at all in the collective life, urbanites must pursue their interests in a fragmentary way. (The Chamber of Commerce, for example, may satisfy an individual's commercial interests, but not his religious needs; the latter would require joining still another specialized organization.) Participation therefore means the subordination of individuality. At the same time, such participation is effective in ameliorating certain kinds of alienation. Neal and Seeman report, for example, that feelings of powerlessness are significantly lower for members than for nonmembers of voluntary associations.[34]

THE REFERRANTS OF URBANISM

One problematic issue in both the ecological and interaction approaches to the study of cities involves whether the emphasis should be on variations within or between societies. Wirth's use of rural-urban differences illustrates the within-society emphasis. Attention is drawn to patterns of social organization that are distinctively urban. By contrast, his recognition that the influence of cities transcends their physical boundaries introduces the between-society emphasis. Based upon variations in overall patterns of urbanism within nations, entire countries are expected to differ systematically from one another on dimensions related to urbanism. Both of the examples from Wirth should suggest that stress on within- or between-society differences is not tied to the ecological or the interactional

[34] Arthur G. Neal and Melvin Seeman, "Organizations and Powerlessness," *American Sociological Review,* 2, 1964.

approach; it is a distinct emphasis that can be employed in conjunction with either.

The differences between the two emphases can be further clarified with a concrete example. Secular rather than religious orientations have often been thought to be associated with urbanism. Leaving aside the difficult problems of how secularism should be conceptualized and measured, a within-society approach could test for a relationship by comparing religious orientations in urban and rural settings. A number of studies have used this approach to study not only religious differences, but differences in attitudinal permissiveness, confidence in institutions, and so on. In some cases the expected differences have been obtained, but they have typically been rather small, and sometimes there have been no differences at all.

From a between-society perspective, the absence of rural-urban differences is hardly surprising, because patterns of activity and orientations that may originate in cities soon spread to the countryside as well. Impersonal controls such as clocks may initially be more prevalent in an urban context. But farmers also carry watches and must follow formal time constraints when they go to town to keep an appointment with the local banker or quit harvesting in order to watch their favorite television show. Thus, the historic pattern of urbanization in a country, or its degree of urbanization, may be related to between-nation differences where no rural-urban differences exist within a nation.

In addition, urban sociologists have recognized that patterns of commerce and travel in the contemporary world involve relationships between cities in different countries. Wheat may be shipped from Toronto to Moscow; international travel links New York and London; and so on. Patterns of subordination and dominance between nations thus involve major cities. Similar patterns occur within nations—meat products travel from Omaha to Chicago and steel moves from Pittsburgh to Detroit. The possibility of rural-urban differences within nations presents a number of interesting questions, although exclusive concern with them can mean disregarding equally interesting questions involving interurban relationships.

PROSPECTUS

In the chapter that immediately follows, we will examine the historical development of permanent settlements, from villages and towns to medieval and colonial cities. In Chapters 3, 4, and 5, urbanization and industrialization—as mutually reinforcing processes—will be examined throughout the world. One major objective in these chapters will be to assess the impact of the forces that have helped to produce industrial-urban cities, forces such as war, commerce, population growth, and complex divisions of labor. We will focus on the historical development of urban social and spatial organizations from London to Tokyo to Stockholm.

Chapters 6 and 7 will deal with the United States and with the demographic, industrial, and spatial forces that molded American cities. Specific topics will include regional and rural-urban differences, racial and ethnic ghettoes, and the neighborliness of communities. In Chapter 8 we will again extend our perspective and examine residential patterns in American cities in relation to those of Rome, Madrid, Cairo, and other cities of the world.

Chapter 9 presents an examination of the social integration of urban life, with the focus on the institutional and normative problems distinctive of urban social organization. Rural-urban differences in alienation and anomie will be examined, and urban life will be viewed as the generator of "deviant" life styles. In the last three chapters our attention shifts from cities to metropolitan areas. Focusing predominantly upon the United States, we will examine types of suburbs, the relationship of suburbanization to transportation developments, and the ensuing problems of integrating metropolitan areas. We will study the fiscal, racial, and political impediments to metropolitanization, but we will also see that contemporary urban problems—such as mass transit and air pollution—intrinsically seem to require metropolitan-level planning.

Cities first formed when agricultural production was sufficient to support both farmers and nonfarmers in relatively dense settlements (Cuernavaca, Mexico).

2 The History of Cities

Our 6,000-year journey through urban history begins in ancient Mesopotamia, moves through Greece and the Roman Empire, the decimation of urban populations in the Middle Ages, European cities in the seventeenth and eighteenth centuries, to the development of colonial cities. Unlike some historical accounts, we will try to analyze as well as describe; to infer some general relationships between the development of cities and politics, warfare, trade, and markets.

ANCIENT CITIES

To talk about the original city is presumptuous, implying as it does a false certainty about origins. There is a degree of consensus, however, that the first cities probably emerged in the ancient country of Mesopotamia (later called Iraq) and perhaps in the fertile river basins of southern Mesopotamia along the Tigris and Euphrates Rivers. In an interesting way this river valley, watered by running streams, resembles the legendary Garden of Eden, where "a flood was rising from the earth and watering all the surface of the soil."[1]

In any case, cities were able to develop here somewhere between

[1] In the Book of Genesis, the Tigris and Euphrates Rivers are specifically described as flowing out of Eden and bathing the garden. When man was expelled, he was sent out of the naturally irrigated garden to "till the soil."

19

3500 and 4000 B.C. because of cereal agriculture, based upon irrigation. Reliable harvests could be produced independent of fluctuations in rainfall, and the system of irrigation could be geographically expanded to support an increasing population.[2] These places are called cities today because they were relatively permanent and densely populated settlements that included some specialized nonagricultural workers.[3]

The most widely accepted theory of the emergence of cities was originally presented in the late 1930s by the archeologist V. Gordon Childe and later developed by the historian Ralph Turner.[4] Their basic thesis is that urbanization requires the development of technological skills sufficient to produce a surplus of food in order to support a settled population. In Mesopotamia, the farming system—based upon irrigation—was capable of producing such a surplus.

There is at least strong circumstantial evidence that the kind of population density associated with cities could not have occurred in earlier hunting or food-gathering economies. Allan estimates that the latter require about sixteen miles of land to support each individual. Given the usual hunting-gathering techniques, such an extended territory had to be worked to provide subsistence. By contrast, even with the poorest soils and no other implement than an ax, cultivation can support about forty times as many people on the same amount of land.[5] In addition, Allan points out, the valleys and deltas watered by running streams would have "naturally" created the conditions for further population concentration. Middle East wheat production on seepage sites, for example, is still twelve times greater in yield than neighboring crops grown under rain-fed conditions. Thus, the cultivation sites would have been logical centers for rapid population growth.

In the Childe-Turner thesis, a near-perfect correspondence is presumed among agriculture, sedentary (nonmigratory) life, and villages. The villages (communities of several hundred persons) are seen as evolving, in turn, into cities (communities of several thousand persons including nonagricultural specialists). Flannery, however, argues that the dependence of villages upon agriculture and sedentary life has been exaggerated. Recent archeological evidence indicates the existence of sedentary communities in the Near East prior to domestic crops (or animals). And in Mesoamerica (Mexico and Central America), there were apparently plant cultivators who were also nomadic. Perhaps the relationship between agri-

[2] A. L. Oppenheim, "A Birds-Eye View of Mesopotamian Economic History," in Karl Polanyi et al. (eds.), *Trade and Market in Early Empires* (New York: Free Press, 1957).
[3] These are among the characteristics emphasized by Gordon Childe. See "The Urban Revolution," *Town Planning Review,* 21, 1950.
[4] For a discussion of their thesis, and further references, see Paul Meadows, "The City, Technology, and History," *Social Forces,* 36, 1957.
[5] William Allan, *The African Husbandman* (London, 1965).

culture and village life does not uniformly hold true. In order to support this possibility, Flannery presents an interesting comparison of early permanent settlements in the Near East and in Mesoamerica.[6]

At the end of the food-gathering period in the Near East (up to 10,000 B.C.), subsistence was based on the skilled hunting of sheep, deer, and other animals and supplemented by fish and fruits. In Mesoamerica the late food-gathering era (up to 5000 B.C.) involved the harvesting of wild plants during the rainy season and limited hunting. During the dry season, groups dispersed and depended upon limited wild plants. In the Near East, these pre-village settlement patterns, according to Flannery, involved greater population densities and were also more permanent than in Mesoamerica. Thus, the origins of sedentary life, he concludes, are tied to hereditary ownership[7] of "high resource potential" land areas, regardless of whether the areas are cultivated or hunted. It is also true, however, that naturally watered valleys would be viewed as areas of great resource potential.

Early permanent settlements in the Near East, not based on crop cultivation, tended to be circular in form. Specifically, huts were small and circular in construction. They housed a single individual or served as a granary. Individual huts were arranged in a circle enclosing the headman's hut and granaries. Somewhere around 6000 B.C. in the Near East, and several thousand years later in Mesoamerica, villages of rectangular houses emerged.

The rectangular houses were larger, probably accommodating entire families rather than individuals, and containing their own storage areas. Households had apparently become units of production. This is also suggested by the fact that individual courtyards (used as work areas) were often walled in. A major feature of the rectangular ground plan was that, unlike circular huts, rooms could be added as families grew. Also, unlike the circular compound, these villages themselves could more easily expand. According to archeological evidence, though, the circular type of hamlet settlement never appeared in Mesoamerica. The absence of circular compounds in Mesoamerica is due, Flannery concludes, to the existence of the family as the unit of production long before agriculture began.

The ultimate size, even of these villages, was very limited. According to traditional theories, they could not outgrow their agricultural production potential. According to Flannery, they were limited by the absence of political leadership that could prevent disputes from leading to fragmentation once villages grew too large.

---

[6] Kent V. Flannery, "The Origins of the Village as a Settlement Type in Mesoamerica and the Near East," in Peter J. Ucko et al. (eds.), *Man, Settlement and Urbanism* (Cambridge: Schenkman, 1972).
[7] Given the absence of written deeds, the burial of ancestors is a people's best proof that land has belonged to it "since time began."

Once villages form, security threats stimulate their growth and the formation of other villages. In Mesopotamia, nomadic groups surrounded the settlements, and a state of almost perpetual warfare characterized relationships between them and the villagers, and later the townspeople.[8] People moved to existing villages for protection, or else formed their own settlements. This situation was also true centuries later in Greek and Roman cities. Ancient cities were thus often enclosed by walls, since one of their primary reasons for being was to serve as fortresses.

Warfare and defense also have important consequences for further political and economic development. For example, they lead directly to the emergence of certain nonagricultural specialists, such as weapon makers and administrative recordkeepers. This type of specialization is, of course, identified with the transition from village to city. In addition, it seems to provide the conditions most closely related to political development. Evidence for this (and similar) conclusions comes mostly from anthropological studies of more recent preindustrial societies. It requires an inferential leap to generalize from these societies to the villages of antiquity. The compatibility of such generalizations with archeological and other historical data, however, provides at least tentative justification for the inferences.

In one study of a sample of preindustrial societies, political development was measured by the presence or absence of a headman, the number of jurisdictional levels, and other related considerations. As measured, political complexity was correlated with population size and density, economic development, the degree of social differentiation, and a number of other variables. The strongest relationship occurred between political complexity and differentiation. This suggested that the greater the degree of specialization within a society, the greater the pressure to develop a formalized political unit to provide for mobilization, regulation, and control within the social group. Sheer growth in population size that does not result in increased social differentiation does not create comparably strong pressures for political development.[9]

Fear of attack leads to larger permanent settlements and social differentiation. Both of these lead to political development, which in turn permits further growth and specialization. Under certain conditions, conquest also encourages the development of cities. In the Roman Empire, for example, conquered territories became military encampments and then

---

[8] Stuart Piggot, "The Role of the City in Ancient Civilization," in E. M. Fisher (ed.), *The Metropolis in Modern Life* (Garden City, N.Y.: Doubleday, 1955).
[9] Mark Abrahamson, "Correlates of Political Complexity," *American Sociological Review,* 34, 1969. (Similar results, for an African sample, are reported by S. N. Eisenstadt, "Primitive Political Systems," *American Anthropologist,* 61, 1959).

cities as the conquerors set up markets and administrative centers. (Paris, London and many other great European cities began in this way.)

The relationship between warfare or fear of invasion and development of the political system is not entirely so one-sided, however. In many ancient societies as well as in more recent "primitive" societies, warfare is best described as ritualistic. Confrontations between persons representing different groups or societies result in loss of face or loss of life. But they do not result in subjugation or territorial invasion, and so there is no change of regime.[10]

The kind of warfare that can lead to conquest seems to require a previously existing degree of political development, though it is also clear that conquest can lead to political complexity. Which happens more probably varies according to the developmental stage of the society as suggested by the following generalizations:

1. Forming a permanent settlement is a stimulus to task and role differentiations (that is, it leads to the development of nonagricultural specialists).

2. Social differentiation tends to produce internal problems of task and role coordination, stimulating the development of formal political institutions to provide regulation.

3. The development of a political institution permits the mobilization of an army that is capable of conquering territories.

4. When the more "advanced" society wins a confrontation (which is more often the case than vice versa), superimposing the victor's political system over that of the losers results in a more complex arrangement for the losers. (This is obviously not true when the barbarians win.)

5. Administering an occupation army, collecting taxes or tribute, and the like encourages further development of the victor's political institutions.

6. Assimilating conquered people who have distinct specializations of their own results in still greater differentiation for the now enlarged society that further stimulates political development.

These propositions may in some cases describe actual sequences of development. But this sequence is not the only one possible, and events presented as separate steps (such as items 5 and 6) may in fact occur simultaneously.

Even in the Roman Empire, where all roads led to Rome, the apex

[10] Andrew P. Vayda, "Primitive Warfare," in D. Sills (ed.), *International Encyclopedia of the Social Sciences*, vol. 16 (New York: Crowell, 1968).

of ancient cities, there was a clear relationship between political development, urbanization, and military conquest. The empire was a confederation of political states held together by the military forces of the central government in Rome. And the movement of agricultural foodstuffs from the provinces was necessary to support that army.[11]

TRADE AND MARKETS

Archeological evidence indicates that the Mesopotamian cities were divided into a "town proper" and a "suburb." There was also a port or marketplace for intercity trading, but it was set apart in a temple or palace. Because most of those who lived in the city were self-sufficient farmers, there was little trade *within* the city. The "sheltered" marketplace was not part of most townspeople's daily lives.[12]

The Mesopotamian settlements qualified more as cities by population criteria than by marketplace development. Archeological estimates of the size of various cities vary to a maximum of 24,000 in Ur, the largest. Its walls enclosed about 220 acres, giving it a relatively high density for an ancient city. All these population estimates, however, based as they are on *assumptions* of persons per household, amount of land to support a person, and the like, produce estimates that are often of dubious value.[13]

[11] John Sirjamaki, *The Sociology of Cities* (New York: Random House, 1964).
[12] Oppenheim, *op. cit.*
[13] For further discussion of population estimates, see Amos Hawley, *Urban Society* (New York: Ronald, 1971), pp. 32–35.

Agricultural life with infrequent market contact still characterizes many people who live outside of cities (the "Friday Market" in Toluca, Mexico).

In the Greek and Roman cities, and particularly in Athens and Rome, trading functions became substantially more pronounced. Before the Golden Age of Athens in the fifth century B.C., for example, the notion of a purely economic exchange hardly existed. As described by Polanyi, transactions were public acts designed to reinforce the status of the parties involved.[14] Brides, slaves, and plots of land were among the objects exchanged, and the laws of reciprocity that governed the transactions tended to be embedded in the kinship organization. Because of this kinship context, such exchanges are better viewed as gift-giving than as trade. Their primary function is to enhance solidarity rather than to redistribute wealth. Since these are the same terms anthropologists use to describe exchange in primitive societies, we can use one such analysis to illustrate the pre-Athens situation. A historical study of the Tiv in Central Nigeria by Paul Bohannan is particularly instructive.[15]

The Tiv, like most premonetary peoples, had a "multicentric" economy. That is, the goods exchanged fall into mutually exclusive spheres, each of which is governed by a different set of values. One was a subsistence sphere involving foodstuffs, livestock, household utensils, and some agricultural tools. These goods typically exchanged hands within a marketplace, but trade was in the form of barter prior to the introduction of European money. A second sphere involved prestige items, such as slaves, cattle, medicine, and brass rods. These items were typically exchanged in public ceremonies, and kinship considerations influenced what was traded and to whom. Even though supply and demand principles may have affected some prestige exchanges, these items never entered the market and the traders were apparently not consciously pursuing a profit motive. In addition, exchanges almost never occurred between spheres. No one traded slaves for food, or brass rods for farming tools. In fact, there was no way for such exchanges to occur. Items were considered to belong to different moral categories, and without money there was no way to determine the worth of an item in different spheres.

The third and final sphere involved woman-rights in marriage. According to Tiv values, only a woman could be exchanged for another. Thus, an ideal arrangement would be for grooms to exchange sisters. When this was precluded, which was often, there would be delayed reciprocity. A man would get his wife now and pay for her with some other woman later. In the interim, a man could demonstrate his good faith with gifts from the prestige sphere—brass rods, or sometimes cattle. These "gifts" did not wipe out the debt, however; only another woman could.

[14] Karl Polanyi, "Aristotle Discovers the Economy," in Polanyi et al. (eds.), op. cit.
[15] Paul Bohannan, "The Impact of Money on an African Subsistence Economy," Journal of Economic History, 19, 1959.

Using this description of exchange in Tivland as the background, we can see Aristotle's analysis of the market in Athens and Greece in perspective. From a contemporary economic viewpoint, Aristotle's preference was for that which ought to be rather than that which exists.[16] He condemned the taking of interest, for example, and argued that a fair price should reflect the parties' social positions (who they were rather than what they were trading).

In a market economy, prices are determined by supply and demand, the laws of the marketplace. Individual participation is governed by the profit motive rather than kinship obligation, supplication of deities, or the like. With respect to the operation of a marketplace, Aristotle's economics have been considered naive. Polanyi asserts that historians have attributed an exaggerated development to marketplaces up to, and including, Athens. The existence of an autonomous economic institution and the corresponding development of purely economic orientations were, according to Polanyi, just emerging in Athens. Aristotle's economics, with its disregard of scarcity and profits, is therefore an account of the emergence of the market.

Other descriptions of the Greek city-state fit this one, for they indicate how defense and conquest led to a politically unified empire, but not to a modern economically sophisticated city. As late as the fifth century B.C. Athenian cosmopolitanism was reflected by trade throughout the world; but there was little development of a market orientation *within* the city. Most residents lived off their landed estates, most buyers and sellers exchanged goods directly rather than through an impersonal marketplace, and extensive exchanges throughout the metropolis were all but precluded by narrow, crooked, and poorly paved streets.[17]

The dual economy

The separation of a modern marketplace in Athens from the routine, everyday life of its inhabitants illustrates what is generally called a *dual economy*. A similar separation among contemporary "underdeveloped" countries typically entails a rural-urban distinction: a market economy in the towns, a subsistence economy in the rural areas.[18] In the latter, agricultural products, which are the major output, are largely consumed by the producers. What exchange there is ordinarily involves barter rather than

---

[16] Polanyi, *op. cit.*

[17] Alfred Zimmern, *The Greek Commonwealth* (New York: Modern Library, 1931).

[18] For further discussion and additional references, see Bert F. Hoselitz, "Development and the Theory of Social Systems," in Manfred Stanley (ed.), *Social Development* (New York: Basic Books, 1972).

money. (The mutually exclusive spheres of a multicentric economy generally correspond to the different sectors of a dual economy.)

For the most part, the ancient cities thus far considered seem to be characterized more by subsistence than by market economies. It is generally assumed, as Aristotle commented, that subsistence economies function to enhance solidarity. There is correspondingly little economic growth. In market economies, by contrast, the primary function of exchange is adaptation to an environment. A redistribution of wealth characterizes market economies, which are also assumed to be more dynamic.

Although these categories do correspond to differences between types of societies, they are—like many dichotomies—somewhat exaggerated. One influential early study, for example, was Malinowski's analysis of the *kula* ring in Trobriand society—the exchange of arm shells and necklaces.[19] A young man received a starting supply of these objects from his father and proceeded to begin trading them with partners previously established by the father. An arm shell went to this one, a necklace was received in return; then the necklace went to another in return for an arm shell. The overriding norm was equal reciprocity; that is, an exchange of trinkets of equal value. The absence of money as a fixed medium of exchange led to a small amount of haggling over what was really equal. Malinowski, however, emphasizes the way in which the ceremonial exchanges led to bonds of trust among partners and strengthened the solidarity of Trobriand society, though nobody benefited in an economic sense.

A more recent analysis by Uberoi devotes more attention to the other side.[20] The ambiguity of nonmonetary exchange, he proposes, enabled a more ambitious individual to trade his way "upward" in Trobriand society. This primarily involved power and prestige. The more *kula* partners an individual possessed, the more his potential supporters. Thus, as in our own society, building a base of support can be translated into power. In addition, the bonds of trust created by *kula* trading facilitated later exchanges of nonritual items that were more purely economic in nature.

Subsistence economies, then, are not exclusively oriented to solidarity, nor are market economies directed solely at adaptation. Consider, for example, the exchange of Christmas cards in our own society.[21] The relative absence of economic growth in subsistence economies therefore need not be attributed entirely to the (presumably) different functions of sub-

[19] Bronislaw Malinowski, "The Primitive Economics of the Trobriand Islanders," *Economic Journal,* 31, 1921.
[20] J. P. Uberoi, *Politics of the Kula Ring* (Manchester: Manchester University Press, 1962).
[21] For additional examples and further clarification of types of economies, see Neil J. Smelser, *The Sociology of Economic Life* (Englewood Cliffs, N.J.: Prentice-Hall, 1963).

sistence and market economies. It may also be due to the absence of money, which inhibits nonritual trading, or to limited technology that cannot prevent the spoiling of foodstuffs which could otherwise have been used like money.[22] Note that Aristotle was sensitive to the introduction of money into the Greek economy and critical of its possible effect on the solidarity that had been produced by a subsistence economy.

The dominance of the marketplace

It was probably during the expansion of the Roman Empire, shortly before the birth of Christ, that a widespread market economy became more dominant. In Rome, shoppers crowded marketplaces and there was a full spectrum of nonagricultural occupations, from shoemaking and tailoring to money lending and bookkeeping. It was a congested city, but the total population was probably less than 350,000 inhabitants.[23]

The dominance of the marketplace and its profound effects on the totality of Roman life were the subjects of a famous nineteenth-century sociological work by Sir Henry Maine.[24] Until the early days of Rome, he argued, individuals were imbedded in a kinship system that both regulated and limited the kinds of relationships into which they could enter. Matters of personal property, inheritance, and the like were all fixed by lineage positions. Correspondingly, law in ancient societies emphasized status—family positions, set by birth. In a heterogeneous city such as Rome became, however, the marketplace encouraged more individualistic, more autonomous negotiations. The idea of a blood feud, for example, is inconsistent with the notion of let the buyer—as an individual—beware. This "freeing" effect of the market is reflected, for Maine, by a changing emphasis in the law to matters of "contract."

The Maine thesis is that the marketplace generates new conceptions of man as an individual negotiator. These replace the previous conception of man as a part of a lineage or family. Spreading out from the marketplace, this new orientation becomes part of a general social pattern and is finally embodied in the law. The transition from status to contract law thus indicates a more general change in social relations.

Prior to the time of the Roman Empire, then, cities contained ports or marketplaces, but economic orientations to a marketplace did not predominate. Most city inhabitants were self-sufficient farmers, and the bulk

---

[22] Cyril S. Belshaw, *Traditional Exchange and Modern Markets* (Englewood Cliffs, N.J.: Prentice-Hall, 1965).
[23] See Hawley, *op. cit.*
[24] Sir Henry Sumner Maine, *Ancient Law* (London: Oxford University Press, 1931). Originally published in 1861.

of the items they exchanged did not pass through a market. The exchanges enhanced solidarity, but did not lead to economic growth and did not encourage ideas of individuality. As a final postscript, however, we must question the assumed stability of subsistence economies. One type of stability involves an absence of change in system properties—the gross national product, for example, in today's terms. A second type of stability entails an absence of change among the components of a system—redistribution of wealth within a society, for example. Premarket subsistence economies tended to have stability of the first type, but not necessarily of the second.[25]

AFTER ROME

Europe

The general decline in the population of Europe after the breakup of the Roman Empire, which lasted until about the tenth century, was also reflected in the decline of cities. Outside Europe, however, a few major cities developed during this period. Baghdad, for example, reached a population estimated at 300,000. (Paris, by contrast, did not reach a comparable size until at least the sixteenth century.) New cities in Europe and elsewhere tended to form around former Roman army camps, at river crossings, or at high grounds which could be more easily defended. Warfare was common and cities, again, were largely armed fortresses.[26]

Beginning in the tenth century, and continuing at a slow rate for several hundred years, the European population began to grow, and with it the cities. For the most part, however, medieval European society lacked the technology and knowledge necessary to prevent various types of disasters to which concentrated populations were particularly prone—earthquakes and fires, for example, and the rampant spread of epidemics.

The single worst epidemic, called the Black Death or the bubonic plague, ravaged Europe between 1348 and 1350. It began in the ports of Italy, probably carried by merchant seamen, then spread to France, England, and across all Europe. At least one-quarter of the entire European population died, but the figures are much higher proportionately for the crowded and unsanitary cities of the time. The plague claimed about one-half of the population of Florence, two-thirds of that of Hamburg, and so on.

[25] For further discussion, see Mark Abrahamson, "On the Structural-Functional Theory of Development," in Stanley, *op. cit.* In the same volume, see Bert F. Hoselitz, "Comments on Abrahamson."
[26] Robert C. Cook, "The World's Great Cities," *Population Bulletin,* 16, 1960.

The panic and terror that seized urban populations are easily imagined. After being stricken came a few days of high fever, agonizing pain, and hemorrhages in the skin. Death occurred within five to six days. People of course fled epidemics when they could, and both literal and figurative witch hunts were common. The Christian majority also commonly blamed Jews (for poisoning wells), physicians (for their impotence), and anyone else who was handy. There was also an apparent lowering of restraints as people indulged in alcohol and sex to blot out the suffering.[27] Boccaccio's *Decameron,* for example, describes a group of revelers in a country house outside plague-swept Florence. In the cities, gangs were murdering the sick and robbing the dead, and people were either packing into churches or turning to witchcraft. After the fourteenth century there were a number of locally severe epidemics, such as those that claimed over one-fourth of Venice's population of 160,000 in 1576 and almost half of Marseilles' population of 90,000 in 1743, but none equaled the toll of the Black Death of 1348–50.

Japan

In Japan at this time fires and earthquakes brought comparable disasters. Throughout the sixteenth and seventeenth centuries, for example, Edo (Tokyo) was ravaged by terrible fires. If they followed a prolonged period of drought, and if strong winds happened to be blowing when they broke out, the results were particularly disastrous. Just such a fire began in Edo in 1657. It raged out of control for several days, and was finally extinguished by a change in the weather that delivered a major snowstorm. However, the break in the weather was hardly a blessing, since much of the population was homeless by then. An estimated 108,000 deaths resulted from the fire and cold. In one of the single most tragic episodes, prisoners were released to escape the flames, but an erroneous message of escape was relayed to the nearest gatekeeper, who responded by securing the gate. People fleeing the blaze were trapped, and 10,000 bodies were later counted at that gate alone.[28]

There was an elite group of volunteer firemen in Edo, but its technique of knocking down structures adjacent to fires was only of limited success. The group's rather elaborate water works (completed in 1654) from the Tama River to the outskirts of Edo was inadequate except for extinguishing very small fires.

Although natural disasters ravaged the population of Tokyo and other Japanese centers, the main reason for their lack of further development as cities was probably the isolationist government policies that began in the

[27] William L. Langer, "The Black Death," in Kingsley Davis (ed.), *Cities* (San Francisco: W. H. Freeman, 1973).
[28] Kazuo Nishida, *Storied Cities of Japan* (Tokyo: Weatherhill, 1963).

Because of their dense populations, cities historically have been prone to such disasters as the mid-nineteenth-century Chicago fire.

sixteenth century. During the last half of that century, the population of London nearly doubled, and commercial activities in English, Spanish, Dutch, and other cities were being aided by the "fruits" of colonization. Japanese seamen were all over Southeast Asia in the sixteenth century, but when foreign traders were expelled from Japan, the merchant marine was also brought home. Isolationism probably cost Japan the opportunity to colonize in Australia, New Zealand, and elsewhere.[29] Japan's military headquarters were moved to the castle town of Yedo, an immense fortress surrounded by walls, moats, and thirty-six gates, symbolizing Japan's isolation from the rest of the world.

THE GROWTH OF LONDON

Trade and markets grew rapidly in Europe after the fourteenth century, but it took two hundred years to replace the population lost in the great plagues. Cities were increasingly dominated by markets and market orientations. London in the middle 1500s was described as a commercial city; the pomp and ceremony of the Middle Ages was disappearing. The Queen remained largely outside the city (in Somerset and Whitehall), and it was remarked that "Londoners know no king but their Mayor."[30] Paris was

[29] Richard Storry, *Japan* (New York: Oxford University Press, 1965).
[30] Martin Holmes, *Elizabethan London* (New York: Praeger, 1969), p. 5.

similarly becoming more autonomous. During the sixteenth century, its "sheriffs" were given jurisdiction over commercial activities much like that of the Lord Mayor of London.

The dominant European cities of this time shared a number of other characteristics in common. Paris, London, the Rhine-Ruhr agglomeration (including Bonn and Cologne), and others had all been former Roman encampments originally settled because of their favorable locations with respect to river transportation. London's growth prior to the Industrial Revolution is particularly interesting, though.

The main features of London in 1600 were still largely determined by the Roman settlement pattern of more than a thousand years before. The wall, bridge and tower that had dominated London continued to be both the major symbols of the city and its ecological constraints. London had originally been designed for defense with the Thames River to the south, a marshy meadow to the north, easily monitored plains to the east and west, and its semicircular wall.[31]

Houses, shops, and warehouses lined narrow streets that bustled with activity. Pack animals carrying goods shared the right of way with pedestrians, horsemen, and open gutters. To widen the streets would have cut into properties on either side, and it was successfully resisted because the proliferating commercial activity was greatly increasing the value of inner-city property. London Bridge, a timber and stone span constructed in the twelfth century, made London the "first great cross-roads of England."[32] Craftsmen and merchants were thus selling both to local and outside buyers.

In order to attract customers, merchants found it efficient to display goods of the same type in close proximity to one another. Street markets came to be known by their products, which in turn gave streets names such as Grocers' Court and Poultry (which still exist). A number of foreign groups had also settled together in various parts of the city, and were often associated with distinct occupational pursuits. Wealthy Dutch merchants engaged in international trade had settled in North London, just within the walls. Less well-off merchants settled closer to the Thames, and to the Customs House in particular. Also in this area were a large number of Italian wine merchants and the English boatmen at Billingsgate, to their west. On the opposite side of London Bridge were a smaller number of German grain merchants. And a rather sizable French settlement ("Petty France") was just beyond the wall to the east.[33]

These areas are shown in Figure 2–1, a map originally published in 1572. The streets of London were crooked and narrow, and the

---

[31] George V. Zito, "The Sociology of Shakespeare" (Unpublished Ph.D. dissertation, Syracuse University, 1972). See also George V. Zito, "A Note on the Population of Seventeenth Century London," *Demography*, 9, 1972.
[32] Holmes, *op. cit.*, p. 30.
[33] Zito, *op. cit.*

The concentration of similar commercial activities, characteristic of seventeenth-century London, has continued (the 47th Street Diamond Exchange in New York).

Thames's role as the major transportation artery is clear. The river was lined with small boats that took passengers up and down stream. However, the infamous tides prevented easy passage during many parts of the day, particularly around London Bridge. Its piers also prevented large ships from passing under it, so cargo was unloaded onto barges near the Customs House. (The bridge was not demolished until the nineteenth century.) The similarities between London and Paris again are striking. The importance of the Seine for commerce and transportation rivaled that of the Thames, and early development of the city on the left and right banks of the Seine was similar to London's concentration along the Thames.

In the middle of the sixteenth century London was still full of clear streams and water from the Thames was still considered "sweet" to drink. Over the next century or so, however, this picture changed substantially. Estimates for this period are of course crude, but the population within the walls probably tripled, from somewhere around 150,000 to nearly 500,000. Since the enclosed area comprised approximately one square mile, the congestion was extreme. Estimates of the population outside the walls are still more crude, but perhaps another 25 percent lived in these areas around 1600. The principal settlements were Southwark, across the Thames; Petty France, to the east of the wall; the manors of Northbank, north of the wall. And an estimated 6.000 migrants per year were settling largely in the growing area just west of the wall.

An enclosed city, whose dominant landmarks had been laid 1,500 years earlier, was straining to accommodate a rapidly growing and increasingly commercial population. With its "suburbs" and its immigrant groups, London of the seventeenth century was beginning to resemble a modern city. The resemblance also included serious pollution problems. The streets of London were infected with dead dogs, pitch bonfires were lit

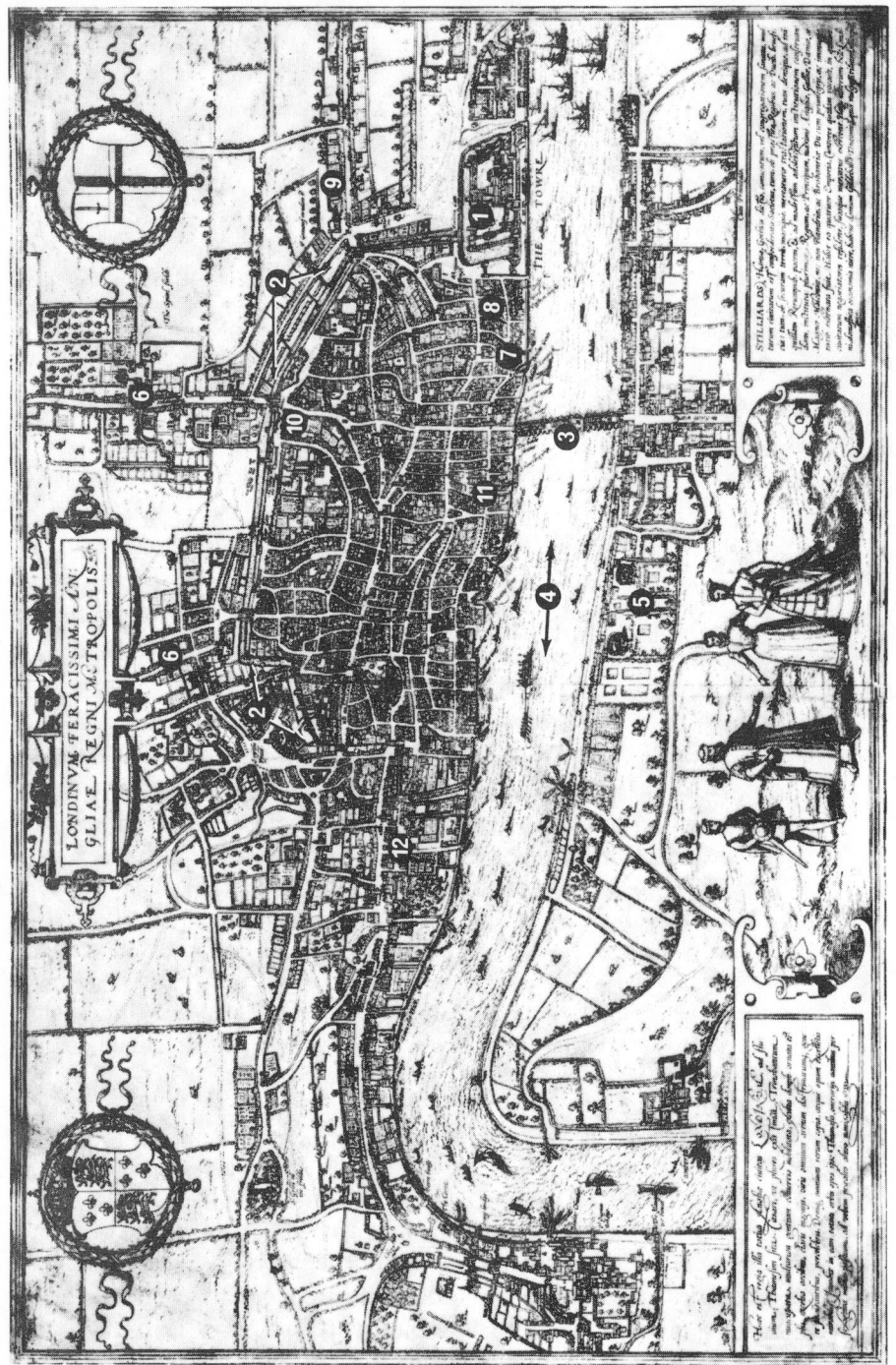

1 – The Tower
2 – The Wall
3 – London Bridge
4 – Thames River

5 – Southwark
6 – Northbank manor
7 – Billingsgate
8 – Area of Italian wine merchants

9 – Petty France
10 – Area of wealthy Dutch merchants
11 – Area of German grain merchants
12 – Area of rural immigrants

FIGURE 2–1   Map of London first published in 1572.

34

twice a week in an effort to "cleanse the air," and fishermen were concerned with how pollution of the Thames was killing the fish.[34]

By the seventeenth century it was possible to recognize a general and substantial domination of England by London. The bridge over the Thames, as pointed out previously, made London the great crossroads of the country. This contributed to London's own commercial development and made it into the center through which all England was connected to world markets. And a market orientation, with all that it entails, spread outward from the city.

London's influential role was not confined to economics, however. It became dominant culturally as well, determining forms of artistic expression. The talented, such as Shakespeare, soon found their way to London no matter where they were born. So too did persons of all sorts, as evidenced by an estimated yearly arrival of 6,000 migrants from the countryside. The observation that all roads led to Rome was probably an accurate description of that historic city, but it became even more true (both literally and figuratively) in London and other great European cities after the turn of the seventeenth century.

They had become what are generally termed *primate* cities, cities that dominate a country. The movement of foodstuffs, of raw materials, and of migrants all tends to go in one direction: to this city. The one-way flow so monopolizes resources that the existence of a primate city tends to inhibit the development of other cities within an extended geographical area. London, Paris, and Stockholm are all examples of a single city dominating a country to the relative exclusion of all others. After industrialization, other cities did tend to emerge and grow in other parts of the larger countries; for example, Birmingham in northern England. Such primate cities, however, are still in evidence in less developed countries of the world, where an original "capital city" tied a colony to a mother country and then functionally expanded to dominate all other activities.[35]

COLONIAL CITIES: TODAY'S THIRD WORLD

The colonial practices of the great European nations during the fifteenth, sixteenth, and seventeenth centuries furthered their economic and com-

---

[34] *Ibid.*
[35] Philip M. Hauser, "The Social, Economic, and Technological Problems of Rapid Urbanization," in Bert F. Hoselitz and Wilbert E. Moore (eds.), *Industrialization and Society* (New York: UNESCO, 1963).

Cortez at Vera Cruz, enslaving the Indians (from a mural by Diego Rivera).

mercial development. The British Empire, for example, benefited from American grain and African minerals, and the international trading position of London in particular was enhanced. Dutch, French, Spanish, and Portuguese cities were similarly developing as international ports of trade as the result of colonial empires. In North and South America, Africa, and elsewhere, cities were emerging both as colonial administrative centers and as fortresses to defend the materials that were being shipped back to the mother countries.

Spanish-American cities in Latin America, for example, established primarily during the sixteenth century, were all substantially alike and functionally very limited. As a result of Spanish colonial policies, which prevented the development of indigenous manufacturing and emphasized mining, all the wealth of the country went to Spain.[36] Colonial centers developed in two types of places: in seaports along the coast, where shipping connected Spain and the New World (for example, Vera Cruz in Mexico); and inland, where areas were being worked under Spanish domination (for example, Lima in Peru). Both types of cities were substantially alike, how-

[36] T. Lynn Smith, "The Changing Functions of Latin American Cities," *The Americas*, 25, 1968.

ever, in that they were heavily fortified garrisons without markets. In addition, as Smith points out, the inland centers were typically not favorably located with respect to transportation facilities. They were intended primarily as inaccessible fortresses, and in this respect differed greatly from the many European cities that developed along established trade routes. It was not until the twentieth century that the social and economic functions of the Latin American cities began to modernize.[37]

Under British rule, by contrast, the North American colonies developed initially as both garrisons and markets. Although the development of British-administered marketplaces in Nigeria did not occur until later, the general cultural effects of colonization in Tivland in Nigeria are interesting to look at here. The arrival of the British, according to Bohannan, put an end to warfare among tribes, and the combination of safety and new road networks led to more trade and more markets. Trading companies in northern Nigeria put Tiv in contact with the world economy. The major effect on Tiv culture, however, came as a result of the introduction of European money.[38]

A basic characteristic of money is the fact that it is all-purpose; that is, it provides a standard medium of exchange for transactions of all types. Traditional Tiv exchanges, it will be recalled, were differentiated into three spheres: subsistence goods, prestige items, and woman-rights. Until money was introduced, there was no way to convert items between spheres. After it was introduced, Bohannan states, it created "its own revolution." The Tiv now buy their wives and sell their daughters, for example, and the marketplace considerations of supply and demand determine the price. Money also produces its own kind of debt and credit. Exchange ceases to be tied to kinship and status, and becomes rather a matter of personal and individual contract.

As is usually the case, money in Tivland converted a multicentric economy into a unicentric one, but cultural values lag behind the transformation. The Tiv find it demeaning to buy and sell wives for cash, but money has so permeated their society that there is no longer any other way. In essence, then, money helps to create a unicentric market, but *perceptions* of the market are slower to change. Similarly, the marketplace creates its own psychology within a traditional culture, so that it becomes possible to talk about inflation of bride prices in the Tiv marriage market.

Many of the former colonial countries are today viewed as "underdeveloped." They are the nations of the Third World. In Africa, Asia, and Latin America they belong to the twentieth century in some respects, but

---

[37] *Ibid.*
[38] Bohannan, *op. cit.*

traditional patterns persist and they are plagued by deficient resources, civil wars, political fragmentation, and a host of other problems.

Colonization by European countries, in most cases, is the source of many of the current obstacles to development. National unity, for example, can be obstructed by the creation of "artificial" states. The countries formed by colonization in all of Latin America and most of the Afro-Asian world were not national entities prior to colonialization.[39] And the boundaries laid down by the European powers rarely coincided with the actual ethnic or linguistic distribution of the natives. In addition, colonial control often lasted for as little as a few decades (such as in sub-Sahara Africa), insufficient time to create a sense of national identity.

The resultant lack of national unity combined with the frequent occurrence of border clashes and civil wars discourages capital investment by more industrialized nations and also diverts national resources away from housing, educational, and economic reforms. It is an economic, political, and social vicious circle. For both selfish and altruistic motives, however, the more developed nations are vitally concerned with modernization of the Third World. Questions of their political-economic development have become so transcendent, Cox notes, that the motto of the United Nations could be changed to "Peace through Industrialization."[40]

In the contemporary Third World Nations, two master trends are evident: industrialization and urbanization. The latter is conventionally defined by the increasing percentage of a nation's population that lives in urban rather than rural areas. Industrialization involves the increasing use of electrical, steam, and other inanimate sources of power. (By contrast, animate sources of power—human and animal—are associated with pre-industrial production.) Later stages of industrialization entail changes in the nature of raw materials and the ways they are processed, but we will not be concerned with these aspects until Chapter 6. The term Industrial Revolution is actually a misnomer, since "revolution" connotes a rather abrupt break with the past. Industrialization, however, has been occurring for the past two centuries, though at markedly different rates in various parts of the world.

There are a number of intimate links between industrialization and urbanization. Most apparent is the fact that both typically involve the movement of populations out of agricultural occupations. The nature of salaried work in industrial occupations and life in an urban context are also thought to have a number of other similar consequences, such as more

[39] Fred R. von der Mehden, *Politics of the Developing Nations* (Englewood Cliffs, N.J.: Prentice-Hall, 1964).
[40] Oliver C. Cox, "The Preindustrial City Reconsidered," *The Sociological Quarterly*, 5, 1964, p. 134.

achieved and impersonal systems of stratification, a decline in extended family living, and so on. In the following chapters our attention will be directed at the changes in social organization that are associated with both industrialization and urbanization.

Brooklyn, New York.

3 Population, Specialization, and Location

URBANIZATION has historically occurred in relation to population growth. It involves both the direct growth of cities and the growth of nations that provides a surplus of potential migrants to cities. Third World cities are currently experiencing the type of growth that was characteristic of American and European cities in the nineteenth century. As we shall see, however, a number of subtle differences in birth and death rates have led to the association of current population growth with a number of more serious societal problems.

As cities have grown in size, their populations have typically become more densely settled as well. Because size and density are important antecedents to specialization of labor, we will examine changes in the division of labor in the following section. Specialization is associated, in turn, with transportation and communication developments that alter the spatial features of cities, our topic in the final section of this chapter.

THE DEMOGRAPHIC TRANSITION

From the Middle Ages until the Industrial Revolution, the populations of cities were exposed to a variety of hazards. Congestion favored the rapid spread of contagious illnesses, and cities' roles as trade centers meant that new diseases were regularly introduced. In the contemporary Third World, illness and disease continue to decimate urban populations, and it is not uncommon for nearly half the infants born to die before reaching one year of age. Some of the effects of epidemics and pollution were discussed in Chapter 2. Let us look more closely at the degree of health risk actually experienced by populations in early cities.

It was apparently not uncommon for the death rate in a major city (for example, Stockholm) to be about twice as high as the death rate in rural areas of the same country. Calculating a death rate means simply counting the number of persons per thousand who die. It is a "crude" rate that can be misleading. A more sophisticated measure involves adjustment of the age categories involved so that they are more directly comparable. Specifically, we know that persons who migrate to cities tend disproportionately to be young adults. Older persons, probably because they are more committed to tradition, are less likely to leave their villages. Married persons with children tend to be "locked in" more than unattached persons. So migrants are typically young adults without children.

Because of these selective aspects of migration, the population of growing cities tends to differ from rural populations in the same country. Of most direct relevance, in developing cities there are relatively more young persons whose mortality rate is lower than that of older persons. A crude rate misses this difference in populations. By comparing the actual death rates of each age category, we get an adjusted rate which shows that the crude estimate of rural and urban differences is underestimated. The age-adjusted death rates of cities were probably more than double those of the countryside.

Not only were city death rates very high; they also exceeded birth rates. Thus, cities experienced a net loss in their "natural" (births minus deaths) rate of population growth. Representative figures from Stockholm's vital rates are presented in Figure 3–1.[1] These are the crude rates, and so they underestimate the death rate. Similar reasoning indicates that the age-adjusted birth rate is overestimated because migrants to the city are at peak child-bearing ages. The sketchiness of data from the eighteenth and nineteenth centuries makes it impossible to calculate precise age-adjusted rates (even the crude rates are not precise). If age-adjusted rates could be calculated, the discrepancy between births and deaths in these cities would be still greater.

This general point can be made quite dramatically by comparing crude and adjusted death rates where figures are available. In 1954, the crude death rate in Taiwan was 8.2 per 1,000. In the United States, it was 9.2 per 1,000. Thus, it appears that the death rate in the United States was higher than in Taiwan! Given the general relationship between socio-economic development and death rates, however, we should be skeptical of the apparent difference. In fact, if the United States' death rate is standardized by Taiwan's age distribution, the American death rate is only

1 From Kingsley Davis, "The Evolution of Western Industrial Cities," in Davis (ed.), *Cities* (San Francisco: W. H. Freeman, 1973), p. 103.

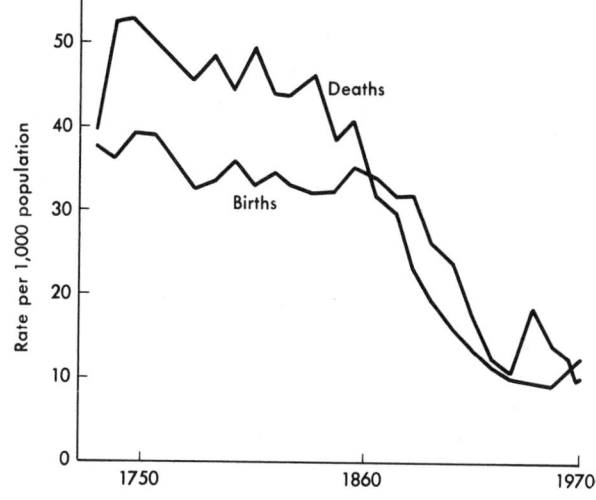

FIGURE 3–1 Stockholm's vital rates, 1720–1970.

5.0, appreciably lower than that of Taiwan.[2] How this is calculated is shown in Table 3–1.

Examination of the figures indicates that low death risk age groups (ages 1–4) comprise a larger percentage of the population in Taiwan than in the United States. Correspondingly, higher risk groups (over 65 years) are relatively overrepresented in the United States. Thus, a crude rate and an age-adjusted rate provide very different pictures, regardless of whether births or deaths are being compared.

[2] Data from William Pooler, "Death Rates and Age Distributions." Department of Sociology, Syracuse University. *Mimeo.*

TABLE 3-1 Adjusted death rate.

Age in Years	Age Specific Death Rate		Age Distributions		Age Adjusted U.S. Rate (2) × (3)
	Taiwan (1)	U.S. (2)	Taiwan (3)	U.S. (4)	
Under 1	32.2	30.2	4.2%	2.2%	1.27
1-4	11.9	1.2	14.8	8.8	0.18
25-29	2.6	1.4	7.8	7.3	0.11
40-44	5.9	3.8	4.9	6.8	0.19
Over 65	70.2	59.7	2.5	8.4	1.49

Data from William Pooler, "Death Rates and Age Distributions." Department of Sociology, Syracuse University. Mimeo.

Lowering the death rate

Despite their net natural decline in population, Western European and American cities were growing in size during the eighteenth and nineteenth centuries. London's rapid growth during this period was described in Chapter 2. Stockholm grew as well, from about 45,000 inhabitants in 1720 to about 100,000 in 1850. Obviously, in all such cases it was a very high rate of rural to urban migration that both offset the deficit in the natural rate and resulted in a net surplus of persons.

In preindustrial countries, there is typically a very high rate of both deaths and births. The death rate is high for previously discussed reasons. The birth rate is high largely due to the relative absence of birth control techniques and contraceptive knowledge. The two rates balance each other out, resulting either in no natural increase or in an actual decline in natural growth. In demographic transition theory, these are *stage one* societies and, like the preindustrial category, they include an assortment of countries cutting across diverse historical periods and geographical areas.

Stage two is defined by a declining death rate with a relatively unchanged birth rate. The death rate falls because of technological innovations, such as autoclaves for baby bottles, or new knowledge, such as learning to keep infants away from diseased persons. As these examples illustrate, the initial great strides in lowering the death rate occur with respect to infant mortality. Infants are a high death-risk category in stage one societies, but some relatively minor innovations can drastically alter their mortality rate.

Most of the Third World nations are currently in the midst of the very prolific population growth experienced by stage two societies. In fact, cities in Latin America and Asia may actually be growing faster than Western European countries of the early nineteenth century because there is some evidence that the former entered stage two with a higher birth rate than the latter. Some comparative figures are presented in Table 3–2.[3]

Currently developing nations differ in still another important respect. Rural to urban migration in nineteenth-century Europe did not involve the same population pressures on the land. People migrated primarily because they were attracted by the probability of finding work. There was no push to leave the rural land, because the excess population was emigrating to the United States. Today, the growth of stage two has led to rural population growth despite rural to urban migration. Thus, even though the rate of industrialization has often lagged behind population growth—so that there are not enough urban jobs—land pressures continue to force rural to urban migration. Spiraling urban unemployment and poverty are the result.[4]

[3] From United Nations, *Demographic Yearbook* (New York, 1965).
[4] Ned Levine, "Old Culture—New Culture," *Social Forces*, 51, 1973.

TABLE 3-2   Birth rates of selected countries.

Country	Period	Birth Rate
France	1821-30	31.0
England and Wales	1841-50	32.6
United States	1871-75	37.0
Ceylon	1960-64	34.9
Egypt	1960-64	42.8
Mexico	1960-64	46.0

As a general rule, death-control techniques precede birth-control techniques. In terms of cultural values, there is simply less resistance to the former. For contemporary Third World nations, antibiotics and anti-malarial DDT sprays are readily available from the developed nations and have resulted in much more rapid declines in mortality than were previously experienced in stage two by the now developed nations.[5] The innovation of birth control techniques, however, lags behind because it violates conceptions of masculinity or is offensive to religious beliefs, and so on. Creating more equality among nations with respect to death rates therefore has the initial effect of increasing differences in growth rates, with the poorest nations growing the fastest. As a result, stage two societies are characterized by overcrowding, hunger, and poverty, though these are familiar problems in all the cities of the contemporary world.

Further consideration of the demographic consequences of declining infant mortality makes it apparent that it is the same as a further increase in the birth rate. If 400 per 1,000 infants die before they are one year old (a not unrealistic figure in stage one) and this is reduced to 200 per 1,000, the effects are the same as increasing the birth rate by one-third. When birth rates are already very high, then a tremendous economic burden is placed on parents who may be trying also to support their own elderly parents. In addition, the high birth rate and low infant mortality produces a disproportionately young population who soon reach child-producing age themselves. The population growth thus becomes cumulative.

Lowering the birth rate

The lag between death and birth control, another way of viewing stage two, is not uniform throughout a society. Like most innovations, birth control tends to be adopted first in cities, and the time of its adoption in cities is related to people's involvement in the industrialization process. Adoption then spreads outward from the city to the countryside according

[5] George J. Stolnitz, "A Century of International Mortality Trends," *Population Studies,* 10, 1956.

to degree of urban contact and proximity. This pattern is true for virtually all types of technological or material innovations.

The diffusion of technology from a central market to outlying areas is illustrated by a study of modern milking techniques in Mexico. Since World War II, the demand for milk in Mexico has steadily increased. A major supplier of powdered milk, the Nestlé Corporation, was forced by the urbanization of Mexico City to seek supplies farther to the north. In 1958 the company set up a collection depot just outside the city of Aguascalientes and tried to induce farmers to switch from growing corn and beans to dairy farming. The company offered free technical assistance, agreed to pay transportation costs for delivering milk, and offered a payment that would exceed the return from corn and beans. Over the next ten years, initial reluctance was slowly replaced by a willingness to convert to dairy farming, until virtually all had made the change.

In explaining the process of conversion, Brown and Lentnek[6] emphasize distance from the market. It is accessibility to the market and information about the innovation that most determine who will or will not adopt, and both variables correlate highly with distance from the market. The personal characteristics of farmers (education, age) are not initially related to adoption differences. Among farmers equally close to the market, however, older ones tend to adopt more quickly. This is not explained by the investigators, but age of the farmer is correlated directly with size of the family at the time of adoption, so economic need may differentiate between farmers with equal access. Over time, the area of adopters widens; that is, it spreads out farther from the market. As it does, a new group of farmers have increased access to information and the number of adopters increases. Again, age is related to time of adoption within an area of equal access. In a similar way, information about, and access to, birth control techniques diffuse from a city to a countryside.

The use of legal abortion is a well-studied means of controlling births, and it clearly illustrates the basic diffusion pattern. In Hungary, for example, few legal abortions were permitted prior to about 1954. Then government policies became more liberal, partly in response to the Russian decree of 1955 giving women the right to decide themselves the question of motherhood. After 1955 the rate of legal abortion increased rapidly until by 1961 it exceeded the number of live births by about 20 percent.[7] The figures are presented in Table 3–3.

The consequence of this decline in live births is easily underestimated until it is realized that slight differences in rates of population growth have cumulative effects. If a population grows at a yearly rate of 0.7 percent, for

[6] Lawrence A. Brown and Barry Lentnek, "Innovation Diffusion in a Developing Country," *Economic Development and Culture Change,* 21, 1973.
[7] Christopher Tietze, "The Demographic Significance of Legal Abortion in Eastern Europe," *Demography,* 1, 1964.

TABLE 3-3 Legal abortions and live births in
Hungary, 1949-1961.

Year	Legal Abortions (1,000)	Live Births (1,000)
1949	1.6	190.4
1951	1.7	190.6
1953	2.8	206.9
1955	35.4	210.4
1957	123.4	167.2
1959	152.4	151.2
1961	170.0	140.4

*From Christopher Tietze, "The Demographic Signifi-
cance of Legal Abortion in Eastern Europe,"* Demography, *1, 1964.*

example, it will double its size in about 100 years. If that rate is cut to
0.3 percent, it will take over 230 years to double.[8] The live birth rate is, of
course, only one of the variables determining the overall rate of growth of
a population, but it is an important one, and even small changes may have
great repercussions on further growth.

The urban to rural diffusion of abortion, like other means of controlling births, can be seen in Hungary by looking at differential rates of
utilization in any given year. The figures for 1960 (per 1,000) are 27.3
legal abortions and 8.8 live births for the city of Budapest, 21.7 and 10.4
for greater Budapest, and 14.3 and 16.1 for the rest of the country.

With the legalization and liberation of abortion in many states in
the United States beginning in the late 1960s, there has been a similar lowering of fertility rates. In Maryland, for example, laws governing abortion
were substantially liberalized in mid-1968. Fertility rates in that state had
been declining since 1960, at about the same rate as in the remainder of
the United States. After 1968, however, Maryland's rate declined more
steeply, as indicated in Table 3–4.[9] Clearly, legalization and liberalization
of abortion appears to lower fertility rates to a dramatic degree.

As observed in Hungary and elsewhere, the immediate utilization of
abortion was greater in urban than in rural areas. Specifically, between
1960 and 1968, reductions in fertility rates were about the same in metropolitan Baltimore as in the nonmetropolitan areas of the state—30 and
29 percent, respectively. Between 1968 and 1971, however, fertility in

[8] U.S. Bureau of the Census, *The Methods and Materials of Demography* (Washington, D.C.: GPO, 1971), Figure 13–5).
[9] Ira Rosenwaike and Robert J. Melton, "Legal Abortion and Fertility in Maryland,"
Demography, 11, 1974.

TABLE 3-4 Fertility rates per 1,000 population, 1961-1971.

Year	Maryland	Total U.S.
1961	116	117
1963	109	109
1965	99	97
1967	88	88
1969	83	87
1971	74	82

From Ira Rosenwaike and Robert J. Melton, "Legal Abortion and Fertility in Maryland," Demography, 11, 1974.

metropolitan Baltimore declined another 11 percent compared to only 4 percent in the nonmetropolitan areas.

These rural to urban differences tend to persist. A Gallup poll of female students in the United States, for example, showed that into the 1960s family size preferences were still highest in rural areas. The daughters of farmers and farm laborers, for example, continue to want the largest number of children.[10]

Birth control and modernization

Within developing cities, involvement in the modernization process is directly related to time of birth control utilization. Among better educated women, women who own modern appliances, and so on, a higher percentage use some type of preventive technique and have correspondingly lower birth rates. This is particularly true of women in their late thirties, whose children are older and more likely to survive. The fear of infant death makes younger women more alike; they *all* are less likely to use birth control, since their children still are threatened by the infant mortality rate. Representative findings are presented in Table 3–5 from Freedman's study of family planning in Taichung, the capital of Taiwan.[11]

Examination of column 1 in Table 3–5 shows that differences in family size preferences are not very large. The better educated and more involved women do want fewer children, but the differences in actual numbers of live births (column 2) are much larger. Differences in the

[10] Judith Blake, "Demographic Science and the Redirection of Population Policy," in Thomas R. Ford and Gordon F. DeJong (eds.), *Social Demography* (Englewood Cliffs, N.J.: Prentice-Hall, 1970), Table 6.
[11] Ronald Freedman et al., "Fertility and Family Planning in Taiwan," *American Journal of Sociology*, 69, 1964.

TABLE 3-5   Births, preferences, and prevention.

Women's Characteristics	Children Wanted (Avg.)	Live Births (Avg.)	Percent Using any Preventive Technique
Primary education or less	4.3	5.4	38
More than primary	3.5	4.1	71
Never read newspapers	4.4	5.8	32
Read at least sometimes	3.8	4.4	64
One or less modern objects	4.9	6.4	25
Two or more	4.1	5.0	54

utilization of any kind of preventive technique (from condoms to abortions) are probably responsible for the greater differences in actual births. Thus, a decline in birth rates is not primarily due to a change in values; it is due more to innovations (birth control techniques) that bring values and reality into closer accord.

Effects of demographic changes

To appreciate these demographic factors fully, they must be seen in relationship to the pressures they place on an entire society. Economic development, for example, generally requires mass education, which is expensive. How expensive depends on the number of students and the ratio of students to persons gainfully employed in the labor force. This ratio is, in turn, determined by fertility and mortality rates as well as by immigration.

In order to demonstrate the relationship between demographic stages and educational costs per worker, Arriaga has compared Latin America with the United States and Sweden.[12] Each shows a markedly different demographic history. In Sweden, there has been a long period of slowly declining births and deaths; in the United States there has been a rapid decline in fertility, but high net international migration; in Latin America, the fertility rate has remained high while mortality has rapidly declined. As a result of these differences, the costs of education per worker have been lowest in Sweden and highest in Latin America. And the greater the degree of overall education, the greater are the cost differences, as indicated in Table 3–6. Note that educational attainments are standardized

[12] Eduardo E. Arriaga, "Impact of Population Changes on Education Cost," *Demography,* 9, 1972.

Translated, the sign on the wall states: "To want a child is to educate him." Such signs are placed throughout Mexico by its federal government.

across nations. Low attainment characterized Sweden and the United States in the mid-nineteenth century and Latin America in 1930. High educational attainment characterized Sweden and the United States in the 1960s; it is projected for Latin America in the year 2000.

What the figures in Table 3–6 illustrate rather dramatically is that increasing educational attainment always increases costs per worker, but especially in countries demographically like Latin America. Under the same educational and labor force conditions, intermediate education, for example, would have cost nearly 50 percent more in Latin America than in Sweden. The projection to the year 2000 shows still greater differences even if Latin America drastically cuts its fertility rate. The differences would remain because of the large numbers of youngsters already born who would still have to be educated.

TABLE 3-6 Educational costs and demographic trends.

| | Education Costs per Worker | | |
Educational Attainment	Sweden	U.S.	Latin America
Low	0.62	0.73	0.73
Intermediate	1.96	2.15	2.90
High	8.88	10.39	15.93

In sum, high degrees of educational attainments are tremendously expensive for the labor force to support. In the U.S. and in Sweden, spiraling costs have been partially held down by lower fertility and by expansion of the labor force. In Latin America, costs have taken off because fertility rates have remained high and have not been counteracted by labor force expansion. Thus, poverty and low educational attainment become parts of a vicious circle in societies demographically in stage two.

Stage three of the demographic transition involves a decline in the birth rate to approximately equal the death rate. Population size is again relatively stabilized as in stage one, but this time both rates are low (at about 10 per 1,000). Until quite recently, stage three was more of a demographic projection than a reality. And parity of birth and death rates has as yet been attained by only a few of the most industrialized nations. The remainder are in stage two, along with most of the contemporary Third World nations.[13] Because the actual rates of such stage two societies differ so much from each other, the process of transition described here has been treated as involving five stages by the Population Division of the United Nations. In the latter, the three middle categories involve variations of stage two.[14]

The transitions between these stages, however, involve more than just changes in the gross birth and death rates. The entire demographic structure of a nation (or city) is modified. For example, entering stage two is associated with a larger percentage of young children; entering stage three is associated with a larger percentage of older persons. With these changes there are corresponding changes in the causes of deaths. Preindustrial (or stage one) people die more from infectious diseases, whereas later in stage two or three, people live longer and die more from degenerative diseases. As American Indians have modernized, for example, their illness-specific death rates have mirrored these trends.[15] Table 3–7 shows the changes from 1955 to 1967.

With modernization there is not only an increase in deaths from degenerative diseases, but an increase in deaths due to what may be termed "strain-induced" causes. This includes: cirrhosis of the liver (associated with high alcohol consumption), suicide, and accidents. Initial exposure to modernization, in fact, often results in rates of strain-induced deaths far higher than those recorded in more modern societies. Again, the American Indian's experience is illustrative.

[13] A few are still primarily in stage one. Into the 1960s, death rates in the African countries of Dahomey and Gabon, for example, remained almost 30 per 1,000. United Nations, *Demographic Yearbook* (New York, 1966).

[14] For further discussion of the five categories, including a possible sixth, see Dennis H. Wrong, *Population and Society*, 3rd ed. (New York: Random House, 1967), chap. two.

[15] Robert A. Hackenberg and Mary M. Gallagher, "The Costs of Cultural Change," *Human Organization*, 31, 1972.

Stage three of the demographic transition is associated with older populations and with an increase in deaths due to degenerative and strain-induced illnesses (Toronto, Ontario, Canada).

In order to further examine the relationship between modernization and strain-induced deaths, Hackenberg and Gallagher studied the Papago Indians of southern Arizona. Different sections of the reservation were unevenly exposed to outside influences, permitting the investigators to rank each of the four regions in terms of modernization. The ranks were associated with the percentage of residents in modern occupations, education, and religion. Thus, the most modern region had the highest percentage working in factories or in clerical jobs, the most with at least some high school education, and the most non-Catholic. In the least modern section there was the largest percentage of persons working in agriculture or arts and crafts, the fewest educated, and the most traditional Catholic.

The most common treated injuries among the Papago involved falls, collisions, vehicles, burns, and so on. They were combined into a compo-

TABLE 3-7   Causes of death among American Indians (per 100,000).

Cause	1955	1965	1967
Infectious Diseases			
Influenza—pneumonia	90	65	54
Tuberculosis	55	19	16
Gastroenteritis	36	21	15
Degenerative Diseases			
Cancer	59	65	71
Heart disease	134	134	140
Stroke	46	49	49

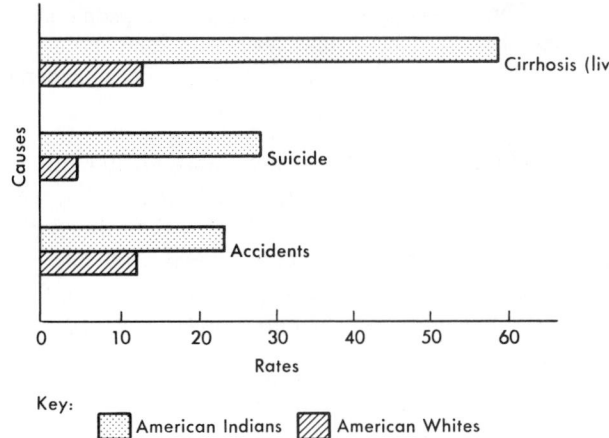

Key:

FIGURE 3–2 Age-Adjusted Death Rates (1967).

*Data from Robert A. Hackenberg and Mary M. Gallagher, "The Costs of Cultural Change,"*Human Organization, *31, 1972.*

site accident rate for 1960 to 1970 and correlated with the modernization rate of each region. The results are indicated in Figure 3–3. Initial exposure to modern technological artifacts probably accounts for part of the increase in motor vehicle accidents, burns, and so on. High alcohol consumption probably also contributes to accident proneness. In addition, however, the investigators conclude that accidental injuries are also a symptom of the stress experienced by people attempting to adjust to a more modern way of life.

Taking still another perspective on demographic changes, it is clear that as the population grows, so too in most cases does the degree of population density. As the degree of density increases, institutionalized patterns of behavior change in response. For example, in the middle of the seventeenth century, Sir William Petty observed that density leads to what Veblen was later to popularize as conspicuous consumption.

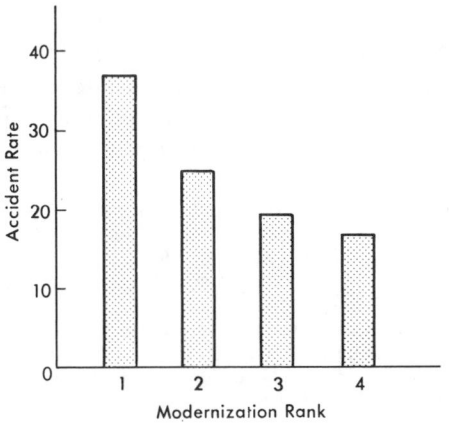

FIGURE 3–3 Papago accident rates (1960 to 1970).

> When England shall be thicker peopled . . . the very same people shall
> spend more than when they lived more inurbanely . . . and more out
> of sight . . . of each other; every man desiring to put on better apparel
> when he appears in company.[16]

With a greater density of people there is almost invariably greater differentiation within a population. If the population in a fixed area rises it will
have to become more specialized, simply to survive. Even a Saturday night
party illustrates the basic process. The first guests to arrive, Mott has observed, form a single, undifferentiated group. As others continue to arrive,
more and more of the guests divide themselves into more specialized sub-
groups.[17]

THE DIVISION OF LABOR

Most sociological treatments of the division of labor begin with the
seminal work of Emile Durkheim. Around the turn of the century, the
dominant theorists of his day viewed social change as analogous to a
process of natural selection. Durkheim rejected the oversimplified and
ethnocentric view that societies were moving unavoidably toward a
"higher civilization" that would be the pinnacle of social evolution. He
argued that the comforts and satisfactions associated with civilized society
were actually mixed blessings.[18]

Durkheim was not immune to the then pervasive interest in the transformation of societies, however, and his writing on the division of labor
followed this line of inquiry. In small and dispersed societies, he said, there
is relatively little specialization. There are few categories of persons who
regularly perform tasks that require special preparation denied to others
of the same age or sex. Values in such societies are widely shared because
of the absence of specialized groups that could develop distinctive views.
Unification of the components of these societies is based on homogeneity,
and Durkheim called this "mechanical solidarity."[19]

Population growth and its attendant consequences were viewed by
Durkheim as breaking down mechanical solidarity. Specifically, population growth resulted in greater physical density; that is, more persons per

[16] Sir William Petty, *Political Anatomy of Ireland*, 1672. Quoted in Paul F. Lazarsfeld, "Notes on the History of Quantification in Sociology," in Harry Woolf (ed.),
Quantification (Indianapolis: Bobbs-Merrill, 1961).
[17] Paul E. Mott, *The Organization of Society* (Englewood Cliffs, N.J.: Prentice-Hall,
1965).
[18] Durkheim also failed to distinguish clearly more than two types of societies, and
his theory was correspondingly incomplete in analyzing stages of development. See
George Simpson, *Emile Durkheim* (New York: Crowell, 1963).
[19] Emile Durkheim, *Division of Labor in Society*, trans. George Simpson (New
York: Macmillan, 1933).

mile. Increased physical density, in turn, produced increased social or moral density. What Durkheim meant by this has been subject to a variety of interpretations; it probably refers to the intensity of interaction within a population. In contemporary United States, for example, it has been measured by the percentage of a city's labor force that is employed in communication and transportation.[20]

Proliferation of specialized groups is characteristic of larger and more dense populations. In other words, for Durkheim the division of labor involves more distinctive positions into which people are sorted. Rival conceptions and values then result from the relatively unique experiences of specialized groups, and the number and intensity of shared sentiments shrink correspondingly. Shared religious values come to embrace an increasingly smaller part of social life; law and morality become increasingly separate; and so on. But the functional dependence of specialized positions on each other is very great, and this dependence provides the basis for a different type of solidarity. Durkheim labeled this solidarity "organic."

In clarifying Durkheim's contribution, Kemper questions his initial assumption that "earlier" societies (those based on mechanical solidarity) do not possess a functionally interdependent division of labor. Kemper argues that some division of labor has always existed, but that Durkheim failed to recognize three distinct forms it could take:

(1) A "parallel" form: people perform similar tasks and pool their efforts.

(2) A "sequential" form: people perform either similar or different activities, but in a serial order.

(3) A "reciprocal" form: people perform different tasks and pool their efforts.

The first type is Durkheim's simple form, but still a type of division of labor. The third is the complex form, and the second type has been largely ignored.[21]

Links between specialization and other changes

Using primarily the third of these forms, sociological studies have related increasing complexity of division of labor to a variety of presumed consequences of urbanization and industrialization. The results have been strik-

[20] Frank Clemente and Richard B. Sturgis, "The Division of Labor in America," *Social Forces,* 51, 1972. In this study of American communities, social density was found to be the most predictive antecedent, though variations in communities' divisions of labor were apparently quite small.

[21] Theodore D. Kemper, "The Division of Labor," *American Sociological Review,* 37, 1972.

ingly consistent: almost uniform findings of strong relationships between social differentiation (division of labor) and variables such as family patterns, secularization, rates of social mobility, and others.[22] Empirically, it is virtually impossible to separate the division of labor from industrialization (or the technological complexity in general). It is the means and the overall system of production that primarily determine the complexity of the division of labor. Theoretically, however, Durkheim's perspective provides great insight into the effects of more complex divisions of labor, even if they are technologically induced.

Focusing on the nature of differentiation can also clarify the links between technology and changes in dominant cultural values. This is illustrated by Nisbet's work, which has traced the social history of many roles.[23] The role of the man of knowledge, for example, was originally subsumed within other roles, such as prophet or magician. Knowledge was important to these roles, but secondary to other functions. It is only when knowledge is valued for its own sake, Nisbet argues, that philosophers, scientists, and other men of knowledge roles can emerge. Thus, the differentiation is greater, indicating how a more complex division of labor is related to both technological developments and emerging cultural values.

The relationship between technology and the division of labor, particularly with respect to urbanization, has been the subject of several investigations by Gibbs and Martin. Their basic thesis is that the population of a city is dependent on the transportation of materials from outside its boundaries. Food is an obvious example, but in an industrial city various raw materials and energy sources must also be imported either from other regions or other nations. In order to transport such items, often across great distances, an advanced technology and a specialized division of labor are necessary.[24]

Technological development is required simply to transport objects of trade, and specialized occupations related to transportation and communication must necessarily emerge. There are also likely to be such other specialists as traders and brokers, who manage the actual process of exchange. Once set in motion, the process of differentiation almost seems to feed on itself. Consider, for example, the particular local purposes to which imported raw materials are put. Steel can be used in one locale to build industrial tools, in another to make cars, and so on. Each involves a unique pattern of occupational specialization associated with technological developments in each new industry.

[22] See Robert M. Marsh, *Comparative Sociology* (New York: Harcourt, Brace, 1967).
[23] Robert A. Nisbet, *The Social Bond* (New York: Knopf, 1970), pp. 163–180.
[24] Jack P. Gibbs and Walter Martin, "Urbanization, Technology and the Division of Labor," *American Sociological Review*, 27, 1962.

Urban populations are dependent upon the extensive transportation of food and materials from outside the city (Brooklyn, New York).

Gibbs and Martin analyzed a sample of forty-five nations to test the hypothesized links between the transportation of materials, technology, specialization, and urbanization (indicated by the percentage of the country's population living in a metropolitan area). On this measure (circa 1950), the least urban country was Pakistan (5 percent) and the most urban was the United Kingdom (72 percent). From United Nations data on each country they obtained information on occupational specialization (indicated by amount of industrial diversification),[25] technological development, and external trade (amount imported times distance traveled).

Subsequent analysis showed generally strong and positive relationships among the above three variables and between them and urbanization. The higher a nation scored on any one, the higher that nation tended to score on all others. One way of seeing these relationships is by comparing countries of similar and dissimilar degrees of urbanization. This comparison is presented in Table 3–8.

The data in Table 3–8 show that there are exceptions to the general pattern. Though it was only a moderately urbanized country in 1950, note that France scored more like the highly urbanized countries on all variables. The expected relationships were typically quite strongly confirmed,

[25] The division of labor, or occupational specialization, was measured by the diversification of industries; for example, the distribution of the labor force in manufacturing, commerce, transportation. It is apparent, though, that people in different industries may still do the same things (e.g., accountants). Therefore, it is not an ideal measure of the division of labor, but it will differentiate predominantly agricultural societies from others.

TABLE 3-8   The industrial correlates of urbanization.

Country	Occupational Specialization	Technological Development	External Trade
Low (less than 20% urban)			
Columbia	.66	.3	119
Egypt	.64	.2	143
Haiti	.30	0	46
Thailand	.27	0	35
Moderate (20-40% urban)			
Cuba	.74	.5	248
France	.81	2.0	360
Greece	.71	.2	235
Japan	.71	.8	164
High (over 40% urban)			
Australia	.83	3.1	1457
Canada	.82	6.5	1373
Netherlands	.81	2.0	655
United States	.81	7.7	381

Data from Jack P. Gibbs and Walter Martin, "Urbanization, Technology and the Division of Labor," American Sociological Review, *27, 1962.*

however. (Rank-order correlations among the four variables, in the entire sample, range from .79 to .91.)

The kinds of urban area, however, can be very different. Cities range in population from those with a few thousand inhabitants to those with hundreds of thousands or millions. The need to import materials, and the corresponding technological and occupational developments, should certainly be greater the larger the city if the Gibbs-Martin theory is correct. To demonstrate this contention, they examined the correlations among these variables according to the size of urban areas in each country. The results show, as expected, that technological development and occupational specialization are more strongly related to large-scale than to small-scale urbanization.

USES OF PHYSICAL SPACE

Thus far in this chapter, we have considered the effects of technology, division of labor, external trade, and population growth on urbanization and industrialization. If the physical results of these processes were periodically examined with aerial photographs, they would display a changing geographical pattern. In part, the ecological redistribution of activities and people is a consequence of the social processes described previously. But spatial considerations also interact with these variables to determine the ultimate form of urbanization and industrialization.

Central place theory

Walter Christaller's highly influential central place theory assumes that the geographical distribution of towns and cities will be formed according to various criteria of expedience. In his view, marketing and transportation needs will lead to a concentration of activities in the most accessible locations—that is, locations that minimize transportation and marketing problems.[26] The utility of Christaller's straightforward assumptions can be seen in geographer Brian Blouet's analysis of settlement patterns. From a number of actual studies he has generalized a settlement pattern that would fit most regions (northern Nigeria, southern Illinois). It begins with a simple situation in which there are not yet any villages or towns, but "natural variations" lead the farmers of the region to produce surpluses of different commodities. For them to trade with each other—a logical desire given different surplus items—would require extensive traveling on everyone's part. A centrally placed village is then likely to develop because it will reduce everyone's trading effort. This centrally placed market will in turn facilitate the emergence of commercial specialists to "manage" the exchange process, and also create opportunities for various types of more specialized craftsmen to sell their products.[27]

Thus far we have been talking about a single village, but similar processes throughout a region are simultaneously leading to the development of other villages. In order to minimize travel costs and difficulties, and because of competition, it is further assumed that the villages will be equally spaced from each other. Figure 3–4 shows how the distribution of villages might look in the region at this time.

Next we assume that simple differences in natural resources alone will produce surpluses within the region that are scarce in an adjoining region. Supply and demand dictate that interregional trading will occur. Perhaps this other region is located to the northwest of the one illustrated above, and the easiest access point from region 2 into region 1 is at vil-

[26] Walter Christaller, *Central Places of Southern Germany,* trans. C. W. Baskin (Englewood Cliffs, N.J.: Prentice-Hall, 1966).
[27] Brian W. Blouet, "Factors Influencing the Evolution of Settlement Patterns," in Peter J. Ucko et al. (eds.), *Man, Settlement and Urbanism* (Cambridge: Schenkman, 1972).

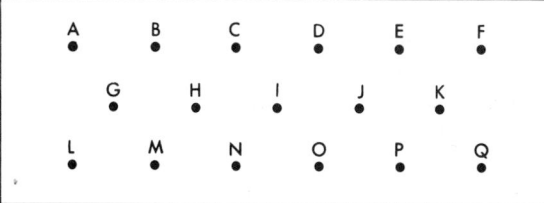

FIGURE 3–4 Region 1, initial location of villages.
From Brian W. Blouet, "Factors Influencing the Evolution of Settlement Patterns," in Peter J. Ucko et al. (eds.), Man, Settlement and Urbanism *(Cambridge: Schenckman, 1972).*

lage A. It has a locational advantage as the point of shortest distance from region 2. As a result, village A may become a trading center. From A, however, the items imported from region 2 must be distributed elsewhere in region 1. (It is unlikely that A can consume everything.) This may work to the advantage of village I, because it has the highest overall degree of "connectivity" for intraregional exchanges. Other goods may also be entering this region from still other regions. Their points of origin into the region may be at villages L, F, or Q, which in turn may become trading centers.

Each of the villages involved is also likely to attract complementary economic activities. If wheat is being shipped into village A, for example, then granaries and mills are likely to be attracted to A. Village I serves as the distribution center for wheat because of its intraregional connections. However, its experience as a wheat distribution center along with its centrality make I the logical distribution center for items entering at L, F, or Q too. In this hypothetical region, villages like A and I are likely to grow and to become dominant centers within sections of their region. At this point, according to Blouet, villages are being transformed into towns that display the characteristics of preindustrial cities. The smaller and less advantageously located villages correspondingly tend to decline in importance.

Now let us introduce some raw materials into the region, such as coal, and the technological capacities to mine it. (This is, of course, the energy source associated with the Industrial Revolution.) The hypothetical coal field may be located in the northwest corner of the region, in the middle of a triangle formed by villages A, B, and G. Mines will be dug right at the source of the raw material. So, a new mining town might spring up. If the coal is to be an important source of energy for production, it must be transported to a production site where labor is available. Transportation expedience, a major consideration, equally favors A, B, or G. But availability of labor and financial skills favor the already more developed A as the likely site. This means still more jobs for A, with the likelihood of more migrants. In fact, it may continue to grow at the further expense of B and G. A has developed from a village to a town to the beginnings of an industrial city.

Meanwhile, if the coalfield is a rich one, it is producing enough for the entire region—and perhaps even other regions, though this real possibility may be ignored. The immediate problem is how to distribute the coal within the region. Entrepeneurial market skills have already been developed at I, so it is a logical choice for a coal distribution center. I is, of course, becoming a major urban center. In Christaller's terms, it is developing as a "central place" that dominates the economic life of an entire region.

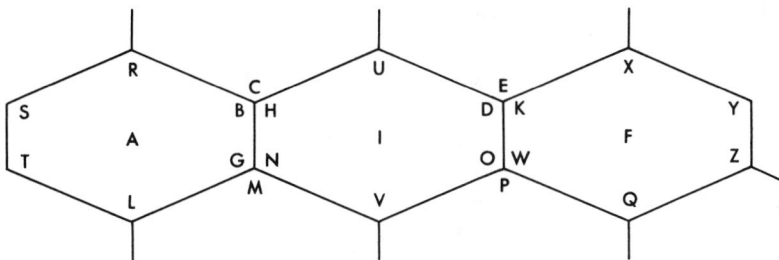

FIGURE 3–5 The new regions, wherein R, S, T, U, V, W, X, Y and Z are new towns not in the original region. A and F are central places in their hexagons, and I is *the* central place (i.e., in the middle of the central hexagon).

Losch's modification of Christaller's theory leads to the expectation that there will be a hexagon-shaped configuration of cities, with increasingly more dominant cities in the middle of more centrally placed hexagons.[28] Figure 3–5 shows how the original region might now look. According to Losch, the most efficient way for the market needs of an entire area to be served is by this six-sided distribution of cities and towns. The smallest towns at the periphery of a hexagon (S or K) offer the least specialized, or most mundane, services—for example, food stores. In the center of peripheral hexagons are larger cities (A or F) in which all the services of the peripheral towns are duplicated, but more specialized ones are also provided—for example, banks.

The services hierarchy continues up to the middle of the central hexagon, the central place (I). It is the only city in which a large number of services are located. It may be the seat of government or a transportation center, in addition to providing all the services found in cities and towns below it on the hierarchy. In societies like our own, vastly different constellations are possible—for example, a clustering of small farming towns around Cortland, New York; or large national configurations with cities like Chicago or New York as their central places.

It should also be clear that Losch's hexagon distribution is not the only type of configuration consistent with Christaller's central place theory or the principles of accessibility. Even in preindustrial cities, for example, a rhombial pattern involving intersecting rectangular distributions has been inferred, with a central place and large towns at the corners of each rectangle. The latter was presented by Johnson from archeological evidence concerning settlement patterns in Iraq around 3000 B.C.[29]

[28] August Losch, *The Economics of Location,* trans. W. H. Woglom (New Haven, Conn.: Yale University Press, 1954).
[29] Gregory A. Johnson, "A Test of the Utility of Central Place Theory in Archeology," in Ucko, *op. cit.*

PRIMATE CITIES AND CENTRAL PLACES

At the end of Chapter 2, seventeenth-century London was seen as a primate city, the city that dominates a country to the virtual exclusion of all others. In some cases, primate cities have literally been geographically central as well—Madrid and Tokyo, for example. In many other cases, primate cities are central only if the geography of the country is viewed functionally. Many primate cities, for example, developed on the coasts of countries engaged in international trade. These primate cities are not central to the entire country as it now exists, but they were central for overseas trading. Examples include Lisbon and Stockholm.

With increasing industrialization and urbanization, the primacy of a single city tends to be replaced by a hierarchy of dominance among several cities.[30] The ensuing spatial distribution of relations among cities becomes one useful way of assessing degrees of urbanization and industrialization. As we have seen, however, there does not appear to be any one spatial form corresponding to the "pecking order" pattern of relationships among cities in a more urban, industrial country. In addition, there are marked differences between countries both in city dominance and in urbanized patterns. New Zealand, for example, never had a primate city, and no clear pattern of dominance characterizes relationships among New Zealand's four contemporary metropolitan areas (each of which has a population over 100,000 persons).[31]

With a current population of slightly less than 3 million persons, New Zealand is a relatively small country. However, other countries of comparable size with similar degrees of overall urbanization have had dominant cities—Montevideo in Uruguay, for example. The difference, according to Gibson, lies in New Zealand's long, narrow shape. It is almost all coastline, 2,500 miles long, with inhospitable terrain. As a result, intercity relations were minimized and no strong pattern of intercity dominance developed. Uruguay, by contrast, is rounder in shape with a total land area about one-third smaller than New Zealand's. The population of the two countries is similar in size and the overall degree of urbanization in both has historically been similar. Both have long coastlines and export pastoral products in return for manufactured goods. However, Uruguay's coastline is only 400 miles long (compared to New Zealand's 2,500 miles), and given its rounder shape, despite its coastal location, Montevideo is no more than 350 miles from any other place in the country.

[30] The most relevant study is Brian J. L. Berry, "City Size Distribution and Economic Development," *Economic Development and Cultural Change,* 9, 1961. For a discussion of mitigating factors in Berry's study, see Amos Hawley, *Urban Society* (New York: Ronald, 1971), pp. 278–279.
[31] Campbell Gibson, "Urbanization in New Zealand," *Demography,* 10, 1973. The four metropolitan areas are Auckland, Wellington, Christchurch, and Dunedin.

Population growth and increasing specialization interact with geographical locations to produce a pattern of urbanization within nations. In many cases, a single city developed first, often in a functionally central location. The geographical and topographical characteristics of a nation, however, obviously influence the chances that a central primate city will emerge. With increasing population, urbanization takes different forms. The primate city may continue to grow at the expense of other possible cities, resulting in continued dominance. This seems particularly likely to occur in small nations (for example, San Juan in Puerto Rico, Monrovia in Liberia). In larger and/or more industrialized nations, other cities are likely to develop, though the original primate city may also continue to grow. Total domination then gives way to a hierarchy of dominance (for example, London-Birmingham-Manchester in England). In the highly industrial nations, however, modern systems of transportation and communication permit intercity hierarchies to take a variety of spatial forms.

Social stratification as viewed by the Mayan Indians (Central America).

4 Industrial-Urban Stratification

In Western Europe and the United States, urbanization and industrialization have followed parallel lines. Their relationship is less uniform in contemporary Third World nations, where urbanization has sometimes outstripped industrialization and resulted in the congestion and poverty of cities growing in size but not in work opportunities. Nevertheless, the historical relationship between urbanization and industrialization has been sufficiently strong that in studying their consequences it is difficult to assess where one leaves off and the other begins. One potentially useful approach to this question involves differentiating between the social organizations of pre- and post-industrial cities. This is an ambitious effort because it attempts to generalize across diverse cultures and different historical periods in order to arrive at uniform categories of cities that differ only in degree of industrialization.

THE PREINDUSTRIAL CITY TYPOLOGY

By the middle 1950s, a number of studies of contemporary non-Western cities suggested that their structure and organization strongly resembled that of medieval European cities. Sjoberg in particular was struck by the similarities and offered an influential synthesis in his description of pre-industrial cities.[1] His basic goal was to construct a typology of cities with preindustrial as one type and industrial as another.

[1] Gideon Sjoberg, "The Preindustrial City," *American Journal of Sociology,* 60, 1955, and *The Preindustrial City* (New York: Free Press, 1960).

Ethnic segregation

The first dimension of difference he emphasized was ecological. In all pre-industrial cities he noted a tendency for rigid segregation of ethnic groups into separate sections of the city. In some cases, groups are actually walled in or kept apart by locked gates. In colonial cities, historical animosities among groups artificially thrown together could account for the segregated pattern. However, even in sixteenth-century London there was a fairly typical pattern of segregation—Petty France, the Dutch and German settlements, and so on. Distinctive trades are also frequently associated with each ethnic group, so that sections of the city simultaneously attain ethnic and occupational identities. This pattern, which characterizes contemporary preindustrial cities such as Kabul in Afghanistan, was also illustrated in the preceding discussion of sixteenth-century London.

The relationship between occupation and ethnicity is primarily the result of kinship-based recruitment into various trades. In other words, young men follow in the occupational footsteps of their fathers. In addition, much of the routine work is performed in, or near to, the family residence. Kinship influence over work is therefore pervasive, and ethnicity provides the overarching link between similarly engaged family units.

Although Sjoberg emphasizes ethnic segregation as a characteristic of preindustrial cities, similar patterns are also associated with industrial cities. There are Harlem and Watts in contemporary United States, for example, and numerous Jewish and Italian ghettos. But ecological segregation need not be related to ethnicity. In many contemporary Latin American cities, for example, there are shanty towns inhabited by poor, illiterate immigrants who do not differ ethnically from the native urban population. Here the relationship between area of residence and social characteristics is unmistakeable. To illustrate, the shanty town outside Buenos Aires is topographically lower than the rest of the city. This makes it a distinctly undesirable area because it is particularly prone to flooding. Locally, the shanty town area is known as *el bajo* ("the lower"). This designation accurately reflects its topology, its residents, and its deprived condition (no roads, no sewers).[2]

Social mobility

Ecological segregation is not a unique characteristic of preindustrial cities, but the social class structure and the social values of these cities combine to give patterns of ecological segregation somewhat different consequences. Stratification tends to entail two major categories: a literate elite who occupy positions of great power, and the illiterate masses. (The latter may be further subdivided, but their similarities exceed their differences.) Be-

[2] Alison M. MacEwen, "Stability and Change in a Shanty Town," *Sociology,* 6, 1972.

cause a middle class, which predominates in industrial cities, is virtually unknown, social mobility for the segregated groups is precluded; there are no positions into which they could be mobile. Values in preindustrial cities reaffirm the historic legitimacy of the existing stratification. People, in other words, know their place. Unlike the case of some shanty-town youngsters seeking industrial job opportunities in Buenos Aires, ecological segregation in preindustrial cities is a more enduring phenomenon, supported by traditional values. In addition, there are some indications that kinship and ethnicity are more consistently and more pervasively involved in the preindustrial pattern. The political system, for example, also tends to be based largely on kinship. A representative situation is presented by the Yoruba cities of Nigeria.

In a typical Yoruba city[3] it is possible to designate nine social strata. The upper strata are extremely exclusive, with about 95 percent of the population contained in the five lowest. Membership in these strata is based almost completely on kinship lines; that is, youngsters inherit their family's social standing. Within a city the class-linked lineages are organized politically into permanent precincts, and the heads of each lineage constitute a precinct council. One representative from each of the city's precincts in turn make up the ward council. Finally, a chief from each ward serves on the king's council. Thus every type of political or economic relationship between individuals of different lineages is determined by the relative rank of their lineages. "The individual counts for little," Bascom concludes, "except as a member of the lineage."[4]

According to Sjoberg, relationships within lineages are formally patterned by age and sex. Youngsters are strictly subordinated to parents as well as to other adults. Power and age are highly correlated in the kinship system and therefore throughout the preindustrial city. Because the male lineage is emphasized in most cases, privileges are passed from father to son, and to the eldest son in particular. Women are in a clearly subordinated position, first in relation to their fathers and then to their husbands. As would be expected, women's activities are almost exclusively confined to domestic duties within the home. In nineteenth-century Seoul, Korea, for example, women were not permitted even to leave their homes during the day.

Political influence in preindustrial cities is also frequently in the hands of guilds, economic organizations that include all craftsmen of a given type. In addition to conventional craftsmen, such as weavers or blacksmiths, Sjoberg points out that even beggars and thieves have been

---

[3] In the official 1952 census, the largest Yoruba city, Ibadan, had a population of nearly one-half million. Lagos, the second largest, had over a quarter of a million inhabitants.

[4] William Bascom, "Urbanization among the Yoruba," *American Journal of Sociology,* 60, 1955, p. 450.

organized into guilds. These organizations are virtual monopolies, setting prices for services and controlling access to an occupation, usually with kinship as a primary criterion. Historically, guilds were also forerunners of modern political parties. In medieval Florence, for example, two coalitions of guilds became dominant factions. One was composed of entrepreneurs and professionals, the other of small tradesmen and artisans. During the fourteenth and fifteenth centuries, these two groups competed for municipal power.[5] Guilds in preindustrial cities also engaged in a variety of noneconomic activities. For example, they had their patron saints (or equivalents), around which they organized major religious festivals. They also provided economic assistance to members, thereby functioning as an early type of social service agency.

The economic organization of preindustrial cities, however, is characterized by a relative absence of specialization. Craftsmen tend to manufacture complete articles, unlike modern workers who make small contributions to total products such as automobiles. And the craftsmen themselves market the products they produce. Middlemen do not mediate between producers and consumers, buyers and sellers. Using contemporary standards, Sjoberg also characterizes economic activity by a low degree of rationality. Weights, measures, and even money are often unstandardized, making trade chaotic. Thus, in the Yoruba cities Bascom describes the selling of "watered down" wine and the near-perfect counter-

[5] Max Weber, *The City,* trans. Don Martindale and Gertrude Neuwirth (New York: Free Press, 1958). See also Gabriel A. Almond and G. Bingham Powell, Jr., *Comparative Politics* (Boston: Little Brown, 1966), pp. 255–259.

Painters, plumbers, carpenters, and other craftsmen congregate daily at a main plaza and wait for customers (Mexico City, Mexico).

feiting of government currency.

That the Yoruba buyer had to beware is illustrated by the popular "money doubling machines." The gullible (up-country) investor would put his shillings into this marvelous Western gadget, and twice the amount would be returned. Most investors would begin with very small amounts, but initial skepticism can be replaced by greed in the best of men under these conditions. When everything was finally invested for the big killing, the machine would inevitably become stuck. The operator would explain that it would take overnight for the machine to double such a large amount. By morning, both man and machine would have moved on.[6]

Summary

Sjoberg, then, viewed the preindustrial city as a conceptual category to be analyzed in relation to industrial cities. The overriding similarities of these cities in different time periods and different cultures suggested, for Sjoberg, the usefulness of the preindustrial category. Given the similarities in social and economic organization despite the cultural differences, he was led to conclude that technology provided the best explanation for them. Technology was specifically defined as "the available energy, tools and know-how associated with these. . . ."[7]

Industrialization, in other words, requires a definite type of social structure that it also helps to generate. The demands of a preindustrial system of production are simply different and result in a different institutional configuration. In summary form, the major differences are presented in Table 4–1.[8]

[6] Bascom, *op. cit.*
[7] *The Preindustrial City, op. cit.*, p. 328.
[8] From the conclusion to "The Preindustrial City," *op. cit.*

TABLE 4-1 Industrialization and social structure.

Preindustrial Cities	Industrial Cities
Unstandardized, quasi-autonomous market places	Rational, centralized economic organization
Occupational recruitment and social rank tied to pervasive lineages	Stratification based on achievement, with flexible, limited kinship systems
Elite education to maintain privileged statuses	Mass education to prepare individuals for industrial employment
A small elite and disadvantaged masses	A predominantly middle class society

Though it provides some distinct insights, Sjoberg's theory shares one important and much-criticized feature with other theories of social change —the proposing of "ideal types." In an analysis of ideal types, an investigator tries to generalize from observable manifestations to the pure (unadulterated) form of a phenomenon. Sjoberg's industrial cities, as a type, do not correspond perfectly with any existing city. In that sense, his typology is a deliberate exaggeration designed to clarify the pure form of industrial cities. Although they have not explicitly said so, Sjoberg and others have actually viewed the United States as presenting the industrial prototype. Poor, "underdeveloped" countries are conceptualized at the other extreme.[9] Then development is seen as the process by which preindustrial cities come increasingly to resemble those of the United States.

At the heart of the criticism of ideal type approaches is the claim that they are implicitly ideological, that they lead to a view of the world in relation to the United States, with the United States as the psychological center of the universe. The criticisms tend to be equally ideological, though they are at least more openly so. Sociologists' use of the ascriptive-achieved continuum has been used to indicate how such invidious judgments are made.

The continuum is an attempt to differentiate between earned and unearned rewards, between those based on personal qualities (age, sex, race), informal contacts, or family connections and those based on objective performance. To Sjoberg, for example, the importance of kinship makes preindustrial cities *ascriptive*. Other sociologists have viewed *achievement* as a distinctive characteristic of industrial social organization. According to Frank, however, American sociologists have distorted reality in order to differentiate societies in this way. Thus, Latin American political leadership that is based on military coups is called ascriptive; so too is financial success that depends on extortion. In both cases it should be called achieved, he argues, but the ideological biases of American sociologists prevent them from recognizing this.[10]

If the basic distinction is to be made at all, Frank continues, it is necessary to qualify further what is based on achievement. In the United States, he concedes, the rewards given to people after they are in a position are predominantly determined by their achievements. However, recruitment into high level business positions is often based very much on race, sex, or a variety of other ascribed attributes. In Japan, by contrast, the situation is often reversed. Recruitment tends to be based on achievement

[9] This is described as the "index" method by Manning Nash, "Approaches to the study of Economic Growth," *Journal of Social Issues*, 29, 1963.
[10] Andre Gunder Frank, "Sociology of Development and Underdevelopment of Sociology," *Catalyst*, 2, 1967.

(for example, academic performance), but rewards based on an individual's age and familial obligations, can be highly ascriptive. It is therefore an overgeneralization, Frank argues, to talk about Japan as more ascriptive than the United States or as becoming more developed because recruitment is more achievement-based.

Frank concludes that ideal type approaches are theoretically worthless, empirically false, and lead to imperialistic policies. Some of Frank's arguments are well taken, in my judgment, because they sensitize sociologists to their generalizations. We will soon consider a number of other perspectives that also suggest Sjoberg's conception of preindustrial cities to be overgeneralized. Frank, however, is also grinding an ideological ax, which may account for the factual errors of which he appears guilty. In criticizing the association of large middle classes with industrial cities, for example, he cites Hoselitz's finding that Argentina has one of the largest middle classes in Latin America.[11] Frank argues that Argentina is not the most developed. But of the seven Central and South American countries studied by Gibbs and Martin, Argentina is, in fact, first in urbanization and first in technological development.[12] Frank's own ideological position is well illustrated in his discussion of the relationship between large middle classes and industrial cities. For him, the middle classes in Latin America resemble those of Nazi Germany and Fascist Italy in providing the popular support for military dictatorships. The growth of a middle class leads not to development, he concludes, but to "the further underdevelopment of the majority." (Of course Frank's premise is questionable, as industrial cities are presumed to lead to a larger middle class, and not vice versa.)

There have also been a number of explicitly cultural criticisms of the preindustrial typology which have argued that Sjoberg has described what is a uniquely Western pattern. These arguments focus primarily on the potential for industrialization, or technology in general, to "generate" cultural forms. We will return to these broader issues in the following chapter. To review for a moment, however, most of the issues we have been considering have related to stratification in pre- and post-industrial cities—the size of the middle class, opportunities for social mobility, and so on. In many respects, therefore, the preindustrial city typology is a theory about changes in stratification systems.

One major assumption—for which there is substantial support—is that occupation determines social status more than anything else in an industrial city. Thus, a family's income, their general prestige in the community and the kind of community in which they live, their children's educational opportunities, and so on, are all strongly related to the occu-

---

[11] Bert F. Hoselitz, "Economic Growth in Latin America," in *Contributions to The First International Conference in Economic History* (The Hague: Mouton, 1960).
[12] Jack P. Gibbs and Walter T. Martin, "Urbanization, Technology, and the Division of Labor," *American Sociological Review*, 27, 1962.

pation of the husband and/or wife. Our initial goal, therefore, is to examine the general process by which occupation becomes a dominant status in an industrial-urban society.

THE LONG ARM OF THE JOB

One of the best descriptions of how occupations affect all aspects of life was provided by the Lynds and called "the long arm of the job." In their study of the midwestern town fictitiously called Middletown, they walked around the streets of the community at six o'clock on winter mornings. They observed two different kinds of homes: "the dark ones where people still sleep, and the ones with a light in the kitchen where the adults of the household may be seen moving about, starting the business of the day."[13] The former were identified as business class families and characterized by a father who worked with other people as a salesman, manager, and so on. The latter, where household activity had already begun, were called working class families and characterized by a father who worked primarily with machines and tools. (These are, of course, essentially the same distinctions as blue and white collar or manual and nonmanual.)

Neighborhoods could similarly be differentiated according to whether they were predominantly composed of working or business class occupations. And from these differences in the occupationally based rhythm of life, the Lynds went on to describe a number of other, more subtle, differences. In the spring of 1925, for example, Middletown was in a controversy over Daylight Saving Time. The working class was generally in favor of moving the clock forward in order to have an extra hour of cooler morning sleep before going to work. The business class, however, wanted to move the clock backward to make their time congruent with Eastern businesses and to have an extra hour of daylight at the end of the day for golf. "Each group," the Lynds report, "thought the other unreasonable." They also report on a public speech by a prominent (business class) citizen of Middletown. He proposed that the solution to the generation gap problem (Yes, they thought there was one in the 1920s) was to make breakfast "a time of leisurely family reunion." He simply did not realize, nor did the enthusiastic business class audience, that in about two-thirds of all the homes fathers were at work hours before their children were awake.

Inkeles places this description of Middletown in a larger theoretical context by asserting that men are shaped by the institutions in which they live. Their outlooks and values differ because of their different positions in the institutions that shape their lives. In modern societies, he concludes,

---

[13] Robert and Helen Lynd, *Middletown* (New York: Harcourt, Brace, 1929), p. 53.

the industrial-occupational institution is the most important "shaper." It has created "industrial man," a man whose experiences, perceptions, and values are most directly influenced by his occupational status.[14] To illustrate, Inkeles presents the results of surveys conducted simultaneously in a dozen different nations. In virtually every country, the results show that persons of higher occupational standing (professional or executive) differ in a consistent way from the middle scoring persons (white collar), who in turn differ from low scorers (laborers). The higher the occupational status, the greater the satisfaction with progress in life, the more likely people are to have laughed in the last twenty-four hours, the less likely they are to have cried, and the less likely they are to feel that life has more pain than joy.

Thus, occupations in an industrialized society produce differential rhythms of life that are related to differential status, and differential satisfactions that are correlates of status. The importance of occupation is made sharper by the anonymity and impersonality that appear to be characteristic of cities. In small towns or villages, by contrast, it is possible for people to rate each other on the basis of long-term, intimate associations. Individuals are less able to manipulate status symbols deliberately where everyone is well known to everyone else. In a small rural community in Missouri, for example, West describes a stratification system in

[14] Alex Inkeles, "Industrial Man," *American Journal of Sociology,* 66, 1960.

With modernization, the social standing of people is inferred more from occupational indicators than from personal knowledge (Mexico City, Mexico).

which ratings are based on such considerations as family background, religiosity, and morality.[15] It obviously takes a degree of intimacy even to know these things about another let alone evaluate them as a basis for conferring status.

To illustrate the contrasting nature of urban stratification, Form and Stone interviewed a sample of adults in a middle-sized Michigan city.[16] Respondents were asked how they would judge the social standing of people they might meet in the downtown area. The answers indicated a general tendency to rely heavily on occupational indicators. For example, "working class" persons would be identified by uniforms, lunch pails, and so on. In addition, respondents were given the following hypothetical situation: "Suppose your daughter told you she was in love with a man you did not know. What is the first thing you would ask her about him?" His occupation, as would be expected, was near the top of everyone's list.

We have thus far argued that occupations become increasingly more important determinants of status as both industrialization and urbanization occur. Industrialization results in a greater proliferation of occupations, making an occupational rating possible. In a farming community, the absence of differentiation precludes such an evaluation. Correspondingly, an urban way of life places a premium on characteristics that can be impersonally "objectified" and evaluated without additional, more intimate knowledge of another person. Occupation is clearly more suitable for this purpose than family background, moral propriety, or other considerations that require extensive personal knowledge.

In order to clarify these processes further, Table 4–2 compares the relationships between an individual's occupational status and a wide variety of other statuses in a number of cities. The original data for this examination are reported in a study by Artz et al.[17] It included six cities varying in size from about 5,000 persons to over half a million. Half the cities were in Arizona, the other half in Indiana. They assessed a total of seventeen variables, including education, house and neighborhood ratings, friends' occupations, and income. Table 4–2 shows the average (mean) correlation between occupation and all other variables in the six cities.

The overall trend is for the magnitude of the correlation to increase with city size. Theoretically, this may be interpreted as indicating the greater importance of occupation with increased urbanization. It is also clear that the amount of change between cities of different size is greater in Indiana than in Arizona. From our perspective, this may be attributable to differing degrees of industrialization in the two states. The largest cities included

[15] James West, *Plainville, U.S.A.* (New York: Columbia University Press, 1945).

[16] William Form and Gregory P. Stone, "Urbanism, Anonymity, and Status Symbolism," *American Journal of Sociology*, 63, 1957.

[17] The data used for this analysis are reported by Rita D. Artz et al., "Community Rank Stratification," *American Sociological Review*, 36, 1971.

TABLE 4-2 Average correlation between occupation and all other status variables.

Approximate City Size	Cities in Arizona	Cities in Indiana
5,000	.38	.36
25,000	.38	.44
700,000	.41	.52

in the table, for example, are Phoenix and Indianapolis. If we take the percentages employed in manufacturing as an index of industrialization, the Indiana city scores substantially higher than the Arizona city: 31 percent to 22 percent. Occupational statuses therefore become increasingly important as a function of both urbanization and industrialization.

One significant aspect of the relationship between occupation and urbanization-industrialization is the type of cross-national similarities that emerge. Despite historical and cultural differences, urbanization and industrialization produce marked similarities in the occupationally dominated stratification systems of different countries. In addition, rates of mobility in a society become correspondingly linked to the same factors. We will examine each of these processes in turn.

THE DEVELOPMENT OF OCCUPATIONAL STRATIFICATION

With industrialization there is an initial demand for factory workers, clerks, and a variety of other skills that simply did not exist previously. A new frame of reference for evaluating career possibilities must be established, particularly for young persons. This process has been examined by Wood and Weinstein in a study in Uruguay.[18] Because of the great variations in its cities and towns, Uruguay is an excellent subject to study. It contains a number of small, rural, and somewhat isolated towns in which little industrialization has occurred. The seaport capital of Montevideo, by contrast, is an industrialized city of a million persons. There are also intermediate types. Wood and Weinstein's investigation was carried out in seven cities varying from most to least industrialized.

In terms of its traditional values, Uruguay is representative of Spanish culture. There is a disdain for manual labor of any kind and an orientation toward noneconomic "self-improvement" (for example, a cultivated use of leisure, an emphasis on nonutilitarian intellectual development, and

[18] James R. Wood and Eugene A. Weinstein, "Industrialization in Uruguay," *American Journal of Sociology*, 72, 1966.

like sentiments). In contrast to the orientations toward hard work and economic profit often associated with industrialization, traditional Uruguayan values would seem to present a barrier to industrialization. To focus on this possibility, the investigators distributed about five hundred questionnaires to students in the seven Uruguayan cities. All were finishing their final year in secondary school and nearly all would then enter the labor market. Thus, questions about choice of occupation were highly relevant.

They were presented with thirty paired occupations, one modern, one traditional. Each student was then given a total score indicating his relative preference for either traditional or modern occupations. In addition, the investigators administered an attitude scale dealing with the general acceptance of traditional values—willingness to work with hands, importance of leisure, and the like. The results showed that in communities with higher concentrations of factories, students were more likely to prefer modern rather than traditional occupations. But there was virtually no relationship between industrialization of the community and the students' general affirmation of traditional values. There is an apparent contradiction in these results that makes them very interesting. The traditional cultural values—the broad evaluative categories—did not vary in response to industrialization, but the evaluation of specific occupations did. Wood and Weinstein resolved the apparent contradiction by proposing that occupational evaluations change in response to direct exposure. As students and other young people observe the rewards of modern occupations, their evaluations change. Not so their cultural values, however; these are probably the last to change.

The general conclusion which emerges is that industrialization increases the exposure of young persons to good-paying modern jobs. Their evaluations of the occupations change accordingly, ultimately producing a modern type of occupational prestige hierarchy. Broad cultural values seem much more resistant to change, although evidence from other countries indicates that they do eventually change. In Japanese cities, for example, industrialization has probably been more pervasive and of longer duration than in Uruguayan cities. Correspondingly, studies indicate that quite different cultural values coexist in Japan. In the more industrial urban centers, industrial values predominate, but traditional values remain quite salient in rural sectors.[19]

The studies suggest that as countries become more industrial, essentially the same occupational prestige hierarchies develop. In order to test this assumption directly, Hodge and his associates analyzed a sample of twenty-three countries.[20] The sampled nations differed substantially from

[19] David M. Lewis and Archibald O. Haller, "Rural-Urban Differences," *Rural Sociology,* 29, 1964.
[20] Robert W. Hodge et al., "A Comparative Study of Occupational Prestige," in Reinhard Bendix and Seymour M. Lipset (eds.), *Class, Status, and Power* (New York: Free Press, 1966).

each other in degree of industrialization, ranging from the Belgian Congo and India to the United States and the Netherlands. From each, the investigators obtained a ranking of occupations. The same (or highly similar) occupations were rated in all the nations and the similarities and differences examined. They found that the more industrialized the nation, the more alike the occupational prestige hierarchies. Physicians, executives, and teachers uniformly were accorded high prestige; clerks and salespersons were in the middle; unskilled workers and laborers at the bottom. Even among countries dissimilar in degree of industrialization, the degree of congruence in occupational prestige was still very high. Finally, the rankings were quite similar even among nations whose levels of economic development (as measured by gross national product) were very different.

The conclusion which follows is that in all but the least differentiated agricultural societies, a degree of industrialization results in certain shared values—for example, that health is important, that education is good, and so on. Correspondingly, the practitioners of such occupations (physicians, teachers) are accorded high prestige. Increasing bureaucratization results in demands for less skilled clerical personnel who are accorded moderate prestige, and so on. The importance of industrialization as a generator of such values is indicated by the apparent inability of different traditional cultures to produce inversions in the prestige hierarchy, except within a very small range. These findings are quite consistent with Sjoberg's emphasis on industrialization as a molder of the social structure. In addition, industrialization is also expected to increase the rate of mobility. It should be clear in this context that our focus will be on occupational mobility as opposed to various other types of possible changes in status.

INDUSTRIALIZATION AND MOBILITY

A basic statement of the expected relationship is that prior to industrialization, rural or urban stratification is ascribed, based largely on location in kinship organizations. Cultural values are assumed to reinforce tradition by stressing the desirability of sons following in their fathers' footsteps. Thus, there is little mobility. With industrialization, however, the tie to tradition is weakened, inherited kinship locations are less salient, and there is a greater probability of mobility occurring.[21] It may also be assumed that changes in degree of urbanization exert congruent influences.

On closer inspection, we can identify two distinct propositions in this statement. First, the hypothesis that rates of mobility vary directly in relation to degree of industrialization, and second, that variations in rates of mobility can be best explained by changes in value orientations gener-

[21] Kingsley Davis, "The Role of Class Mobility in Economic Development," *Population Review*, 6, 1962.

ated by industrialization. The second hypothesis rests on the first. A consistent relationship between mobility and industrialization must be demonstrated before the relationship can be attributed to changes in industrial values. (Viewed conversely, failure to confirm the first hypothesis precludes confirmation of the second.)

Entry into the elite

One limited, but very important, aspect of the first proposition concerns mobility into the ranks of high status or elite groups, because pre-industrial cities are characterized by a highly visible elite. Marsh has studied this type of movement in a preindustrial and in a highly industrial society. The first sample was of about 1,000 government officials in China between 1831 and 1879. The industrial sample consisted of about 2,500 contemporary American engineers, many of whom were high-ranking officials of large organizations.[22]

This approach raises some immediate questions concerning the comparability of the two groups. They are most alike, Marsh states, in their means of entry into an elite group. All the engineers held degrees from the same university and all the officials held degrees from the same government examination system. Further, it would be difficult to find two more comparable groups. Current American government officials would not be more comparable, for example, because their nineteenth-century Chinese counterparts had relatively greater prestige. In addition, those in both samples were divided into three subcategories to permit more precise comparisons of relatively elite groups. For example, the highest American group consisted of engineers who had become company presidents and vice-presidents. They were compared to the highest-ranking Chinese officials.

Marsh first analyzed both groups with respect to intergenerational mobility. He noted the status level of fathers of persons in both types of elite groups, then compared the distributions of the fathers' statuses. The results show a more widely distributed pattern of fathers' status for the engineers than the officials. Specifically, almost three-fourths of the Chinese officials were sons of the highest-status fathers in their society, compared to 40 percent of the American engineers. As expected, intergenerational mobility into elite groups appears to be more open in the industrial than in the preindustrial society.

Marsh then compared the two groups with respect to career advancement; that is, the relationship between the position of origin in the organization and the position eventually attained. In both groups, the influence of family background (as indicated by father's status) is found to be minimal.

[22] Robert Marsh, "Values, Demand and Social Mobility," *American Sociological Review*, 28, 1963.

In other words, although initial movement into the elite group is affected by father's status, this influence stops after recruitment, and this is true in both groups. The similarity of intragenerational patterns among American engineers and Chinese officials is surprising. Marsh states: "In a pre-industrial society like China, with a high degree of kinship solidarity, especially at the elite level, it has often been held or implied that advancement would vary with family background, regardless of similarities in education and in career seniority. But this is not the case."[23]

In sum, father's status exerts a rather small, and approximately equal, effect on promotion within elite groups in contemporary United States and in nineteenth-century China, although recruitment is more affected in the preindustrial than in the industrial sample. Thus, the hypothesis initially presented concerning the relations among industrialization, values, and mobility may be substantially true, at least intergenerationally.

Structural vs. voluntary mobility

It is important to differentiate here between two sources of mobility. One is termed "structural," and it involves the mobility forced or demanded by changes in the occupational structure. With increasing industrialization, for example, the number of clerical workers in the labor force substantially increases. Even if all the sons of clerks followed in their fathers' footsteps, there would be too few clerks. By contrast, the percentage of the labor force working as farm laborers rapidly declines. Even if all the farm laborers' sons wanted to emulate their fathers, there would not be enough jobs for them. Changes in the composition of the labor force thus ensure that some movement of persons must occur. The second type is called "voluntary circulation," and it involves the mobility that occurs in excess of structural demands. Egalitarian values most directly affect mobility, as they influence rates of voluntary circulation.

Applying the structural-voluntary distinction to mobility differences between China and the United States, Marsh found that most of the observed differences in mobility were structural in origin and not primarily due to differences in values. To pursue the matter further, he subsequently analyzed a larger sample of thirty-two nations differing greatly in their degrees of industrialization. Three measures obtained for each nation included (1) degree of industrialization, (2) elite demand (structurally forced mobility into elite positions), (3) elite mobility (the total amount of upward mobility into elite positions). The correlations among all three measures are found to be direct and strong. They are interpreted by Marsh as indicating that industrialization produces both elite demand and elite mobility. However, the strongest (and nearly perfect) relationship is

[23] *Ibid.,* p. 571.

between elite demand and elite mobility. Virtually all the variation in amounts of elite mobility is due to structural modification, or demand.

The conclusion suggested by these findings supports the first proposition, that intergenerational differences in elite mobility are due to industrialization. With respect to the second proposition, however, although achievement values may be strongest in industrial societies, the increased rate of mobility in such societies does not appear to be a consequence of these values. In diagram form, the relationships are as follows:

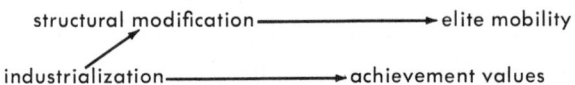

structural modification ⟶ elite mobility

industrialization ⟶ achievement values

The effects of structural influences on rates of mobility are further clarified by Cutright's use of a "Q statistic."[24] Q is a measure of inheritance; thus it represents the complement of mobility. In other words, all sons whose general status—vis-à-vis their fathers—does not change may be said to inherit their fathers' occupational position. A Q value of 1.0 indicates complete inheritance, or no intergenerational movement. A value of 0, by contrast, indicates total movement, or no inheritance. Built into the calculation of Q is a control for the effects of structural changes. If all the observed movement in a society is due to structural modification, the value of Q will be 1.0, indicating no voluntary intergenerational mobility.

In order to measure degree of industrialization, Cutright utilized various indices that actually relate to both industrialization and urbanization. These included technological development, literacy rates, rural-urban population ratios, and family size. All were highly interrelated and combined into a single measure. This industrialization index was then found to be very highly correlated with occupational inheritance. The index accounted for over three-fourths of the variation between nations in inheritance. Further, Cutright was also able to demonstrate that structural modifications rather than value changes were the mechanism through which industrialization affected mobility. This was shown by correlating total mobility from all sources in each society with structural modifications (as indicated in Q). The resultant correlation was almost perfect. Thus, there is further support for the assertion that more egalitarian values are, like mobility itself, a reaction to industrialization (rather than an antecedent to mobility).

The Q values obtained in the sampled countries varied from .61 to .90. When structural changes were held constant, all the societies were more closed than open; that is, inheritance exceeded mobility. Despite this

[24] Phillips Cutright, "Occupational Inheritance: A Cross-National Analysis," *American Journal of Sociology*, 73, 1968.

TABLE 4-3   Variations in occupational inheritance.

Nation	Q Value
Great Britain	.614
Netherlands	.684
United States	.685
Denmark	.689
Norway	.709
Sweden	.735
France	.759
Japan	.768
West Germany	.777
Yugoslavia	.846
Italy	.878
Finland	.883
Hungary	.904

similarity, there were substantial intersocietal differences, as noted in Table 4–3.

Americans might be surprised not to see their country at the very top of the list. Compared with most of the other countries, mobility in the United States is, of course, relatively open. It and the Netherlands are about equal in inheritance, and second only to Great Britain. The high rate of nonstructural movement in Great Britain, the home of the Industrial Revolution, is not surprising in light of other studies. In comparing the fathers of sons in various elite groups, for example, high-status fathers have been found to be more common in the United States than in England.[25] In other words, there is less inheritance of elite positions in England than in the United States.

What the results in general indicate is that egalitarian or achievement values—regardless of their intensity—are not of great *causal* importance for social mobility. This does not mean that variations in the internalization of achievement values will not explain mobility differences between persons *within* a society. As held by individuals, such values are associated with mobility within a society. Intersocietal differences, however, must be explained more by differences in structure than in values.

The forecast

The great observed importance of industrialization as an antecedent to mobility raises an interesting question with respect to the future of mobility in countries like the United States. The greatest acceleration in

[25] Joel Gerstl and Robert Perrucci, "Educational Channels and Elite Mobility," *Sociology of Education*, 3, 1965.

rates of industrialization has probably already occurred in this country. New technological innovations and more automation will surely come, but their relative effects—in terms of degree of industrialization—will necessarily be less than those of the earlier changes. Can we therefore expect a relative decline in rates of intergenerational mobility? To be more specific, a high percentage of the structural modification in preceding decades has involved the displacement of farmers and manual laborers. Although the percentage of the labor force engaged in these occupations may continue to be reduced toward some hypothetical minimum, the rate of decline will necessarily be smaller. In terms of the conceptual dichotomy we have been following, then, rates of mobility should become increasingly dependent on societal values. Voluntary circulation may ultimately account for more of the total mobility than structural modification.[26]

A comparison of the United States with Australia, presented by Broom and Jones, is illustrative of this forecast. There are two important reasons for selecting Australia. First, it is a relatively unique country in that it has traditionally had large-scale agricultural industrialization. There has been little recent agricultural to industrial-urban movement of the labor force. Second, Australia has long been considered highly egalitarian in orientation. Do these conditions result in a higher than expected rate of intergenerational mobility? The two countries were compared according to amount and type of mobility by breaking down total observed mobility into structurally forced and voluntary circulation components. Expected rates of mobility were also calculated, based on the assumption that there would be no occupational inheritance in the society. Finally, observed and expected rates were examined for discrepancies. The resultant statistical summary of mobility in the two societies is presented in Table 4–4.

Examination of the figures shows a greater total amount of mobility in the United States. As a result, the United States' pattern is closer to an

[26] Leonard Broom and F. Lancaster Jones, "Father-To-Son Mobility: Australia in Comparative Perspective," *American Journal of Sociology,* 74, 1969. See also F. Lancester Jones, "Occupational Achievement in Australia and the United States," *American Journal of Sociology,* 77, 1971.

TABLE 4-4 Sources of mobility.

Characteristic	Country	
	Australia	United States
Total observed mobility	42%	49%
Structural mobility	10	23
Circulation mobility	32	26
Expected mobility	62	64
Deviation: observed-expected	−20	−15

open system of mobility (observed minus expected is smaller). More of the total mobility in Australia, however, is due to voluntary circulation, which may reflect the importance of egalitarian values. As the rate of structural change declines in the United States and elsewhere, Australia's situation may foretell a future in which mobility is increasingly dependent on opportunities that are not forced by changes in the occupational structure. Egalitarian values and the opportunities they generate may then be of paramount importance in determining the rate of mobility within a society.

SUMMARY

In this chapter we have begun our investigation into the interplay between industrialization and urbanization. A major difference among cities of varying degrees of industrialization was found to be the nature of stratification and mobility. The preindustrial city appears to be characterized by a small elite and a large illiterate mass. There is little opportunity for intergenerational social mobility because of the strong tendency for sons to follow in their fathers' footsteps. Industrialization leads to a more differentiated occupational structure, however, and both industrialization and urbanization lead to the extraction of occupation from the kinship system and its elevation to a salient position in the stratification system. Correspondingly, comparative studies indicate that rates of occupational mobility increase as a function of the structurally induced changes of increasing industrialization. Egalitarian values are associated with the increased mobility of more industrialized societies, but the relationship between values and rates of mobility does not appear to be a causal one. As the overall structural effects of industrialization decline in the future, however, the strength of egalitarian values may come to play a more important causal role.

In this chapter we have emphasized stratification and mobility changes associated with industrialization. In the following chapter we will continue to contrast pre- and post-industrial cities, but will focus on aspects of social organization other than stratification.

Brooklyn, New York.

5 Industrial-Urban Social Organization

IN SJOBERG'S TYPOLOGY, industrial technology plays an important role.[1] Sources of energy, means of production, and so on generate congruent institutional structures. Industrial cities are associated with less prevalence of extended families, more equality between the sexes, and a pervasive reliance on bureaucratic forms of organization. In this chapter we will examine the degree to which each of these expected changes has actually occurred. First, however, let us briefly examine the nature and background of the technology thesis.

TECHNOLOGY AND SOCIAL STRUCTURE

One of the most influential theories ever offered to account for the role of technology in society was presented by William Ogburn. His began by differentiating between material and nonmaterial culture. Material culture includes artifacts (radios and guns), technology (machines and tools), and their related processes (an assembly line). Nonmaterial culture is all that remains, phenomena such as social institutions, values, and norms. Having dichotomized society in this way, Ogburn proceeded to observe how changes occurred. His famous conclusion was that material culture tends to change first; that nonmaterial culture tends to adjust to it; and that there

[1] See Chapter 4.

is typically a "cultural lag" prior to the readjustment of the nonmaterial culture.[2] Ogburn recognized the similarities between his own theory and Marx's materialistic interpretation of history. Although he expressed an intellectual debt to Marx, his own approach, he argued, did not depend on material changes occurring first. He did, however, conclude that empirical observation suggests the statistical tendency for nonmaterial changes to occur more slowly and in response to material changes.[3]

Approaching the question from an evolutionary perspective, Ogburn noted that there was an obvious accumulation of technology: "The stream of material culture grows bigger." Thus, there could be no cart without the previous invention of the wheel. Because of this cumulative quality, Ogburn described new inventions as growing at an exponential rate. This can, of course, create great strains in a nonmaterial culture trying to accommodate to an accelerated rate of material innovation. The sheer existence of a material invention is, however, not sufficient grounds for inferring a cultural lag. It must first be shown that a material and nonmaterial condition are initially adjusted to each other: for example, simple agricultural technology and extended family households. Next, it must be shown that one of the variables (for example, technology) is changing more rapidly than the other. Finally, it is necessary to show that this differential rate of change has produced a "less satisfactory adjustment" between the material and nonmaterial culture than was formerly the case.

Although recognizing the possibility of cultural lags, theories like Sjoberg's that follow Ogburn assume that in the long run the social organization will accommodate to technology, rather than vice-versa. This premise led to the proposal that because of the general absence of sophisticated technology, substantial similarities should have existed among all preindustrial cities. Murphy, however, argues that the typology was geographically overextended, that technological influences were not the same in all cultural areas. The traditional Asian city, he points out, was more of a political and cultural phenomenon, and less of an economic one, than its Western counterparts.[4] Where trade and markets did develop to comparable degrees in Asia, they were the result of European influences rather than indigenous growth.

Similarly, Murvar argues that the entire cultural configuration of preindustrial cities is different in the West and in the Orient. The context within which industrialization has influenced the social organization is correspondingly different. Secularization, for example, was supported in the West by the Church's separation of its law from secular law. This separation was further strengthened by the rational orientation emanating from

---

[2] William F. Ogburn, *Social Change* (New York: Viking, 1950). Originally published in 1922.
[3] William F. Ogburn, "Cultural Lag as Theory," *Sociology and Social Research,* 16, 1957.
[4] Rhoads Murphy, "Urbanization in Asia," *Ekistics,* 21, 1966.

medieval universities in Italy, England, and elsewhere in the West. Throughout Asia, however, religious and secular law were not similarly differentiated.[5]

The form of preindustrial cities may therefore not be as free of cultural influences as Sjoberg assumed. This is an important point when we recall that Sjoberg emphasized the role of technology because cultural factors appeared not to alter the social structure of preindustrial cities. Cox, among others, has questioned Sjoberg's emphasis on technology from this perspective. He argues that it leaves unanswered too many questions concerning the overall relationship between technology and the social structure. What social conditions, for example, are necessary before an industrial revolution can occur?[6]

From these criticisms it is apparent that any paradigm which focuses on technology as the causal factor of social organization will lead to generalizations that transcend a basis in fact. However, had Sjoberg proposed that all pre- and post-industrial cities were unique unto themselves, an equally strong set of arguments could be presented to indicate that there were uniformities and that the bases for many of the uniformities lay at least partially in similar levels of technology. In addition, the comparative analyses of stratification and mobility presented in the preceding chapter provide highly relevant data attesting to cross-cultural similarities in the effects of industrial technology.

So, where are we? We must conclude that aspects of Sjoberg's paradigm have little support—for example, the notion that rigid ecological segregation is a distinctive aspect of preindustrial cities. We must also conclude that, at least among preindustrial cities, traditional cultural contexts influenced social organization quite apart from the influences of technology. And yet, we must agree that in focusing on technology Sjoberg called attention to an important correlate of some uniformities in the social organization of cities.

EXTENDED FAMILIES

It has often been proposed that in industrial cities the traditional extended family gives way to autonomous nuclear families, and that a more egalitarian position for women is associated with this transition.[7] The logic behind this expectation is that in an agricultural economy, extended kinship

---

[5] Vatro Murvar, "Some Tentative Modifications of Weber's Typology," *Social Forces,* 44, 1966.

[6] Oliver C. Cox, "The Preindustrial City Reconsidered," *Sociological Quarterly,* 5, 1964.

[7] William J. Goode, *World Revolution and Family Patterns* (New York: Free Press, 1963).

groups provide a suitable basis for organizing activities. Extended families are most often patrilineal in structure, so women are in generally subordinated positions. With industrialization, however, the male's industrial employment removes the functional basis of extended families, and job-related mobility may actually separate members of extended families. As the intergenerational tie is weakened, a horizontal tie (between spouses) is strengthened. The less the solidarity of extended families, the more egalitarian the relative position of males and females will be.

Until quite recently, there has been a surprising absence of data on the effects of industrial-urban life on family structure. And as data have begun to appear, they have supported only some aspects of the expected relationships. Analyses of households in India between 1900 and 1950, for example, show no changes in typical size; no tendency for smaller nuclear families to increase as the country industrialized. Correspondingly, a study by Conklin in the Dharwar district of India in 1969 shows that household compositions are the same in Dharwar City (a district capital of 75,000) as in the twenty-six district villages outside the city.[8] Nuclear and extended (intergenerational) families occur with almost identical frequency in both.

Conklin's study does show changes in certain relevant attitudes, however. To illustrate, the best age for a girl to marry is generally considered to be older in the city than the country. This is important because early marriage for a woman is associated with wives' lack of power over household affairs and continued control by the male lineage. (Differences are also related to respondents' level of education; the best age for a girl to marry increases with the education of both rural and urban dwellers). Belief in traditional family norms is also stronger in rural than in urban settings. Rural fathers are more likely to believe that they should select their child's spouse, that widows should not remarry, and that disciplining a son is the father's (not the mother's) prerogative. (These latter differences are due solely to rural-urban residence; level of education is not a factor).

Certain ways of behaving within households are also shown by Conklin to vary from rural to urban contexts. Rural men, for example, are more likely to avoid playing with their children in front of elders, a sign of respect. They also report feeling closer to their mothers than to their wives. With respect to these rural-urban contrasts, education again produces significant differences.

The role of education in shaping family patterns is further clarified in a study of the Bassa in Monrovia, the industrial center of the Republic of Liberia (1970 population, circa 125,000). Particularly since 1950, Handwerker reports, there has been substantial industrialization in this

---

[8] George H. Conklin, "Emerging Conjugal Role Patterns in a Joint Family System," *Journal of Marriage and the Family,* 45, 1973.

city—new iron mines, manufacturing plants, and so on. Working in these industries or in the newly emerging government bureaucracy necessitates education not previously required of Bassa farmers. In Monrovia, Handwerker states, there is now a nearly perfect relationship between educational attainment and occupational standing. The illiterates are unskilled messengers and dock-loaders, the moderately educated are skilled mechanics and clerks, and the best educated are teachers, lawyers, and so on. A person's occupational level is, in turn, highly related to his income.[9]

Residentially unified nuclear families (all members under the same roof) are found to require at least modest incomes. The illiterate, unskilled men cannot earn enough to pay the bride-price necessary to purchase a wife and are unable fully to support children that result from the marriage. Nuclear families are thus highly correlated with the man's education, occupation, and wealth.

The most common household type in Monrovia is the independent nuclear family (31 percent), followed closely by extended nuclear families (29 percent). Most of the remainder are single-person households, mother-child households, and mother-child-mother's parents households. (The latter types are not deviant, and their prevalence is in no way unique to Monrovia. Actually, the mother-child family is prevalent among the poor of industrial nations as well.[10])

Unfortunately, Handwerker presents no comparative or historical figures to indicate whether industrialization has resulted in more independent nuclear families and fewer extended families. However, given the effects of education and wealth, such relationships should not be expected to occur. At least modest wealth is associated with the formation of residential nuclear families, and wealth is also a prerequisite for supporting other members of an extended family. Therefore, there is no reason to expect that adjustment to an industrial-urban way of life, resulting in more education and better jobs, will result in fewer extended residential families in Monrovia.

One additional reason why the decline in extended families does not occur is probably due to an error in the basic premise. The assumption that extended families are prevalent prior to industrialization receives little empirical support. Material presented in Chapter 1 casts doubt on this assumption, as does the historical reconstruction of American family patterns presented by Furstenberg. Prior to the rapid industrialization of the United States in the middle of the nineteenth century, there were no accurate census surveys. The accounts of European travelers, however, present one source of impressions. Although not explicit on the

[9] W. Penn Handwerker, "Technology and Household and Configuration in Urban Africa," *American Sociological Review,* 38, 1973.
[10] Suzanne Keller, "Does the Family Have a Future?" *Journal of Comparative Family Studies,* spring 1971.

matter, the visitors' reports examined by Furstenberg suggest the predominance of independent nuclear families. For example, he quotes Michael Chevalier, a French visitor during the 1830s, on American youngsters: "As soon as they have their growth . . . (they) quit their parents, never to return, as naturally . . . as young birds."[11] Anecdotal evidence such as this does not constitute proof, but it suggests that intergenerational households were not common prior to industrialization.

Cultural patterns and actual practice

Part of the confusion surrounding presumed changes in family structure also stems from a failure to differentiate between actual patterns and normative preferences. In many societies an extended family household, consisting of three generations of directly related males and their nuclear families, is culturally preferred. Its actual prevalence, however, is another matter. In China, for example, such extended households were considered ideal. In fact, they did not predominate, for a variety of reasons: some families had no sons; and among those that did, only the economically most advantaged could afford such households.[12] If the focus is on changing preferences rather than behaviors, then the industrialization-urbanization hypothesis is more clearly supported. Its effects are shown in two ways: by intergenerational differences in family preferences, and by differences between natives and immigrants in industrial cities.

Intergenerational differences are assessed by asking both parents and their offspring how they would feel about living together. In an industrial-urban context, if preferences are changing, then parents should be more in favor of cohabitation than their children. This type of question was put to a sample in the Japanese city of Kanazawa (population 300,000). The replies are shown in Figure 5–1.[13] The basic difference is that over twice as many children definitely prefer *not* to live with their parents (35 to 15 percent).

A comparison of immigrant and local Chinese families in Honolulu shows how extended family preferences change as a function of exposure to an industrial-urban environment. Among the Chinese, extended paternal residences are traditionally valued. This pattern is more often followed by immigrants than by native Chinese-Hawaiians, but the actual differences (15 percent) are not great. Preferences, however, are substantially different. When Young questioned a sample of parents concerning how they would feel if a son of theirs married and came to live with them, there

[11] Frank F. Furstenberg, Jr., "Industrialization and the American Family," *American Sociological Review,* 31, 1966.

[12] Ansley J. Coale et al., *Aspects of the Analysis of Family Structure* (Princeton, N.J.: Princeton University Press, 1965).

[13] Howard Wimberly, "On Living with Your Past," *Economic Development and Cultural Change,* 21, 1973.

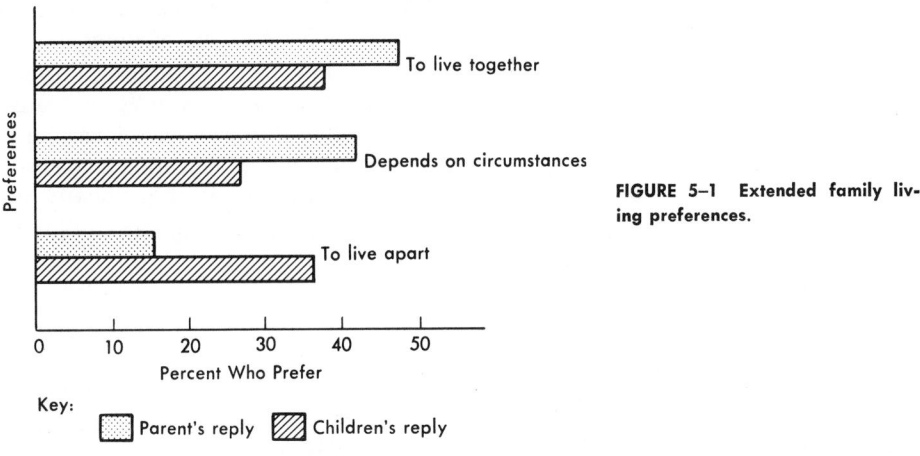

FIGURE 5–1   Extended family living preferences.

Key:

▨ Parent's reply   ▥ Children's reply

were clear differences between local and immigrant families. Specifically, 70 percent of the immigrant parents thought it would be all right as a permanent arrangement. Only 30 percent of the local parents approved on a permanent basis.[14] The conditional nature of parental approval was also shown by these Chinese-Hawaiians when they were asked how they would feel about a married daughter coming to live with them. To these traditionally patrilineal people, both immigrant and local, this was a less desirable pattern. As would be expected, though, living with a married daughter was more acceptable to the immigrant (50 percent) than to the local (25 percent) parents.

There are also a number of other conditional factors. In the study of Kanazawa, for example, Wimberly differentiates between two types of Japanese families. One is the "downtown merchant class" who have traditionally operated small-scale enterprises. For them, the traditional extended family is related to business and household succession. The second type is the "white collar class," typically employed in government bureaucracies. For this group, extended family living is an expedient way to support elderly parents. Thus, one pattern (extended family living) is associated with two quite different functions. There are, correspondingly, different attitudes toward joint family dwellings. Among sons, 50 percent of the merchant class would prefer to live apart from parents, compared to only 20 percent of the white collar. As would also be expected, fewer of the parents (15 percent in each class) than the sons would prefer to live apart.[15]

What we do know is that generalizing about extended family trends is risky. The data indicate that the overall prevalence of joint family house-

[14] Nancy F. Young, "Changes in Values and Strategies among Chinese in Hawaii," *Sociology and Social Research,* 56, 1972.
[15] Wimberly, *op. cit.*

holds does not decline with industrialization and urbanization. It does not decline because extended-family households are part of different cultural configurations that are not uniformly influenced by industrialization and urbanization. In addition, a variety of circumstances mitigate against such residential units even when they are considered cultural ideals. It is preferences that change as industrialization and urbanization appear to bring extended family living into increasing disfavor. In other words, the result of this change is to bring family preferences and actual family patterns into closer accord.

The "culture conflict" theory

Before leaving the matter of extended families, there is one other related issue to be discussed. The "cultural conflict" perspective in part originally led to the expectation that extended families would decline. Urban life styles, with their emphasis on rationality and impersonality, are assumed to be inconsistent with the kinship orientation of nonurban life styles.[16] If newcomers to a city continue to maintain their ties to family and friends back in the village, they will presumably be slower to develop an urban orientation. An alternative theory presented by Levine is that maintaining old ties facilitates making new contacts and adjustments by providing the individual with feelings of security and by providing a frame of reference that enables the individual to judge his own acculturation to the new environment.[17]

In order to test these assumptions, Levine questioned a sample of 400 caretakers in Ankara, Turkey. Ankara has rapidly urbanized over the past forty years and currently has a metropolitan population of over 1.5 million. Most new immigrants move into squatter housing estates in the northern part of the city. The higher class natives live in the south. The caretakers are predominantly relative newcomers to the city, but they reside in the middle-class apartment houses where they provide maintenance, run errands for tenants, and so on. In return, they receive a fee from each apartment that is generally a fraction of the rental cost.

Living in the southern part of Ankara, the caretakers are separated from family and other ex-villagers who, if they move to the city, are likely to be in the squatter estates. Levine questioned them on the degree to which they maintained "old" culture contacts—how often they went home to visit, received letters, sent money, and so on. He correlated this with their "new" culture contacts, indicated by how often they went to movies, read newspapers, listened to news on the radio, and so on. The cultural conflict view leads to the hypothesis that old and new contacts will be inversely

[16] One source of this view is Louis Wirth. See the discussion in Chapter 1 of urbanism as a way of life.
[17] Ned Levine, "Old Culture—New Culture," *Social Forces*, 51, 1973.

Most squatter estates, located on the outskirts of developing cities, eventually are torn down and replaced by modern apartments (Lisbon, Portugal).

related; the more of one, the less of the other. However, Levine obtained a positive relationship (though it was not strong). He also found that the greater the formal education of a caretaker, the more new cultural contacts; and the longer he had lived in Ankara, the more his new contacts. Even when the effects of education and length of stay were statistically controlled, however, old and new contacts continued to be positively related.

Among those more in contact with the urban culture, there were also more urban-oriented attitudes and beliefs; for example, less conservative attitudes towards women's roles and more modern aspirations for themselves and their sons. Those with more contacts also perceived themselves as "better adjusted" to the urban milieu. Thus, becoming urban does not require cutting oneself off from family and old village friends. In fact, adjustments are somewhat better when people do not sever these ties.

The expectation that village contacts will diminish with urban adjustment is also based on an incorrect exaggeration of certain rural-urban differences. In many developing countries today, people live in peasant villages. Economically, they are dependent on urban trade and markets. Culturally, however, they remain tied to traditional ways of life. As described by Foster, they are "incomplete" social units; they have their own traditions and identities, but lack economic self-sufficiency.[18]

---

[18] George M. Foster, "What Is a Peasant?" in Jack M. Potter et al. (eds.), *Peasant Society* (Boston: Little, Brown, 1967).

When people from these distant villages migrate to cities, they tend to reside in close proximity to others from the same village. In effect, they culturally recreate the village within the geographical boundaries of a city. "It would take a keen observer indeed," Abu-Lughod notes, "to distinguish between a village within Cairo and one located miles beyond its fringes."[19] Similar observations have been made in other rapidly urbanizing countries as well as about Puerto Rican and other immigrants in the United States.[20] There is thus an additional lack of support for the cultural conflict view that extended kinship ties will disappear as a function of urbanization.

SEXUAL EQUALITY

It appears that weakening intergenerational bonds tends to create a more nearly equal social role between the sexes. The woman's status is particularly affected because intergenerational families tend to be organized on the male lineage; father-son relationships are the important ties between nuclear families that live together. More direct evidence that industrialization-urbanization changes the woman's role is provided by a study in Brazil reported by Rosen.[21]

Sample families were selected from among rural farm workers and from São Paulo, an industrial city of over 5 million inhabitants. The latter were divided into three groups: recent migrants, established migrants, and permanent residents. In this way, Rosen was able to estimate the effects of varying exposure to the industrial-urban setting.

Parents and children were observed in their own homes by the investigators. Depending upon the ages of sons, families were asked to participate in one of three age-appropriate games. The boys were asked to construct a tower out of blocks or to build a tinker toy design, or the whole family played pick-up sticks. Regardless of the game, the nature of parental help and the interaction patterns of all members of the family were observed and coded. (One advantage of this approach is that it focuses directly on behavior, rather than indirectly on people's perceptions of their behavior.)

The results generally show that the longer the period of industrial-urban residence, the greater the degree of sexual (mother-father) equality. In São Paulo, the equal influence of mothers and fathers in some cases contrasts with the cultural emphasis on the father's decision-making author-

[19] Janet Abu-Lughod, "Migrant Adjustment to City Life," *American Journal of Sociology,* 67, 1961.
[20] Oscar Handlin, *The Newcomers* (Garden City, N.Y.: Doubleday Anchor, 1962).
[21] Bernard C. Rosen, "Social Change, Migration and Family Interaction in Brazil," *American Sociological Review,* 38, 1973.

ity. Women may learn to exert influence in ways that do not openly challenge their husbands' authority, Rosen concluded. "Perhaps urban life makes women more skillful at exercising influence in this type of family structure."[22]

The rate of industrially induced change in women's roles, however, is mitigated by a number of traditional cultural influences. A comparison of the Middle East with Latin America is instructive in this regard. In the Middle East category (including such countries as Egypt, Morocco, Pakistan), family honor is determined by the conduct of the womenfolk. To avoid potentially embarrassing situations, they have generally been kept secluded from contacts with males outside the family. Early marriage is prescribed (about half the women in the Middle East still marry in their teens), and the kinship structure provides for women who become widowed or divorced. As a result, women are currently only 9 percent of the labor force in the Middle East.

In Latin American countries there is a similar traditional view of women's proper place. According to Youssef, however, the Catholic Church historically created legitimate alternative roles for women outside the home, though this was not the Church's intent.[23] The Catholic clergy in Latin America relied on women to be "religious agents," to ensure conformity with Church doctrine in everyday life. To facilitate their role, women were provided with specialized higher education, were permitted to work as religious instructors, did charitable work, and so on. Because of these historically legitimate alternatives, Latin American women have responded more rapidly to the opportunities of industrialization. Women currently comprise about one-third of the Latin American labor force, and only about 16 percent of Latin American women marry while in their teens.

In highly industrial nations battles over the moral propriety of women working outside the home are largely, though not completely, over. But widely held values continue to support the assumption that many occupations are appropriate for men only. The result has been sex-coding of occupations with consequences analogous to those of color-coding. Also like blacks, where women have been able to hurdle occupational and institutional barriers, they have found themselves in lower ranking positions than men. Even when they enter with the same professional credentials as their male counterparts, women hold a disproportionate number of the lowest ranking positions.[24]

---

[22] *Ibid.*
[23] Nadia H. Youssef, "Differential Labor Force Participation of Women," *Social Forces,* 51, 1972.
[24] Randall Collins, "A Conflict Theory of Sexual Stratification," *Social Problems,* 19, 1971.

Industrialized nations are associated with sex-role equality and outside opportunities for women, but women tend to remain in lower status occupations (Toronto, Ontario, Canada—lunch hour downtown).

In different occupations, of course, the degree of resistance to female entry varies substantially. Because different metropolitan areas are characterized by different industrial-commercial mixes, cities and their surrounding areas themselves vary from each other in terms of female opportunities. Bowen and Finegan have scored 100 metropolitan areas on what they term a female-industry mix.[25] This is calculated by taking the national ratio of female employment in each industry and converting it to the total employment of each Standard Metropolitan Statistical Area (SMSA). The resultant female mix is essentially a measure of women's structural opportunities for employment in a local labor force. Table 5–1 presents a sample of SMSAs (as of 1960) varying in their female mix.

One trait that seems to differentiate potential opportunities in a metropolitan area is the concentration of heavy industry. The lowest scoring places are characterized by heavy industry; many of them are thought of as industrial cities. It is the white collar cities, by contrast, that score higher in potential female opportunities. In a subsequent study, this measure of women's potential opportunities was found to be highly correlated with the actual degree of sex-based occupational segregation in a sample of 66 metropolitan areas.[26]

[25] William G. Bowen and T. Aldrich Finegan, *The Economics of Labor Force Participation* (Princeton, N.J.: Princeton University Press, 1969). See Appendix B.
[26] Walter T. Martin and Dudley T. Poston, "The Occupational Composition of White Females," *Social Forces,* 50, 1972.

TABLE 5-1 Women's opportunities by SMSA.

Low opportunity (female mix of 30 and under)		
Bakersfield	Flint	Peoria
Canton	Gary	Pittsburgh
Detroit	Johnstown	Youngstown
Medium opportunity (female mix over 30, less than 35)		
Albuquerque	Hartford	Omaha
Chicago	Los Angeles	Phoenix
Fort Worth	Milwaukee	Salt Lake City
High opportunity (female mix of 35 and over)		
Albany	Columbia (S.C.)	Rochester
Atlanta	New Haven	San Antonio
Boston	Providence	Washington, D.C.

Independent nuclear families, then, may be the predominant type of household in all societies. Prior to industrialization, this form may be common mostly because of concrete circumstances; after industrialization, it may also become the culturally preferred pattern. Certainly there are corresponding changes that appear to be largely attributable to industrialization. The most important of these are sexually more equal nuclear families with higher rates of participation by women in the labor force, and a decline in intergenerational solidarity.[27]

BUREAUCRATIZATION

One of the more basic trends characterizing western societies, as Max Weber saw them, was a "de-mystification of the world." What he meant was that magical beliefs, superstitions, and daily rituals came to play an ever-diminishing role in men's orientations and in their social relations. The concomitant development, in Weber's view, was an increasing rationality, epitomized in the development of modern science and technology. As the social order becomes more dependent on science and technology, the organizational forms of earlier nonsecular (for example, medieval) periods

---

[27] The entire issue becomes still more complex when the possibility of a nonlinear relationship between technology and extended family solidarity is introduced. Some studies report a curvilinear relationship in which as the complexity of production patterns increase, kinship solidarity first increases and then decreases. One explanation stresses the movability of property or wealth. Thus, nomadic hunters and modern urbanites, whose property is highly movable, have independent nuclear families. The in-between societies, with cultivated farming techniques and/or animal husbandry, have the least movable property (for example, family-owned property). It is here that extended kinship seems most pronounced. See Meyer F. Nimkoff and Russell Middleton, "Types of Family and Types of Economy," *American Journal of Sociology,* 46, 1960.

are increasingly less useful. For the most part, authority in large organizations had previously been based either on religious doctrine (the Catholic Church, for example) or else on coercion (feudal armies). The rationality of more contemporary societies required a new organizational form based on a rational-legal orientation.

The generic question to which Weber was addressing himself here concerns the way in which authority is legitimated. Do subordinates comply with the directives of superiors because of the threat of force? of eternal damnation? Bureaucratic organizations, as Weber described them, are based on rational and legal authority; that is, compliance is legitimated by the expertise, or superior competence, of the superior and by clearly defined and limited types of legalistic contracts binding members of an organization.

Charismatic leadership

To appreciate fully the significance of this rational-legal orientation it is useful to examine, as Weber did, its historical development. One of its primary antecedents, he proposed, were associations based upon a feeling of obligation to follow a "charismatic" leader. Rather strictly defined, charisma is the "gift of grace," and charismatic individuals are viewed by their followers as possessing qualities that set them apart from ordinary men.[28] Charismatic leaders were most often great warriors, prophets, or shamans; today they are often the political leaders of Third World nations. It is not that charisma is an undesirable quality in more developed countries; quite the contrary. More bureaucratized political systems, however, do not permit the same degree of flamboyance or personal influence. When a truly charismatic leader has been in office in a modern nation (for example, Hitler), the result has usually been the undermining of the "system."

Third World leaders with access to modern technology often utilize the mass media to create a "personality cult." In Zaïre (formerly the Belgian Congo), President Mobutu is pictured in the opening of the nightly television news floating out of clouds into the center of the screen. His image is that of a traditional tribal chieftain whose status permits excessive material possessions—numerous palaces, a fleet of Cadillacs, and so on. The government press now calls him "Father of our country" (ignoring the first prime minister, Patrice Lumumba). Shortly after he took office, he announced his new and longer name, translated as "Mobutu the peppery,

[28] Max Weber, *The Theory of Social and Economic Organization,* edited by Talcott Parsons (New York: Oxford University Press, 1947), especially pp. 358–392.

all-conquering warrior, the cock who leaves no hen intact."[29] Such tactics, which would seem naive in a modern political system, are remarkably effective when a former colonial area is in the process of becoming a nation.

What all charismatic leaders have in common is the faith of their followers in their ability to perform feats impossible for ordinary men: to work miracles, to save, to heal, or to redress historic social injustices. The origins of such abilities are almost always believed to be in some way divine; thus, they are sacred "gifts." Inherent in the very giftlike bestowal of charisma is one of the features Weber saw as responsible for the almost universal instability of organizations based on a charismatic leader. This is the problem of succession; that is, of replacing one leader with another. The universality of this problem rests on the fact that in at least one way the charismatic are like ordinary men; they are mortal. If charisma could be taught or learned, a successor could be trained. If it were an inheritable trait, succession could fall to an offspring. But as a divine gift, it cannot be imparted to another through any of these means. Thus, Weber observed, associations based on charisma rarely survive the death of the leader.

The personal allegiance sworn to a charismatic leader runs counter to the rational-legal orientation of a bureaucratic organization, in which authority is tied to positions, not incumbents, and to the competence and authority associated with positions. In a fully developed bureaucracy, both permanence and stability are enhanced. By contrast, the more charismatic the leader, the more personal are the relationships and the more problematic is succession.

The instability of charismatic leaders also stems from other sources. For example, followers often will pressure a leader to try to perform beyond his powers. Yesterday's miracles may seem routine today, and they want to be reassured. When he tries to accomplish what is impossible, even for him, he is likely to be discredited and lose his appeal. Charisma is also unstable as a system because such leaders often disdain to create a permanent formal staff. To do so would be to impose restraints on their own freedom to behave impulsively. The absence of a staff creates particularly difficult problems if the charismatic leader is successful and attracts a large following. One man can hardly mediate personally all conflicts over the distribution of valued items, personality clashes, and the like. As a result, followers often become disenchanted and leave. Even if a charismatic leader were inclined to delegate authority, however, the basis of his authority makes this difficult to accomplish. Charisma is the divine gift of the possessor alone. People follow him, not his organization or his lieutenants.

Weber argued that charisma must be routinized if the structure built

[29] "Cock of the Walk," *Newsweek,* May 14, 1973, p. 58.

upon it is to survive. In modern societies, this transformation can occur in only a limited number of ways. One of the most common is the shift to a rational-legal orientation epitomized in the creation of a bureaucracy.

The role of bureaucracy

In Weber's analysis of an ideal-type bureaucracy, he emphasized both characteristics of organizational structure (for example, a hierarchy of authority) and attitudes of employees (for example, orientation to a career). Research by contemporary students of bureaucracy who have wondered whether Weber's ideal type could exist in real life has indicated that several of Weber's primary characteristics do tend empirically to occur together. Combined, they provide the best criteria for determining how bureaucratized any specific organization is.

In a study by Hall, for example, officials of hotels, stock brokerage firms, government agencies, and so on were questioned concerning the characteristics of their organizations.[30] The items most consistently and most strongly related to other presumed characteristics of bureaucracy were the following:

1. A well-defined hierarchy of authority (deans have power over department chairmen, chairmen have power over professors, etc.).
2. A system of rules covering rights and obligations by position (an undergraduate student cannot be punished by a professor for missing a class—but the professor's teaching assistant might be).
3. Procedures governing work situations (to drop a course, a student must petition the registrar).
4. Impersonal relations (whether the student is allowed to drop the course is determined by objective considerations, not by whether his father is a personal friend of the registrar).

This is not a complete listing of Weber's characteristics of bureaucracy, but from an empirical standpoint it provides a minimum set of defining conditions. And every modern organization will not possess all of them. Consider these characteristics as applied to a certain university: if they all fit, that university would be considered highly bureaucratic.

Given modern science and technology, Weber viewed at least moderately bureaucratized forms of organization as virtually unavoidable, and general experience throughout the world largely supports his assertions. To understand the role of bureaucratization in the industrialization-

[30] Richard H. Hall, "The Concept of Bureaucracy," *American Journal of Sociology,* 68, 1963.

Such bureaucratic requirements as typed forms create difficult adjustments when much of the population is illiterate. In Mexico City, street vendors type them for a small fee.

urbanization process, two of its effects must be examined: its role in unifying a nation, and its role in producing rational orientations.

Morocco's experience, which is much like that of other Third World countries, illustrates the role of a government bureaucracy in helping to mold an independent nation. Until 1956, Morocco was a French Protectorate. Under the French, indigenous political parties exerted little influence, but a civil service was established. From 1956 until elections could be held in 1963, the political parties were largely limited to behind-the-scenes maneuvering. It was the bureaucracy, Shuster asserts, that "both proposed and disposed" during this interim.[31] Only it had the necessary stability and continuity to provide administrative control. After independence, one of the first problems was training Moroccans to fill administrative positions formerly held by Frenchmen. This led to a vastly expanded school system, including institutions of advanced training, in which the emphasis was on technical competence and achievement. And due to the rationality of the bureaucracy, Shuster states, it was able to recruit across political, ethnic, and religious lines and thereby unify diverse

[31] James R. Shuster, "Bureaucratic Transition in Morocco," *Human Organization,* 24, 1965. See also Morroe Berger, *Bureaucracy and Society in Modern Egypt* (Princeton, N.J.: Princeton University Press, 1957).

categories of people who would not have been able to fit into more particularistic types of organizations. The government bureaucracy was thus a keystone of political unification and modernization.

Bureaucracies also encourage more impersonal and rationalistic orientations from those who must come into contact with them. In other words, adjustment to an urban context is facilitated by the migrants' confrontation with a rational-legal bureaucracy. One indication that urban dwellers learn how to do this is provided by Danet's analysis of letters to Israel Customs authorities. Written at differing times, there were nearly 900 letters in the sample. All the writers were trying to persuade the Customs authorities. Danet's primary interest was in the nature of their appeals, and the contents of the letters were coded as follows:[32]

1. Impersonal ("As a new immigrant I have certain rights.")
2. Reciprocal ("I filled out all the required forms on time.")
3. Altruistic ("I'm a sick man.")

The impersonal appeals are, of course, most compatible with a rational-legal bureaucracy; the altruistic appeals seem the least compatible.

The ethnic origins and occupational backgrounds of the letter writers were subsequently examined in relation to the types of appeals made. It was hypothesized that bureaucratic traditions were least wide-spread in the traditional societies of North Africa, the Middle East, and Southern Europe. Writers with those origins were expected to make fewer impersonal (and more altruistic) appeals than those from Western Europe, the Americas, or native Israelis. Similarly, regardless of ethnic origin, those employed in government or public service occupations were expected to be more frequently impersonal than those who were self-em-

[32] Brenda Danet, "The Language of Persuasion in Bureaucracy," *American Sociological Review,* 36, 1971.

TABLE 5-2   Differences in types of appeals.

Writer	Appeal		
	Impersonal	Reciprocal	Altruistic
Ethnic Origin			
Native Israeli	25%	30%	45%
Western European	18	31	50
Eastern–Central European	18	27	55
Middle East–North Africa	16	28	55
Employment			
Government–public service	25%	29%	45%
All others	16	26	58

ployed or working on a kibbutz. The results generally confirm the hypotheses, as indicated in Table 5–2.

Bureaucratic organizations therefore provide stable and continuous administrative control over modernization efforts in developing countries. In addition, their rational-legal orientation is highly compatible with the impersonal and achievement orientations of industrial cities. Bureaucratic organizations are not confined to government agencies, however. Because of the compatibility of the rational-legal orientation, industrial, academic and other institutions are equally subject to bureaucratization. Viewed theoretically, changes in the material culture (industrialization) may be viewed as producing changes in the nonmaterial culture (bureaucratic forms of organization) resulting in a new set of personal orientations (rationalistic, impersonal, and so on).

Philadelphia, Pennsylvania.

6 Urbanization in the United States

IN THE PRECEDING CHAPTERS, urbanization and industrialization were examined as general, global processes. In this chapter the focus will be on the United States, and on the specific processes of change as they occurred and are occurring in this country, with the theoretical perspectives we have already considered as a base.

THE DEMOGRAPHY OF URBANIZATION

The historical process of urbanization in the United States can be described in a variety of ways—by changes in population size or density, in occupational specialization, or in cultural values, for example. The easiest way, of course, is to count heads. In the United States, we have made most use of a simple demographic definition: urban places are fixed communities with populations of at least 2,500.[1] Correspondingly, urbanization is the percentage of the population that resides in an urban place.

Probably because of the simplicity of this measure, a number of other countries stress demographic characteristics in officially designating urban places, although the minimum populations required do vary. Only 1,000 inhabitants are required in Canada, for example, but 30,000 is the minimum in Japan.[2] These differences in definitions obviously make it

[1] For a review of different practices, see U.S. Department of Commerce, *The Methods and Materials of Demography*, Vol. 1 (Washington, D.C.: GPO, 1971), pp. 153–161.
[2] United Nations, *Demographic Yearbook* (New York, 1968).

difficult to compare urbanization in different countries. Even within the United States, comparisons are often made difficult by the use of varying criteria with different sets of vital statistics. Precise comparisons require standardization; that is, an adjustment of figures to meet a constant definition. These historical practices, however, raise a number of other issues.

An incorporated area of 2,500 inhabitants, for example, might readily have been considered urban in 1870. If the community still has a population of 2,500 in 1970, has it remained equally urban? Or is it a lot less urban in 1970 than it was in 1870? Comparing the community to other urban (and rural) places at both times suggests that its degree of urbanism has declined. It might also be assumed that there are relatively invariant relationships between population size and density, the complexity of the division of labor, and so on. If such uniform relationships could be assumed, then population size could be used as a relatively permanent indicator of urbanism. Almost no one, however, fully believes such relationships to be completely invariant. It is probably due mostly to convenience and tradition that population size continues to be used almost exclusively.

The nondemographic referrants of urban are, of course, much more difficult to specify precisely, though some nations have attempted to use them. Venezuela, for example, defines urban places as cities and towns with "urban socioeconomic" characteristics; and the Soviet Union, England, and Wales officially designate places as urban in accordance with local

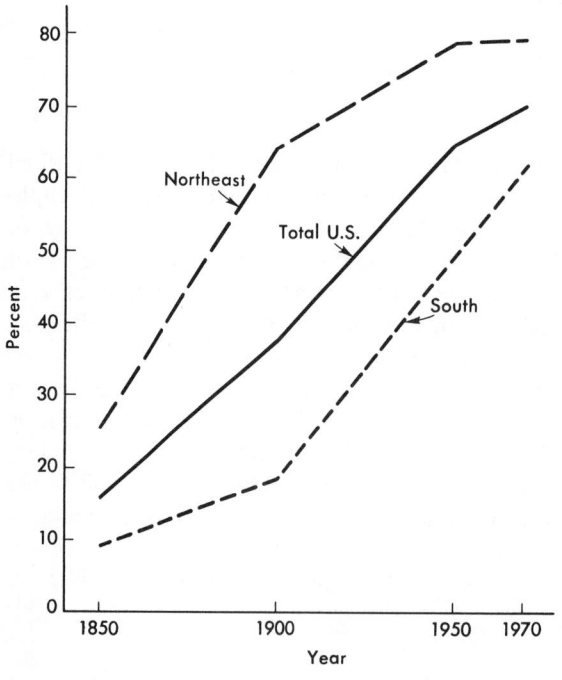

FIGURE 6–1   U.S. Population living in urban places.

Data from the U.S. Department of Commerce, The Methods and Materials of Demography, *Vol. 1 (Washington, D. C.: GPO, 1971).*

TABLE 6-1   Population for United States cities, by region (in thousands).

Region, City	1860	1900	1930	1970
East				
Boston	178	561	781	848
New York	1,175	3,437	6,930	7,868
Midwest				
Chicago	109	1,699	3,376	3,367
St. Louis	161	575	822	622
West				
Dallas	–	43	260	844
Los Angeles	4	102	1,238	3,000*
South				
Atlanta	10	90	270	497
Nashville	17	81	154	425*

Approximate figures.
Source: Statistical Abstract of the United States (*Washington, D.C.: GPO, 1921, 1943, 1971*).

government jurisdictions.[3] A historical examination of the United States, however, necessitates that size considerations be emphasized, at least initially.

Using the conventional definition of an urban place, the most rapid urbanization of the United States occurred between 1850 and 1950. There were large regional differences, with urbanization occurring most rapidly in the Northeast between about 1850 and 1900 and in the South from 1900 to the present. The Midwest and West followed intermediate patterns, though the Midwest is generally more like the Northeast and the West more like the South. These trends are illustrated in Figure 6–1.

Examining the pattern of growth in a sample of cities from different regions of the country further illustrates the different periods of rapid urbanization. Such a sample is presented in Table 6–1. Particularly after about 1850, both rural and urban sections of the United States experienced absolute increases in size because of the rapid population growth. This growth was due to (1) a large natural increase in the population (births minus deaths); (2) a large net migration (immigration minus emigration); and (3) a large natural increase among the immigrants.

Effects of the great immigrant waves

It is generally well known that the largest waves of immigrants came during the last half of the nineteenth century and the early part of the twentieth. What is generally underestimated, however, is the magnitude of their relative contribution to the growth of the country during this period. Illustrative figures are presented in Table 6–2.

[3] *Ibid.*

TABLE 6-2   Immigration to the United States (in millions).

Period	U.S. Population at End of Period	Number of Immigrants	Proportion of Immigrants (%)
1851-60	31	2.6	8.7
1871-80	50	2.8	5.6
1891-00	76	3.7	4.9
1900-15	96	4.5	4.8

Source: Statistical Abstract of the United States (*Washington, D.C.: GPO, 1921, 1943, 1971*).

After 1850 there was no further growth in the land area of the country for over a century. Population growth thus led to increasing density. There were only 6.1 persons per square mile in 1800; it was still under 10 as late as 1840. By 1880, however, it was about 17, and by 1900 it exceeded 25. During the twentieth century population density slowly increased to about 50 per mile by 1950, then remained about the same due to the addition of Alaska and Hawaii, which were more sparsely populated. After 1915 immigration slowed to a trickle because of changes in immigration laws immediately prior to World War I and the subsequent depression. It has increased again since World War II, but its contribution to population growth is quite small.

Like migrants in general, a disproportionately high percentage of those coming to the United States were near peak child-bearing ages. Precise figures for the period are not available, but one indication of their potential fertility was provided by the U.S. Census of 1900. At that time,

In the last half of the nineteenth century, immigration helped to produce great population density in the centers of cities (Chicago, Illinois, circa 1900).

only about one-fourth of the native white population was married. Like most populations in demographic stage two, it was "young." The median age of the native white population was only about 20 years (it is currently a little over 30).[4] As would be expected, the largest percentage of the native population was still single. However, over 60 percent of the immigrants were married, and most of them were of child-bearing age. As a result, the natural increase among immigrants was an important source of population growth. Between 1840 and 1940 the population grew by a little over 100 million persons. The major contributor to that growth was a natural increase among natives—59 percent of the total. Next was net migration, 22 percent, followed by the natural increase of immigrants, 19 percent.[5] Thus, 41 percent of the total population growth during the century is attributable to immigration and the offspring of immigrants.

This 41 percent of the growth is particularly important with respect to urbanization because of immigrants' (and their childrens') preferences for urban rather than rural settlement. In 1900, for example, 40 percent of the total population lived in an urban place. All native groups, whether white or nonwhite, averaged between 20 and 38 percent in urban places. The single category of persons most likely to live in urban places were the white foreign born—66 percent. Thus, the immigrants' preference for urban living accelerated the urbanization of the United States. Many of these immigrants were born or raised on farms in their countries of origin. Compared with natives who were born or raised on farms, however, the foreign-born have historically been more likely to leave the farms. In 1962, for example, 95 percent of a sample of 565 foreign-born men with farm backgrounds were found not to live on farms.[6]

In 1850, about 15 percent of the United States population of 23 million lived in an urban place. By 1950, about 70 percent of a population of 151 million lived in an urban place. And since 1950 the major trend has been toward metropolitanization, the topic of Chapter 10. The population still continues to distribute itself in an increasingly urban pattern. Between 1960 and 1970, for example, the population grew by 13 percent. If that additional population distributed itself according to 1960 locations, then rural and urban areas would each have gained 13 percent. The most rural areas, however, actually lost population, while the urban areas grew disproportionately. This recent trend is illustrated in Table 6–3. From this table it is clear that urban places continued to grow while the smallest rural places lost population. The larger rural areas, with populations just under the size required for urban designations, were growing relative to

[4] The exclusive focus upon native whites in this section is due to the extreme unreliability of census figures for nonwhite groups.
[5] *The Methods and Materials of Demography, op. cit.,* Chap. 20.
[6] Peter M. Blau and Otis D. Duncan, *The American Occupational Structure* (New York: Wiley, 1967).

TABLE 6-3   Location of U.S. population (in millions).

Location & Population	1970	% Change 1960 to 1970
Urban (over 2,500)	149.3	+20.0
Rural (1,000 to 2,500)	6.6	+ 2.5
Rural (under 1,000)	47.6	− 0.7

Source: *U.S. Department of Commerce, General Population Characteristics,* 1970 Census of Population (*Washington, D.C.: GPO, January 1972*).

smaller rural areas, but were not coming close to holding their own. Demographically, the United States continued to become increasingly urban. But what has this entailed in terms of social organization?

URBANIZATION AND CULTURAL CHANGE

The rural-urban continuum

The demographic transformation of the United States has been described in demographic and cultural terms in the "rural-urban" continuum. In this model, rural areas are considered small and sparsely settled, and characterized by lower rates of literacy, less secularization, and so on. Urban places are considered the opposite. To be consistent, however, Dewey[7] argues that the juxtaposition of demographic and cultural variables actually produces four rather than two categories, as illustrated in Figure 6–2.

In this diagram, the rural community is represented by cell 4, the

[7] Richard Dewey, "The Rural-Urban Continuum," *American Journal of Sociology,* 66, 1960.

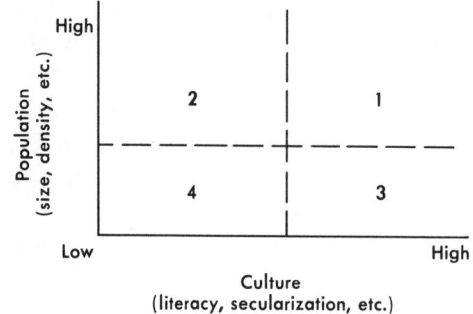

FIGURE 6–2 The rural-urban continuum.

Source: *Richard Dewey, "The Rural-Urban Continuum,"* American Journal of Sociology, *66, 1960.*

urban by cell 1. The remaining two are ignored. The rural-urban continuum would have minimal logical sufficiency, Dewey states, if 2 and 3 were empty cells; that is, if there were no actual communities that could best be placed in either of them. In fact, however, they are not empty cells. Many contemporary college towns, for example, represent cell 3 types. They are small in population, but score highly on all the cultural characteristics associated with an urban place. Cell 2 communities are more difficult to identify, but large ghetto areas could qualify if viewed as separate from the larger city.

Communities that could be placed in cells 2 or 3 indicate the inadequacy of the continuum, because there is no way they can be characterized as either rural or urban. The paradigm is also logically confused by the widespread tendency of its proponents to use time referrants that are not comparable. In his classic essay on urbanism, for example, Wirth began by recognizing that the small, traditional community had little contemporary relevance (in 1938).[8] Yet the historic rural, or folk. community was his implicit point of departure. To compound matters further, the rural-urban theorists commonly viewed the urban form as existing in an emergent state; that is, as an organizational-cultural form that was still in its childhood, if not in its infancy. Thus, they were comparing a rural *past* to an urban *future*.

A comparison of rural and urban places at the same point in time would presumably show them to be substantially less different from each other. The differences have also been obscured, Mann points out, by the "renovation" of rural areas, the superimposing of aspects of urban life styles on top of rural ones. This is illustrated in England, for example, by the "restoring" of rural housing by adding concrete garages; by the appending of resort motels to formerly isolated seaside areas; and so on.[9] Much the same modernization is called "restoration" in the United States as well, and also results in a further blurring of rural-urban differences.

With respect to cultural influences, Dewey rejects the assumption that culture in general moves from urban to rural America. It is clear that jazz and antibiotics have moved from urban to rural, with great consequences for rural communities. At the same time, folk dancing, blue jeans, and tomatoes moved from rural to urban. The result, he concludes, is more like one overall culture than two separate ones. The rural-urban distinction is itself part of "our culture," though, and Dewey concludes by asking if there is not something that can be salvaged. Particularly in conjunction with the effects of industrialization, he proposes that extremes in oc-

[8] Louis Wirth, "Urbanism as a Way of Life," *American Journal of Sociology,* 44, 1938.
[9] Peter H. Mann, *An Approach to Urban Sociology* (New York: Humanities Press, 1965).

cupational heterogeneity may be associated with the continuum, and that urban size may produce differences in anonymity and impersonal relations.[10]

A minimum degree of occupational heterogeneity will almost necessarily exist as a function of sheer size. However, Dewey makes an important distinction between occupational and cultural heterogeneity. With respect to food, clothing, and language, urban America is more homogeneous than was the former rural America. Cultural heterogeneity has actually declined due to a general cultural diffusion. Even several decades earlier, Angell noted a similar decline in the distinctiveness of American communities, which he attributed to improved communication and transportation systems.[11]

Are there rural-urban differences?

Criticisms of the rural-urban continuum are focused on two interrelated issues. Dewey and others are arguing first, that the basic categories of rural and urban are untenable because they assume too much congruence between demographic and cultural characteristics. Second, they are arguing that the categories are relatively useless because they are no longer associated with significant differences. Either national forms of transportation and communication have created a single culture, or whatever cultural-organizational differences may exist do not vary along a rural-urban continuum.

These criticisms are well taken, but they make their points more decidedly than the data will justify. It is true that there is a degree of tension between an emphasis on rural-urban differences and an emphasis on the development of a single urban society. Empirical studies, however, indicate that both are occurring. We will present evidence for both positions, but first we must recognize the logical deficiencies in the demographic and cultural rural-urban continuum. Prior to showing that there are systematic differences between the two types of communities, each type must be adequately defined. One way to do this is to return to the simple demographic criterion and define rural and urban communities by their size alone. Then it is possible to show that there are at least some theoretically important dimensions on which rural and urban communities systematically differ. As an example, let us consider attitudinal tolerance.

Wirth's classic analysis of urban life discussed in Chapter 1 emphasized rural-urban differences in willingness to permit others to pursue varied life styles. (Park, it will be recalled, had earlier stressed essentially the same difference.) Twenty-five years later a former colleague of

[10] Dewey, *op. cit.*
[11] Robert C. Angell, *The Integration of American Cities* (New York: Harper & Row, 1941).

Critics of the rural-urban continuum contend that despite apparent differences in size and heterogeneity, rural-urban cultural differences are exaggerated (Troy, Pennsylvania).

Wirth's, Nels Anderson, still emphasized differences in tolerance in his reexamination of urban life. With respect to tolerance of others, Anderson states that urbanites become accustomed to seeing others who dress and behave differently, look and talk differently, and so on. Although urban dwellers may prefer to avoid others who are different from themselves in certain types of relationships, their toleration of such differences is still expected to exceed that of their nonurban counterparts.[12]

One supportive though now somewhat dated study of tolerance was reported by Stouffer. He questioned a representative sample of nearly 5,000 persons and classified them according to three degrees of tolerance: high, medium or low. Then their views were analyzed in relation to where they lived. A high degree of willingness to tolerate "deviant" religious and political views was found to be most prevalent in metropolitan areas (39 percent). Following in order were smaller cities (30 percent), small towns (25 percent), and rural-farm areas (18 percent). There were also marked regional differences (lower tolerance in the South) and marked educational differences (greater tolerance among the college educated). Basic rural-urban differences, however, persisted even when region and education were held constant.[13]

A decade later, a poll of approximately 2,500 rural and urban youth was conducted by Roper Associates. From our perspective, the most rele-

[12] Nels Anderson, "The Urban Way of Life," *International Journal of Comparative Sociology*, 3, 1962.
[13] Samuel Stouffer, *Communism, Conformity and Civil Liberties* (Garden City, N.Y.: Doubleday, 1955).

vant questions in the survey focused on friends' "doing wrong." Among rural youth, 41 percent said they would try to change their friends or else have less to do with them. Among urban youth, 36 percent felt the same way. Correspondingly, 6 percent of urban youth compared to 3 percent of rural youth said their friends' wrongdoing would not concern them: "it's their life." The differences between the rural and urban samples in this case are small, but they do indicate somewhat greater tolerance in the urban setting; that is, greater willingness to let others "do their thing."[14]

The same trend, but with more marked differences, has been observed in recent Gallup polls that have focused on the moral and political aspects of tolerance. The larger the community, the more people seem to be willing to permit other people to conform to their own standards. In small towns, by contrast, people appear more ready to impose their standards on other people. Some of the reported differences in attitudes refer to situations to which rural people have little direct access. For example, people in rural areas and in small towns are more opposed than big city residents to topless waitresses, nudes in Broadway plays, and so on.

Differences in attitudes of this type suggest a cultural dimension to the rural-urban differences. In other words, the differences probably result from the intergenerational transmission of cultural values rather than from exposure to actual situations.[15] In addition, however, jointly experienced situations and issues are also associated with systematic differences in tolerance, as illustrated in Table 6–4. Further examination of columns 1 and 2 may also be indicative of a more general process of differential

[14] William Osborne, "A Study of the Problems, Attitudes and Aspirations of Rural Youth," in Ruth C. Nash (ed.), *Rural Youth in a Changing Environment* (Washington, D.C.: National Committee for Children and Youth, 1965).
[15] For further discussion of situational versus subcultural explanations, see Louis Kriesberg, "The Relationship Between Socio-Economic Rank and Behavior," *Social Problems*, 10, 1963.

TABLE 6-4 Tolerance and location.

Location–Population	% Opposed to premarital sex 1969	% Opposed to premarital sex 1973	% who feel draft avoiders should return without punishment (1973)
1,000,000 or more	56	34	40
500,000 to 999,999	57	41	34
50,000 to 499,999	66	44	28
2,500 to 49,999	73	50	25
Rural, less than 2,500	80	61	22

Source: *Gallup Opinion Index,* Report #98 *(Princeton, N.J., August 1973). Note that the question of amnesty was assessed prior to the conditional pardon offered by President Ford in 1974.*

change. As attitudes in the society change (regarding premarital relations, for example), there are corresponding changes in both rural and urban residents. Note, however, that they remain about equally different from each other.

The time lag

In the preceding pages we have selected one complex of attitudes relating to tolerance and indicated consistent differences between rural and urban residents. Approval of the government and of specific agencies (such as the FBI), and confidence in various social institutions (such as organized religion) also show consistent rural-urban differences.[16] The larger the community, the more negative or skeptical are individual attitudes toward aspects of the larger social structure. However, all attitudes studied in this manner do not vary in the same consistent way, and this discussion is not intended to imply that they do. The illustrations presented are rather an attempt to correct the overgeneralization that there are no rural-urban differences.

Too much emphasis on rural-urban differences, on the other hand, can obscure other changes related to urbanization occurring throughout the entire society. For example, in his reanalysis of the urban way of life, Anderson emphasized the regulatory consequences of clocks.[17] When cities became important administrative and commercial centers, it became necessary to emphasize time; schedules had to be met, appointments had to be kept. Therefore, clocks were conspicuously located in town squares. Almost four hundred years later, the intensity of urban life demanded the individual pocket watch, and then the still more visible wristwatch. The modern tempo simply requires that individuals know what time it is; such knowledge is indispensable to their daily routine.

As the tempo of urbanism increases, not only does time exert increasing constraints but the significant units of time become smaller and smaller. When two equals meet and one of them is as much as five minutes late, for example, the late party will ordinarily feel obligated to mutter an apology. Two or three minutes' tardiness requires no apology. To be more than a half-hour late, however, may be so insulting that no apology can help. It is only recently, Hall notes, that so short an interval as five minutes has become a "formal set" in our urban society. Twenty-five years ago, a quarter of an hour was the formal set that required an apology.[18]

[16] Gallup Opinion Index, *Report #97* (July 1973) and *Report #104* (February 1974).
[17] Anderson, *op. cit.*
[18] Edward T. Hall, *The Silent Language* (Garden City, N.Y.: Doubleday, 1959). By the same author, see also Chapter 13 in *The Hidden Dimension* (Garden City, N.Y.: Doubleday, 1969).

Behavior in cities is formally controlled by clocks and stoplights
(Los Angeles, California).

Like any other behavioral norm, living by the clock is subject to a range of compliance and results in the experience of different amounts of stress. At the extremely high end of the continuum is the Type A personality, as popularly described by Friedman and Rosenman. This is an aggressive, aspiring individual, found in any occupation, whose daily life is pitted against clocks. Time for such persons ceases to operate as a means of facilitating appointments, schedules, and so on. Rather, it becomes an end in itself; the Type A individual feels compelled to "create deadlines for himself." Time to respond to others in a casual and personal way, Friedman and Rosenman conclude, disappears with the horse and buggy. In a modern urban society everyone experiences some time-related strains on his daily life. Even farmers must carry watches. For the Type A personalities, however, time strains appear to result in markedly higher rates of stress-induced heart attacks.[19]

The kinds of places urbanites in particular seek as refuges also suggest the centrality of time-related stress. Fire Island, Martha's Vineyard, and other urban retreats are places where clocks and watches are neither physically conspicuous nor socially regulative. These areas provide only

[19] Meyer Friedman and Ray H. Rosenman, *Type A Behavior and Your Heart* (New York: Knopf, 1974).

temporary refuge, however, because the commuters must still watch the clock and run for the last ferry back on Sunday afternoon.

In nonurban communities there generally tends to be a more relaxed and casual attitude toward time, with enlarged formal sets that may include days or even weeks. Among the Sioux Indians, for example, there were no words in the language for time, late, waiting, and so on. These concepts simply did not exist in the traditional culture. Correspondingly, for many years there were no working clocks on the reservation and no schedules to be met, by urban standards. This characteristic of Sioux culture seriously impeded modernization efforts. For example, imagine the difficulties in attempting to set up a bus schedule to the reservation school.[20]

Within cities, recent migrants and ghetto residents often display what appears to be a similarly casual attitude toward time. Because their formal sets are different, assimilated middle class observers tend to view their behavior as random and disorganized with respect to time. Scheduled events (a meeting, a party) can occur anywhere within hours of a stated time and not be "late" as perceived by the participants. These differences in time sets form the basis of the distinction between "white people's time" (W.P. time) and "colored people's time" (C.P. time).[21]

As the United States has become more urban, then, certain attitudes and behavior congruent with an urban way of life have become pervasive. Virtually everyone is affected by these changes, and there are few rural-urban differences. In this sense, the United States has become an urban society. At the same time, however, all changes have not occurred at the same rate; several marked rural-urban differences in attitudes continue to persist.

STAGES OF INDUSTRIALIZATION

Viewed in occupational terms, urbanization in the United States involved a movement of the labor force out of agricultural employment. During the final decades of the nineteenth century, roughly 50 percent of the labor force was agricultural; that is, farm owners, farm managers, or farm laborers. With urbanization, total farm employment fell to about 20 percent of the labor force by the mid-1920s, and to less than 5 percent by 1970. The occupations that simultaneously grew were those associated with industrial-urban employment. In 1900, for example, less than 20 percent of the labor force was in the general white collar category of professionals, managers, clerks, and others. By 1970, white collar workers were approach-

[20] Hall, *op. cit.*
[21] Jules Henry, "White People's Time, Colored People's Time," *Trans-Action*, 2, 1965.

ing 50 percent of the labor force. Industrial-urban employment simply demanded their technical, managerial, and administrative skills. And a system of mass education was correspondingly making the attainment of these skills more accessible to the population. Just between 1920 and 1940, for example, the percentage graduating from high school tripled, from 17 to 51 percent.

The occupational transformation

The occupational transformation is one apparent indicator of overall levels of industrialization. Our previous discussions of industrialization, however, have viewed the process in overly simplified terms. In Chapters 3 and 4, industrialization was defined by the transformation of sources of energy; from men and animals to inanimate sources such as electricity and steam. But it is possible to differentiate among three stages of industrialization, each of which corresponds with varying degrees of urbanization.

The first stage entails primary or "extractive" industries. Their distinguishing characteristic is direct involvement with natural resources. Lumber mills or fish canneries are good examples. The next stage involves industries that produce a more refined product from the outputs of the primary industries. Mills that produce paper from cut lumber are a ready illustration of secondary industries. Tertiary industries, the last stage, involve specialized services or research and development functions.

It is possible to view these types of industries as stages because they differ from each other along an identifiable continuum. With respect to relative reliance on labor versus technology, for example, the stages can be hierarchically ordered. Stage one industries tend to be labor intensive. Output is the result of a heavy dose of labor mixed with a small dose of technology. This mixture is largely reversed in ensuing stages, and there is a diminishing direct reliance on natural resources between stages. Primary industries are largely engaged in their extraction, secondary industries tend to begin with already processed raw materials, and tertiary industries are often completely independent of natural resources.

One way to view the progression between industrial stages is to reexamine the redistribution of the labor force, but according to industrial sectors rather than a gross agriculture-industry dichotomy. In Figure 6–3, "agriculture, forestry and fishing" will represent primary industries. Secondary industries will be indicated by "manufacturing" (of both durable and nondurable goods). The tertiary industries will be represented by "professional and related services." Figure 6–3 shows the continual decline in employment in extractive industries. Secondary industries show an initial increase followed by a very gradual decline. Tertiary industries, by contrast, initially grow very slowly and then accelerate.

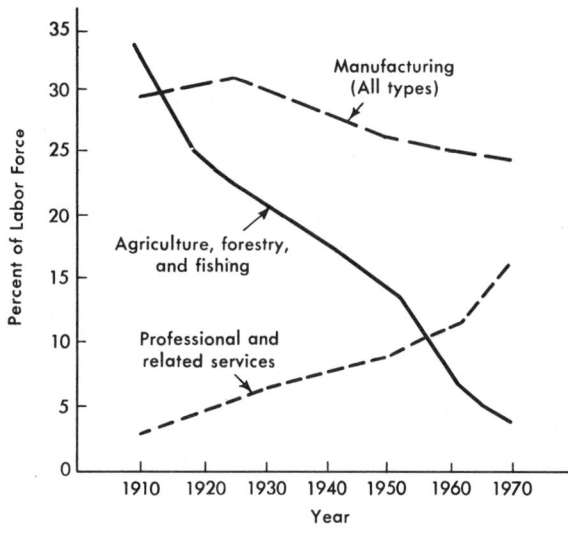

FIGURE 6–3   U.S. labor force by industrial sectors.

Source: *From census publications for indicated years. Historical changes in census definitions of the labor force require caution in interpreting some of the changes between decades. However, the data presented do accurately describe the general trends.*

The output transformation

The shifts between stages can also be viewed as a societal attempt to increase economic productivity by relying on more technologically complex means of production. To provide more products to a growing population, as the United States has done, requires enormous acceleration of economic productivity. From this perspective, the industrial transformation is best viewed by sequential differences in the relative value of each sector's output. Kuznets shows this trend by examining the contributions of each sector to the nation's total product. His findings are presented in Table 6–5. Changes in contributions to the national product (Table 6–5) and in labor force trends (Figure 6–3) are generally congruent, even though the tables involve unequal amounts of time and the industrial types are somewhat differently represented. Nevertheless, both tables show the same sequences.

TABLE 6-5   Contributions to total national product (%).

Sector	Period (1) 1869-1879	Period (2) 1919-1928	Period (3) 1961-63	Change from (1) to (2)	Change from (2) to (3)
Agriculture	20	12	4	−8	−8
Industry	33	40	43	+7	+3
Services	47	48	´53	+1	+5
Total	100%	100%	100%		

Source: *Simon Kuznets*, Modern Economic Growth (*New Haven: Yale University Press, 1966*). *All figures are based on current 1961-1963 prices.*

The consequence of this change in the value of outputs is further explained by Kuznets through "imagining" other types of resource allocation.[22] Suppose, he says, technological improvements were applied only to agriculture and public works. The result would be increased agricultural productivity that would permit larger numbers to build pyramids or temples or have eating orgies. The contribution of agriculture to the total national product, over time, would not show any dramatic decrease. In an urbanizing society, however, more efficient agricultural productivity permits food demands to be met by a smaller percentage of the labor force, the "excess" moving into industrial employment. The economy is then producing more products, even on a per capita basis, resulting in a decline in agriculture's contribution to the nation's total product. Further, the demand for food remains at a relatively constant per capita level, but new demands—for transportation, distribution, and so on—are generated by the urban economy. In order to support urbanization, technological resources are channeled to meet these demands, resulting in relative increases in the value of the activities related to the new demands.

In preceding chapters, industrialization has been shown to affect a society's sex roles by providing increasing opportunities for women to be employed outside the home. Previous discussion of the United States in particular suggested that extended family living was not extensive prior to urbanization, so no further examination of the broader changes in family structure is necessary here. It may be noted, however, that the United States is not an exception to the general relationship between industrialization and women's employment. Women were 15 percent of the labor force in 1880, 19 percent in 1900, 20 percent in 1920, 26 percent in 1940, 29 percent in 1950, 34 percent in 1960, and 40 percent in 1970.[23] (The types of jobs held by women, and a number of related issues, will be further discussed later in this chapter.)

REGIONAL DIFFERENCES IN THE RATE OF CHANGE

In the beginning of this chapter we noted that historically there have been rather substantial regional differences in rapid urbanization. Generally, it occurred earliest in the Northeast and latest in the South (see Figure 6–1). Since about 1950, however, the West and South have been catching up with the rest of the country. Some observers have argued that urbanization and industrialization have "obliterated" regional differences. The United States is now one urban society, they argue, sometimes regretfully, because regional differences involved different ways of life that some people are

[22] Simon Kuznets, *Modern Economic Growth* (New Haven, Conn.: Yale University Press, 1966).
[23] Data are from census publications for indicated years. For further interpretation, see also footnote 11.

sorry to see homogenized. From previously developed theoretical perspectives in which urbanization (and industrialization) generated similar patterns of life even in different countries, a blurring of regional differences would certainly be expected. This interesting issue has been examined in a number of studies with very inconsistent results, however.

The lag in the South

For the most part, regional differences in the United States have involved comparisons of the South with other parts of the country. It has been viewed historically as the culturally most distinctive region, possessing unique values and life styles. Comparative emphasis on the South is also justified by the observable lag in its rates of urbanization and industrialization. Until about 1940, for example, Reissman describes entire southern states (such as Mississippi and Alabama) as being almost exclusively rural.[24] They were perhaps even more completely rural than some northeastern states during the nineteenth century. Over the last thirty years, however, major metropolitan centers—such as Atlanta and Nashville—have developed. These centers now coordinate regional activities, Reissman points out, and provide major links between the South and the rest of the country.

More specifically, McKinney and Bourque argue that the lag is about a half-century in duration.[25] Thus, in 1960, 52 percent of the population in the South lived in an urban place. This corresponds with the rest of the country somewhere around 1910. The percentage of the labor force employed as agricultural workers shows a similar lag. These differences have diminished, but major recent differences between the South and the rest of the country are attributed by McKinney and Bourque to differences in type of industrialization. The South still lags in the development of secondary and tertiary industries. Employment in extractive industries began to decline after 1950. Between 1950 and 1968, however, employment in manufacturing was still increasing by consistent amounts.

This difference accounts for the lower per capita incomes in the South, because the more labor intensive an industry, the lower the average wages. Low wages, they contend, have also lowered the tax base, providing fewer funds for public expenditures. These differences associated with industrial stages are also diminishing with the rapid growth of tertiary industries in the South after 1960. On per pupil school expenditures, for example, the South spent only 41 percent as much as the non-South in 1929–1930, but this increased to almost 70 percent by 1968–1969.

[24] Leonard Reissman, "Urbanization in the South," in John C. McKinney and Edgar T. Thompson (eds.), *The South in Continuity and Change* (Durham, N.C.: Duke University Press, 1965).

[25] John C. McKinney and Linda B. Bourque, "The Changing South," *American Sociological Review*, 36, 1971.

National corporations are making regions look more alike, but a distinctive culture seems to persist in the South (suburb of Savannah, Georgia).

In conclusion, McKinney and Bourque argue, the South is becoming culturally more like the rest of the country as it catches up in urbanization and industrialization. Novelists helped to create a Southern mystique that is slow to die, they contend, but is nevertheless losing its factual basis. In addition, mass national transportation, network television, national wire service distribution to local newspapers, and so on, are making all regions more and more alike. The end of regional differences is viewed as due to the same factors Dewey and Angell saw as responsible for the blurring of rural and urban differences.

McKinney and Bourque, however, make a number of questionable assumptions. To begin with, their data exclusively involved occupation, income, education, and other socioeconomic measures; but their conclusions emphasized attitudes and values. This exaggerates the degree of correspondence between social structure and attitudes and values. For example, Sly and Weller point out that more southern children may be in school for longer periods of time. But is their education the same as in the rest of the country (concerning, say, the Civil War)?[26]

The violent South

To provide a more direct answer to this question requires an explicit focus on components of culture and an examination of whether cultural characteristics of regions have become more alike. One specific charac-

[26] David F. Sly and Robert H. Weller, "Some Comments on the Changing South," *American Sociological Review,* 37, 1972.

teristic of this type that has historically been associated with the South is a code of violence, a readiness to resort to force. As a regional code it was indicated by the persistence of institutionalized dueling long after it had been given up in other areas. And throughout the twentieth century, the murder rate has been higher in the South than in the remainder of the country. The code itself has probably been best described by novelists. Paige Mitchell, for example, describing Mississippi in the 1960s says that changes were pervasive but the code remained: "To master the tools of violence; not for the sake of violence itself, but [for] . . . a code of honor that demands a man . . . be ready to fight with his life. . . . That would make him a Southerner."[27]

Focusing on differences in the murder rate requires that we consider two distinct explanations. One is simply that there is a regional culture of violence in the South and that it accounts for differences in the murder rate. A second possibility is that conditions related to higher murder rates— such as low incomes—are overrepresented in the South. If there are more poor people in the South the murder rate could be higher for that reason, but it should not be attributed to a regional culture. The second possibility is, of course, an unresolvable one. It is always possible that such conditions are present but are not included in investigations. Gastil has attempted to test both possibilities by correlating murder rates with a number of variables previously found to be related to murder rates and with a specifically constructed index of Southernness. This involved giving high scores (30) to Deep South states such as Georgia and Alabama. Moderately high scores (25) were given to states with overwhelming southern backgrounds, such as Oklahoma and Texas. Scores declined in 5-point intervals down to the most non-southern states, such as Maine and North Dakota (scored as 5 points each).[28]

Gastil subsequently correlated homicide rates, by state, with the index of Southernness of that state, and with the scores of other murder-related variables (income, education, and so on) in each state. The results showed that the single strongest relationship was between murder rates and Southernness. Further, when all other variables were held constant (in a multiple correlation), the relationship between murder rates and Southernness remained very high. Fluctuations in rates of murder appear to be attributable directly to this regional code of violence, and not to other variables that are associated with regions. Major metropolitan areas were then given Southernness scores, and the same types of analyses were carried out. Again, Southernness was found to be the best predictor of the murder rate.

These results suggest that although urbanization and industrialization have made the South structurally more like the rest of country, cultural

[27] Paige Mitchell, *The Covenant* (New York: Atheneum, 1973), p. 326.
[28] Raymond D. Gastil, "Homicide and a Regional Culture of Violence," *American Sociological Review,* 36, 1971.

differences still remain. If we are to be cautious in our interpretation, it must again be pointed out that some untested variable might substantially alter the results. Perhaps, for example, differences in murder rates are strongly related to the nature of state laws for the licensing of handguns. If states did vary by region in this regard, it could provide an explanation. We could, of course, still find a cultural explanation persuasive because now we would have to account for regional differences in state laws, and certainly cultural difference could be responsible. In any event, the data to this point are definitely compatible with the cultural interpretation.

It must also be realized, however, that Gastil's data are only for 1960. The previously discussed findings of McKinney and Bourque showed that between 1960 and 1968 some patterns of industrialization in the South changed more than in the twenty years prior to 1960. Looking at differences in 1960, as Gastil did, might just have been too early—that is, too soon for cultural differences to disappear. I wondered about this. Certainly the regional differences relate to a critical theoretical issue involving the relationship between structural and cultural changes. It would be a shame to reach the wrong conclusion on an issue of this magnitude just because of the timing of one sample. So I decided to pursue the question, armed with later data, from 1970. Murder rates for metropolitan areas like those studied by Gastil were taken from 1970 FBI Uniform Crime Reports.[29] Then each metropolitan area in the sample was given a Southernness score, following Gastil's procedure. The 1960 and 1970

[29] The study included a systematic sample of 10 percent of the 157 metropolitan areas with populations of over 200,000 persons in 1970. The murder rate was taken from the FBI's rate of homicide (including nonnegligent manslaughter).

TABLE 6-6   Murder and southernness in 1970.

Metropolitan Area	Southernness Score	Murder Rate
Akron	20	5.4
Atlanta	30	20.4
Boston	5	4.4
Cincinnati	25	6.4
Denver	20	8.3
Ft. Lauderdale	25	14.0
Hartford	5	4.3
Johnstown	10	1.9
Los Angeles	20	9.4
Nashville	30	12.6
Oklahoma City	25	5.9
Portland	15	4.8
St. Louis	20	14.8
Scranton	10	2.6
Tacoma	15	5.8
West Palm Beach	25	12.3

studies were identical except that Gastil sampled from metropolitan areas of over 250,000 population and I sampled from among those with over 200,000, but this should not make a difference. Presented in Table 6–6 are the metropolitan areas included in 1970, their murder rate, and their Southernness.

Examination of Table 6–6 shows that despite some exceptions to the pattern, the relationship between Southernness and the murder rate was still quite strong in 1970. The correlation is .74. For 1960, Gastil reports a correlation of .68. The difference between the two is too small to be of any significance; it could easily be due to chance factors in sampling metropolitan areas. However, the results certainly suggest that despite the existence of structural changes that were increasing the resemblance between the South and the rest of the country, the South was remaining culturally distinct (at least in some ways).

The southern belle

One other central component of traditional southern culture involves attitudes toward the role of women. Thus, part of the regional culture has historically involved a stereotype of the truly southern woman as capable only of staying in the home. The continuing influence of southern culture could therefore be indicated if there were regional differences in women's participation in the labor force.

In Chapter 5, metropolitan areas were differentiated by their employment mix, resulting in different structural opportunities for female employment. The actual degree of women's occupational segregation was subsequently found to be highly related to structurally determined opportunities.[30] The relationship was not perfect, though. Some metropolitan areas appear to segregate females occupationally more than would be expected on the basis of overall employment opportunities. In others, the degree of segregation is less than would be expected on the basis of structural considerations. Because these differences between actual and expected could reflect cultural discrimination, the metropolitan areas were placed in three categories. In the low category, actual segregation was less than would be expected given the structural employment mix. In terms of "cultural discrimination," such areas were scored as low. When segregation exceeded structural expectations, cultural discrimination was scored as high. Finally, a medium category was established for metropolitan areas where actual segregation was about as expected.

The metropolitan areas in each cultural discrimination category were then given a Southernness score, again following Gastil. The results, pre-

[30] Walter T. Martin and Dudley T. Poston, "The Occupational Composition of White Females," *Social Forces,* 50, 1972.

TABLE 6-7 Structure, segregation, and southernness.

Cultural Discrimination*	Southernness Index
Low ($\leq$ 8)	18
Medium (9-16)	21
High ($\geq$ 17)	22

* *This involves actual occupational dissimilarity minus the female mix structure.*

sented in Table 6–7, show that cultural discrimination is related to Southernness in the expected direction, though not strongly. The areas in which there is more occupational segregation by sex do tend to be more southern. The differences in Southernness, however, are not very great, indicating that overall differences in occupational segregation by sex are due less to this cultural consideration than to employment mix structures (where the differences are great). The results again indicate the persistence of regional cultural differences, though to a lesser extent than for the case of murder rates.

One additional and related way to infer cultural differences involves examining relationships between variables in different contexts. If the relationships vary, the operation of cultural influences may be inferred. Particularly with respect to relationships involving race and other variables such as fertility, different patterns of relationships continue to be observed in the South.[31] Findings of this type further reinforce the conclusion that increasingly similar social structures need not produce increasingly similar cultures. Such findings do run counter to numerous theoretical assumptions, however, which suggests the advisability of further examination of the assumptions.

MACRO STRUCTURES, BEHAVIOR PATTERNS, AND VALUES

McKinney and Bourque began their study by hypothesizing that increased urbanization and industrialization would lead the culture of the South to become more like that of the rest of the country. Their theoretical assumptions should have been familiar to the reader; they are essentially the same as Ogburn's theory of technologically induced cultural lags, or Sjoberg's view of industrially determined social organization.

All these theories assume that when the social structure changes, cultural values will also change and in a congruent direction. In some

[31] See, for example, David F. Sly, "Minority Group Status and Fertility," *American Journal of Sociology*, 76, 1970.

cases, empirical research has supported this assumption. For example, some people's preferences for extended family living were seen to decrease with exposure to an urban structure. In other cases, structural changes (such as industrialization) were seen to have substantial effects on behavior (smaller actual families), but only small effects on values (family size preferences). And in some cases, the same pattern of behavior was seen to be associated with different sets of values. For example, extended family households were associated with the support of the elderly by the Japanese civil servants, but for Japanese merchants they were connected with traditions of household and business succession.

Some semblance of consistency to these findings can be inferred if the social structure is analytically differentiated from patterns of behavior. It is true that the latter is often used to indicate the former in sociological theories. However, we can conceptualize a macro social structure—involving type and degree of urbanization and industrialization—as influencing but not determining patterns of behavior. The latter can then be viewed as more or less congruent with the macro structure.

With this distinction in mind, reexamination of the previously discussed findings suggests certain uniformities. Macro structural changes seem to have the most immediate effect on values when such values and patterns of behavior are not in accord with one another. One situation of this type occurs when nuclear family households are the dominant (actual) pattern, but extended families are culturally preferred. With urbanization, a change in the macro structure, the cultural preferences are seen to change in the direction of the actual patterns. Similarly, when women are actually having more children than they desire to have, changes in the macro structure (industrialization) lead to substantial changes in the birth rate, making them more compatible with people's desires. By contrast, when cultural values and behavioral patterns are in prior accord, the direct and immediate effects of macro structural changes appear to be mitigated. Among Japanese civil servants, for example, urbanism induced less change in extended family living than among Japanese merchants.

With respect to the South, if we assume that because of its long period of relative isolation from other parts of the country patterns of behavior and values developed congruently, then macro structural changes could be expected to have less immediate effects. The high rate of murder and the code of violence may present precisely such congruence. Perhaps the most intriguing question that remains is whether the influences of the macro structure can be mitigated indefinitely. The weight of the evidence, in general, suggests a tentative negative answer to this question. However, we must be wary of making too narrow an ethnocentric judgment concerning what kinds of cultural values are congruent with urban-industrial macro structures. What makes for strange bedfellows may seem more obvious to outsiders than to the bedfellows themselves.

Chinatown in Chicago, Illinois.

7 Ethnicity and Race

Beginning in the middle of the nineteenth century, the urban settlement of waves of immigrants has led to a strong historical association between city life in America and ethnic diversity. In this chapter we will examine the assimilation patterns of American cities in three time periods. The first period, from the mid to late nineteenth century, deals with inceasing numbers of Western and Northern European immigrants. Their increasing urbanization appears to be characterized by decreasing amounts of residential segregation. The second period extends roughly from the late nineteenth century to World War I. During this time, immigrants came primarily from Eastern Europe and improved means of urban transportation seem to have resulted in increased segregation. The final period, 1920 to the present, is marked by the South to North and rural to urban migration of blacks. Residential segregation of white ethnic groups declined in the latter period, but black-white segregation appears to have increased. We will also be concerned with patterns of economic organization among racial and ethnic groups and how they varied during the three periods.

NINETEENTH-CENTURY CITIES

The period prior to the Civil War was characterized by extremely high rates of geographical mobility in cities. The native population was young and unattached, and single men moved from city to city in search of better opportunities. The newly arriving immigrants were older, but they too were mobile in quest of the promised opportunities. Even among those who remained in a given city for any length of time, frequent changes of residence were common, mostly because jobs were insecure. Due to limited transportation facilities, people had to live close to their current place of work. Thus, the population of American cities was in a state of constant flux. Between 1830 and 1860 in Boston, for example, about two in five persons changed residence (or left the city) every ten years. Among native-born persons, the rate was only about 30 percent, whereas nearly 60 percent of the foreign-born moved during a decade. The foreign-born mobility rate was therefore about twice that of the native population.[1]

The generally greater tendency for the foreign-born to move within and between cities was tied largely to differences in employment opportunities. The foreign-born were the last to be hired and the first to be fired, a familiar pattern. Employment opportunities expanded rapidly after 1860, however, leading to a marked decline in the difference between foreign-born and native migration. The pattern is clear in Griffen's analysis of Poughkeepsie, New York. In 1850 it was a rapidly growing city, one of only sixty in the country with a population over 10,000. About two-thirds of that population was native-born. The largest immigrant group was the Irish, who in 1850 comprised 60 percent of the foreign-born. The other large ethnic groups were German and English-Scotch. Among both natives and foreign-born, those over 30 years of age moved less than those under 30, and married persons moved less than single persons. The biggest difference, however, occurred between owners and nonowners of real estate, which ordinarily involved a house and lot. "Success for the industrious" meant ownership of land, Griffen states, and those who attained it were most likely to stay, as indicated in Table 7–1.[2] Examination of the table indicates that in both decades owners were more likely to remain in Poughkeepsie than nonowners. With the stabilization of employment in

[1] The city directories from which these figures are computed were particularly likely to exclude foreign-born; therefore, the true ratio was probably greater than 2 to 1. Peter R. Knights, "Population Turnover, Persistence, and Residential Mobility in Boston," in Stephan Thernstrom and Richard Sennett (eds.), *Nineteenth-Century Cities* (New Haven, Conn.: Yale University Press, 1969).
[2] Clyde Griffen, "Workers Divided," in *ibid.*

TABLE 7-1 Residential stability, Poughkeepsie.

Decade	Native Owner	Native Nonowner	Foreign-born Owner	Foreign-born Nonowner
1850-1860	49%	40%	39%	25%
1870-1880	54	35	59	36

the later decade, native- and foreign-born homeowners' rates of stability both increased and became more alike.

The mobility of various nationality groups within cities has frequently been described ecologically as an invasion-succession process. Newly arriving nationality groups would settle near the central city. As its members adjusted to urban American life, the group would slowly move out from the center.[3] At their heels were more recent arriving groups who were invading their former territory. Their movement in turn gave impetus to further movement out of the center city by still earlier arrivals. Specific ethnic groups succeeded each other, but the general pattern was a movement outward of all nationality groups.

This view was rather clearly connected to a concentric circle view of urban growth, and it appears to have accurately characterized cities such as Chicago, which was perhaps the best studied. But there are numerous examples, some of which will be discussed here, of nationality groups that did not initially settle near the center of a city. Their migration patterns did exhibit features of movement as a community, though, and invasion-succession processes were also characteristic. The Norwegian community in New York presents a particularly interesting case.

By 1830, a sizable Norwegian community had settled in Brooklyn, near the East River. They selected this site, according to Jonassen, because its closeness to salt water and ships made them "feel at home." It also put them within easy walking distance of the docks and harbors where many of them were employed.[4] The Red Hook section of Brooklyn became the central shipyard and docks during the 1840s, and the Norwegians initially commuted from their East River community, traveling by horsecar to Hamilton Avenue, where the Hamilton Ferry took them to the docks. The community slowly moved south, closer to work, concentrating around Hamilton Avenue in Brooklyn. By the late 1880s, this was the center of the new community. It attracted other Norwegians from older sections of Brooklyn and became the logical residential choice for newly arriving Norwegians. Young immigrant girls, for example, found jobs as live-in domestics in the more well-to-do homes of the community.

As the Norwegian population became more dense and as southern Europeans began to move in, the Norwegian community continued to move farther south. Density itself was an apparent motivating factor, for the community migrated when parks disappeared and private homes were torn down and replaced by tenements. According to Jonassen, the Norwegians were trying to duplicate the sparsely settled residential pattern of

---

[3] Such a view was presented as the result of observing immigrant groups in Chicago between 1900 and 1930. Paul F. Cressey, "Population Succession in Chicago," *American Journal of Sociology,* 44, 1938.

[4] Christen T. Jonassen, "Cultural Variables in the Ecology of an Ethnic Group," *American Sociological Review,* 14, 1949.

Norway. In 1915 the completion of the Fourth Avenue subway permitted movement still farther south because it provided easy access to Red Hook, which remained the shipping center. Although Norwegians were attracted to the community, other groups were repelled by it. New Englanders, for example, had resided in these areas of Brooklyn prior to the Norwegians, but as the Norwegian community "invaded," they moved farther out. They were succeeded by the Norwegians just as they had succeeded the Dutch who resided in Old South Brooklyn before them. Meanwhile, southern European immigrants, most of whom were Italian, were following on the heels of the Norwegians.

There is a clear tendency for members of an ethnic group to migrate together as a community, but there is also a substantial degree of "slippage." Everyone is not equally attracted to a migrating colony; some remain behind and others scatter in all directions. Some Norwegians, for example, entered nonshipping occupations and left the colony as accessibility to the shipyards ceased to be an important consideration. Generally there is, in addition, interpenetration by other nationality groups. In the case of the Norwegians, this involved overlap with Italians at the rear of the colony, overlap with New Englanders and Dutch at the front of the colony, and general intermingling with Irish and German communities simultaneously moving south.

As immigration continued to increase the relative size of foreign-born populations, mid-nineteenth-century cities in general appear to have become less residentially segregated. That is, Italians became less likely to live exclusively in Little Italy; Germans less likely to reside in Germantown; and so on. This is most clearly reflected in an index of segregation that indicates the percentage of the foreign-born population that would have to move in order to make the ethnic distribution of each section of the city identical. When the value of the index is 0, it indicates no necessary movement, or a complete absence of segregation. At the opposite pole, 100 would indicate complete segregation. Table 7–2 shows an index of segregation for the wards of Boston, along with an estimate of the size of the total foreign-born population.[5]

[5] Leo F. Schnore and Peter R. Knights, "Residence and Social Structure," in Thernstrom and Sennett, *op. cit.*

TABLE 7-2   Foreign-born and segregation in Boston.

Year	Foreign-born	Index of Segregation
1830	5.7%	28.6
1845	23.7	21.0
1855	33.0	22.6
1865	34.2	14.8

TABLE 7-3   Blacks in Boston.

Year	Black	Index of Segregation
1830	3.1%	44
1840	2.3	52
1850	1.5	59
1860	1.3	62

Although the trend is not unbroken, it appears that the degree of residential segregation in Boston declined from 1830 to 1865. At least in part this may have occurred because city growth during this period resulted more in further density than in decentralization. As the population became more concentrated, ethnic groups spilled over into each other's territories. The suburbanization, or decentralization, of cities that occurred later changed the pattern by offering new opportunities for residential segregation.

A quite opposite trend, however, was apparently occurring among the black population of northern cities. Their relative size was declining and their degree of residential segregation was increasing, as the data in Table 7–3 show.[6] Immediately before the Civil War, the degree of residential segregation of blacks in Boston was comparable to the degree of segregation of Italians and Portuguese. It was about five times higher than the least segregated group, the English, and about three times higher than the Irish or the French. But the black population involved relatively few persons in Boston and in other northern cities.

EARLY TWENTIETH-CENTURY CITIES

Between about 1880 and 1920, westward-moving immigrants caused the expansion of a number of midwestern and western cities, such as Denver, Minneapolis, Omaha, and Kansas City. All were medium-sized cities that had been founded as commercial and speculative centers, and all "boomed" between 1880 and 1920. Omaha, for example, grew from about 30,000 to almost 200,000 people during this period.

From descriptions of the population of Omaha, it appears to have been even less residentially stable than earlier eastern cities such as Boston and Poughkeepsie. In any typical five-year period almost half of both the native and foreign-born populations were leaving Omaha. Many, of course, continued to move west in search of better opportunities. Differences within

[6] *Ibid.*

and between groups were very small; the overall norm was migration.[7] In-dexes of segregation by ward in Omaha partially resemble those previously noted in Boston, but also reflect some regional variations in ethnic stand-ings. Some comparisons are presented in Table 7–4.

With the exception of the Danes and other Scandinavian groups not listed, the degree of residential segregation of various ethnic groups in Boston and Omaha was quite alike. This is not surprising, because degrees of segregation reflect degrees of prejudice and such values tend to be widely disseminated. Both cities are also alike in that over time the degree of segregation seems to have declined. In Omaha it is most true of the initially more segregated nationality groups, the Germans and the Italians. The initially less segregated groups tended to remain about the same or to in-crease slightly. (Even when increases occurred, however, the index values indicate very little segregation.)

Using this historical reexamination of Omaha, Chudacoff points out that the degree of ethnic concentration necessary to label an area has been exaggerated. In 1910, for example, approximately 10 percent of Omaha's Second Ward was German. This included about 25 percent of all the Germans in Omaha and was the largest concentration of Germans in any of Omaha's wards. Ten percent of a ward is not a very high per-centage, but it can be sufficient to give an area an ethnic label, especially if no other ethnic group exceeds 10 percent.

With the growth and then the population movement outward in Omaha, he argues, the visibility of many ethnic groups increased. Late nineteenth-century streetcars helped to create small business districts out-side the downtown at the crossroads of major thoroughfares. The commer-cial, social, and religious institutions of ethnic groups tended to cluster at these major intersections, so that streets and neighborhoods became more visibly ethnic. This led to the ethnic labeling of neighborhoods. Three blocks along North 24th Street in Omaha were, in this respect, conspicu-

---

[7] Howard P. Chudacoff, "A New Look at Ethnic Neighborhoods," *Journal of Ameri-can History,* 40, 1973.

TABLE 7-4   Indexes of residential segregation.*

Country of Origin	Boston 1855	Omaha 1910	Omaha 1920
England	12	9	16
Ireland	19	10	12
Germany	33	21	11
Denmark	47	13	12
Italy	57	69	53

* *Boston in 1855 and Omaha in 1910 represent similar stages in the immigrant urbanization of both cities.*

	1912	1916	1920
1102	Jacob Finkenstein	Jacob Finkenstein	Harry Slutzky
1104	Jacob Kaplan	Abraham Stoler	Abraham Stoler
1111	Anshe Sholom Synagogue	Anshe Sholom Synagogue	Anshe Sholom Synagogue
1114	Samuel Krasne, grocer	Simon Krasne	Simon Krasne
			Samuel Cohn
1115	Irene Reber	F. L. Bickford	F. L. Johnson
1117	J. E. Hartman	John Baird	H. C. Orton
1201	Ella Bentley (c)	Wesley Horn (c)	Harvey Williams
1202	Fruma London, grocer	Fruma London, grocer	Fruma London, grocer
1204	Max Fogel, meats	Daniel Hirsch, meats	Daniel Hirsch, meats
			Margaret Egan
1205	Sam Spiegal, junk	Sam Spiegal, junk	Sam Spiegal, junk
1206	Max Hertzberg, baker	Benjamin Blend, baker	C. C. Nerness
1208	Samuel Cohn	Samuel Cohn	Vacant
1210	Max Hertzberg	Everett Brown	J. Ewing
			J. R. Smith
1302		Joseph Margolis, grocer	Joseph Gotsdiner, grocer
1304	Sophia Howard	Max Krasne, shoemaker	Bernie Gault
1304½	Isadore Hurwitz, photographer	Vacant	Thomas Hutchison, billiards
1306	Boyd Burrows, printer	Joseph Bemrose, confectioner	Joseph Bemrose, confectioner
1307	T. H. Weirich, fixtures	T. H. Weirich, fixtures	Vacant
1308	Christian Anderson	Doherty & Mortenson, plumbers	J. W. Wright
1310	E. P. Trumble, coffee house	Samuel Krizelman, hardware	William Mays
1312	Emanuel Thomsen, saloon	Arendt Jensen	J. W. Wright, barber
1314	Louis Pinkovitz, blacksmith	Vacant	C. H. Warden, billiards
1316	Isaac Abramson, feed	Isaac Abramson, feed	Isaac Abramson, feed
1322	T. V. Allison, grocer	Vacant	Belle Christian
1401	Edwin Walker, restaurant	General Scott (c), restaurant	General Scott, restaurant
1402	Joel Bloom, saloon	Joel Bloom, saloon	Sam Flax, grocer
1404	C. J. Olsen	J. C. Carlson, cigars	Mary Glass, restaurant
1405	Hersch Friedman, shoemaker	Isaac Zarinsky, shoemaker	Isaac Zarinsky, shoemaker
	Herman Theodore, tailor	P. H. Miller, upholsterer	
1406			Harry Siref, clothes
1408		Isaac Brooks, shoes	Isaac Brooks, shoes
1410		Samuel Meyer, ladies' clothes	
1412		Jacob Kaplan, second hand goods	
1414	G. A. Walker	Max Rosenbloom	R. H. Robins, grocer
1415	Frank Kellerman		Sarah Shotz
	A. J. Lamb, confectioner	Mushkin & Epstein, meats	Mushkin & Epstein, meats
1417	L. H. Adams (c), barber	Omaha Fish Co.	Max Resick, grocer
	J. L. Kolec, pool	Abraham Goldstein	Eureka Furniture
1419	David Spector, tailor	Paul Eisenmann, baker	R. H. Blend, baker
1421	Jacob Berkowitz	Vacant	S. W. Mills, furniture
	Benjamin Cohn, mens' clothes		
1422	Hersch Friedman	Harry Adelstein	Harry Adelstein
1423	Samuel Babior, meats	Moses Silver, tailor	Herman Gilinsky, secondhand
	Methodist Episcopal Church		goods
1424	C. G. Krasne	C. G. Krasne	Max Kalmonson
1425	Solomon Garmel, grocer	Solomon Garmel, grocer	Kemp Bros., grocers

FIGURE 7–1 North 24th Street.
Source: *Howard P. Chudacoff, "A New Look at Ethnic Neighborhoods,"* Journal of American History, *40, 1973.*

ously Jewish. The names of the inhabitants and their business activities are shown in Figure 7–1, which is taken from the Omaha City Directories of 1912, 1916, and 1920.

To make guesses from the names, it would appear that slightly over half of both residences and commercial establishments were Jewish owned or occupied. But it is easy to understand how these three blocks of North 24th Street would have given an overwhelmingly Jewish appearance to someone riding by in a streetcar. Making further inferences from the names, North 24th Street appears to have remained equally Jewish over the eight-year period, despite a turnover in the population. Jews appear likely to have replaced Jews when there was movement out of the area, and the same pattern seems to have characterized non-Jews. Further, both residential and commercial locations appear equally subject to this replacement pattern.

In summary, between about 1830 and 1880, as increasing numbers of the foreign-born moved into eastern cities, decreased residential segregation appears to have resulted. A similar pattern seems characteristic of western cities some years later, as the foreign-born immigrants moved across the country. In both situations, urban growth resulted in greater population concentration and greater intermingling of persons of different nationalities. Near the turn of the century, however, new opportunities for segregation were created by urban transportation developments that led to increasing population decentralization. The economically more advantaged persons in earlier arriving groups could now more conveniently escape living with newcomers. The streetcar, for example, permitted the Danes to flee Jewish invasions in Omaha, and the Fourth Avenue subway facilitated the Norwegians' movement when Brooklyn was invaded by Italians.

Greater possibilities for segregation occurred almost simultaneously

The first decades of the twentieth century were associated with marked improvements in urban transportation, permitting greater degrees of ethnic segregation (New York City, New York).

with a marked change in the countries of origin of immigrants. Prior to 1883, 95 percent of all immigrants were from northern and western Europe. From 1883 to 1907, however, over 80 percent came from eastern and southern Europe.[8] The later arrivals were of lower ethnic standing in the eyes of the already established northern and western Europeans. The segregation of nationality groups was also reinforced by religious differences tied to countries of origin. Possible relationships between the Dutch and Irish, for example, were impeded by the fact that many of the Dutch were Reformed Protestant and many of the Irish were Catholic. Similarly, many of the eastern European immigrants were also Jewish.

More recent studies of nationality groups in cities generally indicate a relationship between residential segregation and socioeconomic status. The later arrivals tend to be more segregated and, on the average, in less prestigious and well-paid occupations.[9] But, economic interpretations of ethnic segregation are only partially adequate. For example, in Toronto—where ethnic groups are segregated in a pattern resembling that of American cities—differences in income and occupation are not nearly sufficient to explain the degree of ethnic residential segregation.[10] In order to demonstrate this, Darroch and Marston computed expected indexes of residential dissimilarity based on socioeconomic characteristics. In other words, if people were distributed solely on the basis of these status variables, then given between-group differences in socioeconomic status, how much residential segregation would be expected? The expected differences were then compared to the actual index. A sample of the results is presented in Figure 7–2.

The last two bars of Figure 7–2 indicate that some degree of residential segregation would be expected by ethnic group differences in occupation and income. (The investigators also present similar findings with respect to education.) Based on socioeconomic differences, ethnic groups in Toronto would be expected to be segregated in the *order* in which they are actually segregated. However, the actual *degree* of segregation far exceeds the amount expected. It is not clear the degree to which the "excessive" segregation is due to cultural or life style variables, family size considerations, stereotypes or prejudices, and so on. It is clear, however, that the economic basis for the segregation is minimal. Directly comparable evidence from contemporary American cities is lacking, but at least one study of Cleveland in 1930 reported quite congruent findings.[11]

---

[8] Joseph Schachter, "Net Immigration of Gainful Workers into the United States," *Demography,* 9, 1972.

[9] Mary G. Powers, "Class, Ethnicity and Residence in Metropolitan America," *Demography,* 5, 1968.

[10] A. Gordon Darroch and Wilfred G. Marston, "The Social Class Basis of Ethnic Residential Segregation," *American Journal of Sociology,* 77, 1971.

[11] Stanley Lieberson, *Ethnic Patterns in American Cities* (New York: Free Press, 1963).

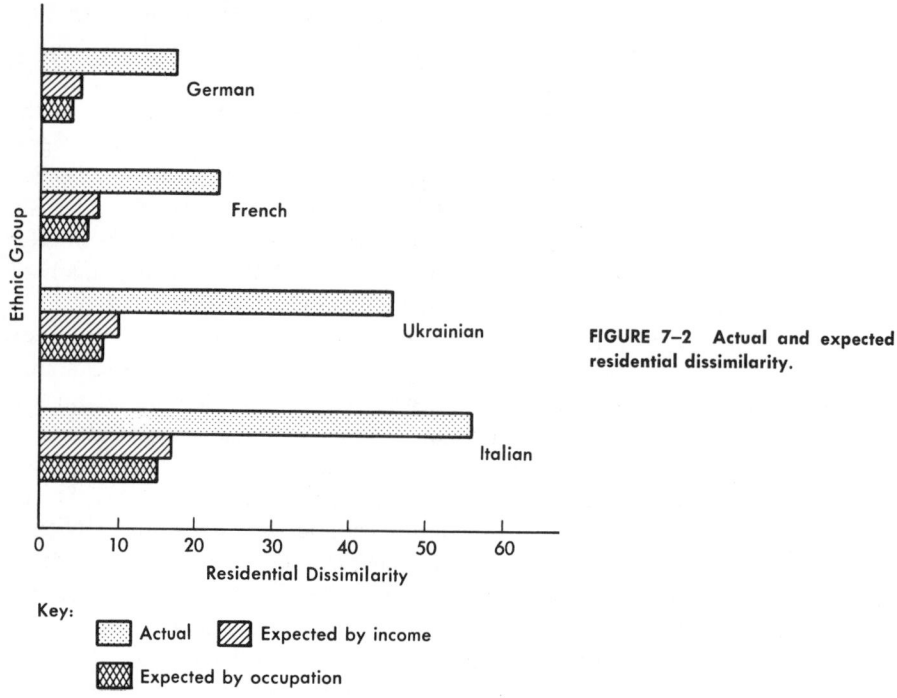

FIGURE 7–2 Actual and expected residential dissimilarity.

Key:

☐ Actual   ▨ Expected by income

▩ Expected by occupation

A socioeconomic view of ethnic segregation has also resulted from the erroneous assumption that from their time of arrival in the United States, later arriving immigrants were less skilled occupationally. If immigrant groups are examined according to their occupational distributions in the United States (as opposed to their countries of origin), just the reverse is indicated. In other words, the later arrivals initially occupied positions of relatively higher standing than the early arrivals.[12] This trend is illustrated in Table 7–5.

[12] Schachter, *op. cit.*

TABLE 7-5 Initial immigrant occupations in the United States.

Occupational Type	1870	1910	1930
Professional-technical	1.6%	2.5%	3.9%
Owner, manager	3.9	4.2	5.9
Clerical, related	2.4	5.7	9.8
Skilled worker, foremen	14.3	15.6	18.9
Semiskilled	59.1	40.2	43.0
Laborer (nonfarm)	n.a.	27.2	18.1
Servant	n.a.	7.7	8.3

When the occupational distributions of the foreign-born are compared with those of native whites, the same trend is indicated. Thus, over time the occupational standing of immigrants increased compared both to former immigrants and to native whites at each time period. This suggests that residential segregation was initially due more to out-group prejudices and/or in-group solidarity than to socioeconomic considerations. We must also keep in mind improved urban transportation, which permitted urban populations to decentralize simultaneously with the arrival of immigrants from southern and eastern Europe.

BLACK MIGRATION

The movement of blacks from south to north, and from rural to urban, did not occur until well after the heavy streams of white foreign-born immigration to northern cities. As late as 1920, for example, the black populations of cities such as Boston, Chicago, and New York were all well under 5 percent.[13] The black population of larger southern cities was relatively larger; cities such as Birmingham and Memphis were nearly 40 percent black in 1920. The southern cities were quite small, however, and the southern black population was predominantly rural.

Black-white residential segregation in the South during this period was virtually without exception. Dollard, for example, describes a small southern city of just over 2,500 persons in 1935 as cut in half by railroad tracks.[14] Whites all lived in the upper half and almost all blacks lived in the lower half. (That way, if there was flooding the black section would go under water first.) Exceptions to the color line were few. There were no whites in the black section. A few cabins occupied by blacks were located behind the houses of their white employers, and two black families had houses that "boldly fronted" a street on the white side of the tracks. As would be expected, differences in neighborhood quality were strongly related to the color of each section. Houses on the white side were large and in good repair, streets were paved and electricity powered fans, refrigerators, and so on. On the black side, homes were small and deteriorating, roads were unpaved, there was no electricity for any modern appliances, and outhouses were common.

[13] In 1860, Boston's population was 1.3 percent black. By 1920 it had increased to only 2.2 percent black. But from 1960 to 1970 it increased from 9.8 to 18.2 percent. Figures from U.S. Bureau of the Census, 1920, 1960, and 1970.
[14] John Dollard, *Caste and Class in a Southern Town* (Garden City, N.Y.: Doubleday-Anchor, 1957). Originally published in 1937.

One effect of the rural to urban, South to North movement of blacks after about 1930 was to decrease the residential segregation of white ethnic groups. In the familiar invasion-succession process, blacks moved into central cities and white ethnics left, scattering in all directions. After about 1930 in Chicago, for example, local white communities became increasingly varied in their ethnic composition.[15] The average family size of the foreign-born became more like that of the native white population and socio-economic differences virtually disappeared. Many of the bases for ethnic residential segregation were rapidly diminishing. The black population, however, became increasingly segregated near the center of the city.

In mid-nineteenth-century cities as the percentage of foreign-born increased, the degree of residential segregation decreased. This pattern changed with improved urban transportation. Among contemporary non-white groups, increases in the size of the racial or ethnic group appear to result in increased residential segregation, especially for blacks. These patterns have been reported by Van Arsdol and Schuerman in a historical examination of Los Angeles County.[16] They divided the county into old and new areas according to time of settlement. Areas built up (with more than two structures per acre) at least twenty years before the date in question were considered old. Generally, segregation of nonwhite groups was lower in newer areas—except for blacks—and higher in older areas—especially for blacks.

Table 7–6 presents figures relating to newness of residential area, population growth, and segregation. The three groups compared are blacks (Negroes), Mexicans (Spanish surname, born in Mexico) and "Other" (primarily Japanese and Chinese). In 1940, minority group members with the exception of blacks were about equally likely to choose old or new areas in Los Angeles (see columns 3 and 4). They aggregated in a few

[15] Albert Hunter, "The Ecology of Chicago," *American Journal of Sociology,* 77, 1971.
[16] Maurice D. Van Arsdol, Jr., and Leo A. Schuerman, "Redistribution and Assimilation of Ethnic Populations," *Demography,* 8, 1971.

TABLE 7-6 Segregation by area.

| | Population (000) | | % in New Areas | | Residential Segregation | | | |
| | | | | | New Areas | | Old Areas | |
Minority Group	1940	1960	1940	1960	1940	1960	1940	1960
Black	75	462	26	26	69	79	84	79
Mexican	59	99	52	42	53	43	50	56
Other	50	122	50	42	50	43	60	56

new areas, then slowly spread out. Between 1940 and 1960, however, the size of the groups appears to have grown more rapidly than members of the groups moved out, because the relative size of the groups in new areas declined. In general, ethnic or racial groups in the old areas remained about equally segregated, while the degree of segregation decreased in the newer areas.

One obvious question raised by these findings concerns why segregation differs by newness of area. If we assume that suburban areas are generally newer than city areas, one possible answer may (again) relate to transportation developments. A study of a dozen metropolitan areas reported by Fine and others indicates that residential segregation—as measured by occupational dissimilarity—is greater in city (older) than in suburban (newer) neighborhoods.[17] Los Angeles, one of the metropolitan areas included, was characterized by an above average difference between city and suburbs in degree of segregation. In general, they suggest, better means of public transportation within the city may permit greater amounts of residential segregation without pushing anyone beyond a reasonable commuting time to work. City-suburban and intersuburban transportation, by contrast, simply may not permit comparable degrees of segregation, and extended commuting in a private automobile may be too expensive. Thus, minority group laborers working on suburban construction projects or service workers—such as janitors in suburban schools—may be pushed to live as close as possible to work.

Effects of black segregation in cities

An interesting related question concerns the effects of minority group concentrations; that is, does the black population (in particular) fare worse in cities where it is more rigidly segregated in central city ghettos? An investigation by Jibou and Marshall indicates that it does not, at least to any appreciable degree. Their results are based on a survey of 74 large cities, all of which have large black populations.[18] The greater the degree of ghettoization, or residential segregation, the greater the occupational and income differences between blacks and whites. But black-white differences due to ghettoization differences were quite small *among* cities. This may be due, Hartley proposes, to the fact that residential segregation of blacks is high in all cities.[19] Because differences in ghettoization are not pronounced, they cannot have demonstrably large effects.

On the other hand, Jibou and Marshall report rather substantial

[17] John Fine et al., "The Residential Segregation of Occupational Groups in Central Cities and Suburbs," *Demography,* 8, 1971.
[18] Robert M. Jibou and Harvey M. Marshall, Jr., "Urban Structure and the Differentiation Between Blacks and Whites," *American Sociological Review,* 36, 1971.
[19] Shirley Hartley, "Comment on Urban Structure and the Differentiation Between Blacks and Whites," *American Sociological Review,* 37, 1972.

within-city racial differences between regions of the country. The relative size of the black population is smaller in southern cities, but racial differences in black-white occupational attainment are more pronounced in southern than in northern cities. When black-white differences are examined in entire metropolitan areas rather than central cities only, the regional differences are still more pronounced. Racial differences in occupation, education, income, and housing are all more marked in southern than northern metropolitan areas.[20]

These regional differences are due in part at least to selective patterns of migration. Blacks who move *between* metropolitan areas tend to be of higher socioeconomic status than black nonmovers, and approximately equal in status to white migrants.[21] The higher-status blacks who migrate are probably selective, moving to cities where employment opportunities are most favorable. Thus, black population growth due to migration has the effect of lowering black-white socioeconomic differences.

Within cities, however, there are quite different patterns of migration by race. The percentage of blacks making long-distance moves (4 percent) is much smaller than the percentage of whites (17 percent) who migrate. The percentage of blacks who move locally (48 percent) is almost double that of the white population (26 percent) moving within the same city.[22] In total, therefore, blacks are more likely to move than whites, but more likely to remain in the same city. These figures come from a comparison of national surveys taken in 1966 and 1969. The findings also indicate that there is no difference in plans to move eventually by race. The suggestion that a greater proportion of black moves may be "forced" is borne out in a comparison of the stated reasons for moves. Slightly over one in five black moves were involuntary, due to destruction of dwelling units, eviction, and so on. Forced moves were the single most common reason offered by blacks but the least common offered by whites, of whom less than 6 percent were involuntarily mobile.

To obtain more space or find a better place to live were other reasons commonly given by both white and black movers. In some cities, this has led the poor and the economically marginal of both races to seek public housing. A decline in private inner city building has also resulted in fewer nonpublic alternatives to central city families who are forced to relocate because of urban renewal projects. In 1971, for example, an estimated 600,000 persons lived in New York City public housing projects, and over 100,000 more were on a waiting list.[23]

[20] Howard M. Bahr and Jack P. Gibbs, "Racial Differentiation in American Metropolitan Areas," *Social Forces*, 45, 1967.
[21] Karl and Alma Taeuber, *Negroes in the City* (Chicago: Aldine, 1965).
[22] Ronald J. McAllister et al., "Residential Mobility of Blacks and Whites," *American Journal of Sociology*, 77, 1971.
[23] However, in other cities—such as St. Louis and Washington, D.C.—crime and vandalism have led to increased vacancies in public housing. Roger Starr, "Which of the Poor Shall Live in Public Housing?" *Public Interest*, 23, 1971.

Central city residents have been forced into public housing as private facilities have deteriorated and not been replaced (Syracuse, New York).

Because public housing is usually desegregated, it offers opportunities for interracial interaction among persons of more nearly equal status than that frequently experienced elsewhere. Theoretically, according to the "equal status contact" hypothesis, this should result in less stereotyping and a greater willingness to form biracial relationships. In a variety of social experiments and surveys conducted during the 1950s and 1960s, this hypothesis was confirmed. As a result of the equal status contact in public housing, whites expressed more tolerant attitudes toward blacks and their objections to integrated living conditions declined.[24]

For the most part, these studies have focused on the reactions of white women to their black neighbors. It was probably an inadvertent racial bias that led many of the investigators to assume that *the* problematic issue was the acceptance of blacks by whites and not the reverse. One of the few studies to surmount this myopia is reported by Ford in an investigation of public housing in Lexington, Kentucky.[25] (Lexington is a "border" city with a 1970 population of 108,000, including 18,000 blacks.) Among the white women in Ford's sample, the previously reported pattern was again confirmed. Among black women, however, racial prejudice toward whites did not diminish. Because of their previous experiences with whites they had developed attitudes that led them to be suspicious and concerned with "subtle condescendence" from whites. The blacks did not

24 For a comprehensive review, see Thomas F. Pettigrew, "Racially Separate or Together," *Journal of Social Issues,* 25, 1969.
25 W. Scott Ford, "Interracial Public Housing in a Border City," *American Journal of Sociology,* 78, 1973.

experience the joint living conditions as equal status contacts, and the ensuing interaction did not lessen their prejudice.

The failure of desegregated living to lessen black prejudices is probably related to the emergence of black pride and militancy in the black community and particularly in the urban black community. Beginning in the 1960s, there was a marked decline in the number of blacks who felt that a servile, humble way of acting toward whites was appropriate. Black was "redefined" as beautiful along with a new and vigorous interest in black (American and African) history. The demonstrations and riots may be seen as an extreme form of racial assertiveness as well as a response to continued residential and occupational frustrations in American cities. Viewing participation in riots as an indicator of black militancy, all the studies are congruent in showing that rioters are more likely to be long-term urban residents. In other words, black migrants are less likely to be militant than black urban natives. In Detroit, in Newark, and elsewhere, blacks who were born in the city were about twice as likely to participate in the riots as those who migrated (typically from the South).[26]

From the late 1960s until the middle 1970s there was a marked decline in violent demonstrations by inner-city blacks, but survey results suggest there has been a "hardening" of black attitudes toward whites. In Detroit, for example, Howard Schuman and Shirley Hatchett assessed black attitudes in 1968 and again in 1971. Their preliminary results show that the percentage who believed riots would increase support from the white community decreased from 58 to 43 percent. However, there was a substantial decline in the percentage who believed whites wanted blacks to "get a better break" and an increase in the percentage who felt they were treated in a discriminatory manner by white sales clerks.[27]

One explanation for riots and hardening attitudes is tied to the economic organization of the black ghetto. It is viewed as economically and culturally different from other types of ghettos, resulting in the frustration of aspirations. In order to assess this view, we must first take a step back and examine the general characteristics of racial, religious, and ethnic ghettos.

GHETTO ECONOMIC ORGANIZATION

A ghetto implies, first of all, a geographical location; that is, a ghetto is ordinarily some part of a city that can be geographically defined by more or less clear boundaries. In this sense it is a "natural" area whose history

---

[26] A review of these studies is presented in Nathan Caplan, "The New Ghetto Man," *Journal of Social Issues,* 26, 1970.
[27] From a preliminary report in the *Newsletter* of the Institute for Social Research, University of Michigan, July 1974.

can be described. What makes an area a ghetto differs from investigator to investigator. For some, it is that inhabitants share a common and distinctive culture that leads to labeling the area Chinatown, Little Sicily, and so on. A ghetto is maintained as a segregated area by the residents' general isolation from the larger city and their insistence on intramarriage.[28] For other theorists, it is the uniformly low socioeconomic position of residents that makes an area a ghetto. According to this view, the distinctive culture of ghetto residents need not be tied to ethnicity or race, but may be generated by their shared economic position. The culture of poverty view is the best example.[29] In general, though, all three characteristics are implied. Ghettos are geographically segregated areas inhabited by people who share a distinctive culture and are uniformly poor. Within the same geographically defined ghetto, however, there are often numerous subghettos composed of different ethnic groups. Each could be called a separate ghetto or, based on their geographical proximity, all could be viewed as parts of a larger ghetto.

Ethnic economic support

Economically, there has been a persistent historical tendency for persons of the same ethnicity (or race) to support each other. Perhaps the most common form involves giving one's business to a "soul brother" or a "landsmann." Neighborhood groceries and bakeries are the best examples. Shops of this type operated by someone of the same ethnicity have historically been the preferred places to patronize. Although the same pattern characterizes all types of commodities, it is probably most characteristic of foodstuffs because of their direct association with a common culture. To a Pole, a German grocer could hardly be expected to know good from bad kielbasa; to a German, a Polish grocer could hardly be expected to carry the right kind of knockwurst.

The dominance of the ethnic grocer in America is well over a century old. In Poughkeepsie, for example, the depression of the 1870s led to substantially higher rates of failure for native-born than for foreign-born grocers. Only 41 percent of the native grocers survived compared with 64 percent of the German-born and 59 percent of the Irish-born. By 1880, about 60 percent of the city's grocers were foreign-born even though the foreign-born were less than 30 percent of the city's total labor force.[30] Similarly, in contemporary Chicago ghettos, Italians continue to shop almost exclusively in the neighborhood stores operated by Italian grocers,

[28] Louis Wirth, "The Ghetto," in Albert J. Reiss, Jr. (ed.), *Wirth on Cities and Social Life* (Chicago: University of Chicago Press, 1964).
[29] For a discussion contrasting economic and cultural views, see Herbert J. Gans, *People and Plans* (New York: Basic Books, 1968), Chap. 22.
[30] Griffen, *op. cit.*

People in cities historically have supported restaurants and food stores of their own ethnicity (above: Miami, Florida; left: Toronto, Ontario, Canada).

and they continue to be serviced by Italian sidewalk vendors who sell Italian lemonade and sausages.[31]

Because of religious prescriptions, a still more extensive pattern of within-group economic activity characterizes the Hasidic community in the Williamsburg section of Brooklyn in New York. Members of this Orthodox

[31] Gerald Suttles, *The Social Order of the Slum* (Chicago: University of Chicago Press, 1968).

Jewish group have bought or rented most of the stores that service the community. Local rabbis supervise, or else lend their names to, the bakeries, butcher shops, and so on. For the purchaser, this ensures that the items and their ingredients are properly kosher. It also indicates the proprietor's routine Hasidic conformity, which earns him reliability; he is an "honest Jew who can be trusted." Even for nonfoodstuffs, where there are no religious prescriptions, members of the Hasidic community feel a sense of responsibility to buy from each other. It is a way of expressing loyalty to the group.[32]

Shopping in one another's stores is one way ghetto residents support others of the same ethnicity. An even more direct way is by providing employment. Among Chinese-Americans, for example, this often takes the form of "partnerships." Those with limited capital will either pool their money to buy a restaurant or hand laundry, or else be permitted to buy into a previously established one. In either case, employment in the enterprise follows, with the individual in the enhanced status of "owner." Even though a dozen or more partners can be involved, it is not common for legal partnerships to be prepared. If disagreements arise, they can be taken to family associations or submitted to the Chinese Benevolent Association for arbitration.[33]

The black economic pattern

For all groups there is a common theme: supportive economic activity is tied to ethnic identity. The Hasidic Jews, the Italians, and the Chinese express their ethnic identities through within-group economic activities. In the black ghetto, by contrast, this has not been the case. Most of the neighborhood stores are white-owned and many of them "import" white employees. There has also been no counterpart to the Chinese Benevolent Association or the Hasidic educational and welfare organizations. The black ghetto has been said to resemble a colony. The schools, welfare agencies, and so on have generally been under the control of whites, and whites who are not ghetto residents. From this perspective, demonstrations and riots in black ghettos can be viewed as analogous to colonial revolutions.[34]

Light points out that retail stores have traditionally been a preferred avenue of social mobility for disadvantaged groups who have experienced discrimination.[35] The underrepresentation of blacks in the proprietary class

[32] Solomon Poll, *The Hasidic Community of Williamsburg* (New York: Schocken, 1969).
[33] Milton L. Barnett, "Kinship as a Factor Affecting Cantonese Economic Adaptation in the U.S.," *Human Organization,* 19, 1960.
[34] Robert Blauner, "Internal Colonialism and Ghetto Revolt," *Social Problems,* 16, 1969.
[35] Ivan H. Light, *Ethnic Enterprise in America* (Berkeley: University of California Press, 1972).

is therefore an anomaly. It is, of course, difficult to do well in a retail business, he points out. Those who have the credentials can usually do better working for the A&P than against it. It is only the disadvantaged who have a "rational motive" for attempting to compete economically with established retail chain stores. Historically, both the foreign-born and black populations have found themselves in this situation. The foreign-born have responded; blacks have not.

One important and relevant difference between blacks and many foreign-born groups, Light points out, lies in the nature of their voluntary associations. Among blacks, the church emerged as the strongest institution after the end of slavery. Its ability to orient blacks to private enterprise was seriously hampered by two problems not experienced by the associations of many foreign-born groups. First, the church faced competition for membership from white denominations, especially for potential middle class members. Thus, many of the black storefront churches developed as fundamentalist and otherworldly institutions to service a predominantly lower class membership. Second, the black church faced the problematic task of attempting to create cohesion within an undifferentiated group. Among Orientals, by contrast, membership in voluntary associations was based on limiting ascribed characteristics, such as surnames. As a result, members immediately possessed a basis of solidarity that permitted the association to concentrate on external efforts such as business enterprises.

The historical absence of large numbers of black-owned businesses has apparently resulted in substantially reduced numbers of jobs for other blacks. An extensive analysis of employment opportunities in the black ghetto has been reported by Aldrich, from a study of over 600 businesses in Chicago, Boston, and Washington, D.C. In each city two areas were selected for analysis. One was a ghetto area, characterized by a high percentage of black residents and low socioeconomic standing. The other site was a nonghetto area.[36]

Aldrich reports that white ownership of neighborhood stores and business predominates even after most of the white population has moved out of an area. The cost of starting over in a new location is apparently prohibitive to white owners, and would-be black owners usually lack the necessary capital. The white owners, however, tend almost always to be absentee owners; that is, to live more than 5 miles away from their stores. The black owners, by contrast, tend to live in the same community. In addition, white owners employ mostly whites, whereas black owners almost exclusively hire blacks. Corresponding to this difference, a higher percentage of employees in white-owned businesses are from outside the community in which the store is located. Many of these differences are summarized in Table 7–7.

[36] Howard E. Aldrich, "Employment Opportunities for Blacks in the Black Ghetto," *American Journal of Sociology*, 78, 1973.

TABLE 7-7   Ownership and employment patterns.

| City | Area Population, % white | | % White Ownership | | % Absentee Owners | |
	1960	1970	1960	1970	White 1970	Black 1970
Boston						
Ghetto	55	28	84	73	86	15
Nonghetto	99	79	100	99	63	—
Chicago						
Ghetto	53	10	68	58	93	29
Nonghetto	97	94	100	100	58	—
Washington, D.C.						
Ghetto	31	17	73	46	72	39
Nonghetto	58	19	85	76	64	29

A comparison of columns 1 and 2 indicates that between 1960 and 1970 all the areas became increasingly black, though this occurred to only a small degree in the nonghetto area of Chicago. Only in the ghetto area of Washington was there a substantial increase in the percentage of black owners, and black ownership of businesses outside the ghettos remained almost nonexistent. From the final two columns it is clear that white owners of ghetto businesses were more likely to live outside the community than either white owners of businesses outside the ghetto or black owners of ghetto businesses.

In sum, Aldrich's findings clearly suggest a pattern in which both business profits and employment opportunities are disproportionately leaving the black ghetto. This appears to occur more frequently than in Italian or Jewish or Chinese or other ethnic ghettos. Differences in voluntary associations may explain part of the reason why this happened. A number of other theories have also been advanced, some of which may provide additional answers. One view is that assimilation into the mainstream of American economic life depends on exposure to northern urban life. Most immigrant groups, it is argued, served their "apprenticeships" in the big cities of the North and then through politics, banking, trucking, or other distinctively urban occupations, moved up. From this view, the time spent by a group outside northern cities simply does not count with respect to economic assimilation.[37] Justifiably frustrated black groups point to their meager gains in more than a century of freedom, but most of that time may be irrelevant sociologically. In terms of migration to northern cities, blacks

---

[37] As discussed in Chapter 6, changes now occurring in southern cities have recently made them more like the types of cities in which minority groups could be mobile.

arrived *much* later than the other ethnic groups to which they have been compared in this chapter.

A POSTSCRIPT

Quite recently, urban blacks have begun to organize themselves into economically and politically more autonomous communities. And in some of these cases, churches have been instrumental, their efforts aided by the larger white community and/or the federal government. Even though blacks are following a well-worn tradition in this regard, the racial pride that is simultaneously expressed in black ghettos has been responded to as threatening by the larger white community. The predominantly black community of East Palo Alto, California, presents an interesting model of the form that future community developments are likely to take.

After World War II, East Palo Alto was a largely suburban and agricultural community of about 8,000 persons, most of whom were white. During the 1950s, real estate agents convinced many owners to sell before an influx of blacks could destroy property values.[38] As a result of successful "block-busting," the neighborhood became about 60 percent black (and 70 percent "non-white") by 1970, with a total population of nearly 20,000.

[38] Phyllis Barusch and Harriet Nathan, "The East Palo Alto Municipal Advisory Council," *Public Affairs Report,* 13, 1972.

Black pride recently has been associated with greater participation in community life (Brooklyn, New York).

During the middle 1960s, East Palo Alto was one small part of San Mateo County and an even smaller part of the nine-county San Francisco Bay Area. Homes were physically deteriorating, high crime rates were forcing businesses out of the community, and there was a great deal of poverty. Worse yet, as an unincorporated area with no political jurisdiction over its own affairs, the community lacked a mechanism for improving its own situation.

In 1967 the San Mateo County Board created the East Palo Alto Municipal Council. It became the first community of its kind to elect a municipal council whose chairman is known as the mayor. Subsequent developments in 1969 and 1970 led to a community-controlled police force, school system, and neighborhood youth program. The staff in all these institutional areas has been predominantly black. And because of the high rate of community participation in decision making, various federal agencies have made unprecedented amounts of money available for diverse projects.[39]

Crime and poverty were not abolished with the formation of a local municipal council; and it is still too early to tell whether they will be significantly reduced. However, East Palo Alto stopped being analogous to a colony and began to take steps that might end the vicious cycle in which poverty, deterioration, and crime feed on each other. The key issue in triggering community participation in the newly independent community involved racial symbols. Youthful proponents wanted to change the community's name to Nairobi as a symbol of pride in their African heritage. Opposed predominantly by older persons in the community, the proposal lost by a 3 to 1 margin. But the issue itself was a catalyst for participation in community affairs. It also stimulated black business—the Nairobi Village Shopping Center, the Black & Tan Barber Shop, and so on.

[39] *Newsweek,* December 18, 1972, p. 67.

Toronto, Ontario, Canada.

8 Urban Residential Patterns

IF YOU WERE TO DRIVE through any large city in the world you would notice some striking differences between the areas in which people live. You might not know exactly where one neighborhood ended and another began, though major avenues or variations in topography would sometimes provide convenient boundaries. One of the first aspects of neighborhoods you would probably notice would be the type of housing (homes or apartments) and its condition (old or new). Then you might notice that some areas had more children playing in front of the houses than others, and that they were younger in age, too. You could probably also identify various racial and ethnic groups in many areas according to the residents' features, the names of neighborhood grocery stores, and the nature of local churches.

Based on these observable aspects, you might make certain additional inferences about the people in each neighborhood. For example, you would probably predict systematic differences in the occupational and educational attainments of residents; in their proximity to extended families; in their participation in community organizations; and so on. On a still more abstract level, you might wonder if neighborhoods of any given type were consistently located in certain parts of cities, and whether there were uniform relationships between adjacent neighborhoods.

This chapter is concerned with *neighborhoods*. Before we can proceed, however, we must examine the very nature of a neighborhood in an urban context.

153

The nature of neighborhoods or communities raises the broader issue of how any residential subarea can be identified in contemporary cities. Ideally, it would be delimited in a way that produced an ecological unit which also corresponded with residents' sentiments and patterns of interaction. It would be a community or neighborhood that simultaneously functioned in a relatively autonomous manner to meet the needs of residents, was viewed as a meaningful social-geographical area by residents; and was characterized by relatively high rates of interaction among residents.

All these ideal conditions cannot of course be met, but many subareas can meet at least some of the criteria and partially qualify as residential neighborhoods. Before reluctantly accepting a somewhat arbitrary geographical definition of neighborhoods, however, let us look at several decades of interesting research that describes the problems of other ways of defining local residential areas.

A historically popular conception of neighborhoods defined them by the homogeneity of residents. Following Park, they were called unplanned "natural areas."[1] Any portion of a city associated with a subpopulation with distinctive needs or specialized services could qualify as such an area. Thus, a locale comprised almost exclusively of the wealthy or of Japanese-Americans could constitute an unplanned natural area—one produced by convenience, economic interest, or the like, rather than by city governments or planning commissions.

The major criterion used in research on natural areas has been rental values, primarily because of the accessibility (and comparability) of such data for all sections of a city. Ethnicity has also been widely used, and for similar reasons. In fact, however, it has been virtually impossible to identify very many homogeneous natural areas or to delineate the boundaries of potential areas. In a study of Seattle, for example, Hatt was able to identify only two very small areas that were homogeneous with respect to rental values. The rest of the city contained interstitial, or mixed, areas. Similarly, the distribution of ethnic groups was found to be widely overlapping and dispersed and therefore inconsistent with the notion of natural areas.[2]

Midtown Manhattan provides an excellent example of the limitations of the natural area approach. This 190-square-block residential area adjacent to the central business district in the middle of Manhattan is characterized by extreme heterogeneity. In this one small area live some of the wealthiest families in the nation, families with social register lineages. There are also very poor immigrant families, living in run-down tenements; and

[1] Robert Park, "The City: Human Behavior in the City Environment," *American Journal of Sociology,* 20, 1915.
[2] Paul Hatt, "The Concept of Natural Area," *American Sociological Review,* 11, 1946.

In parts of many cities, old brownstones and modern, high-rise apartments share the same block (Chicago, Illinois).

the two extremes often are located side by side. Diversity in adjacent types of housing has been increased as developers tear down old tenements in the middle of a block and replace them with lavish high-rise apartment buildings.[3] The same type of "renewal" process in Chicago, Philadelphia, and other cities has made diversity of residents in central city areas a common feature of contemporary urban life.

Another previously mentioned criterion for defining neighborhoods is social interaction. Thus, an area is a neighborhood if there is a high rate of interaction among the residents; and the more homogeneous the residents of a territorial unit, the higher their rate of interaction is expected to be. In addition, a high rate of commitment to the neighborhood is expected to accompany a high rate of interaction. Empirical studies using this approach have shown geographical areas to vary greatly in the degree to which there are interpersonal relationships and involvements, even within relatively homogeneous areas, however.

One relevant study attempted to divide Lansing, Michigan, into 35 "natural" ecological subareas.[4] In each of these areas, there was a degree of homogeneity with respect to the percentage of foreign-born residents, prevalent types of land use, the value of homes, and so on. Residents of

[3] Leo Srole et al., *Mental Health in the Metropolis* (New York: McGraw-Hill, 1962). See especially vol. 1, pp. 69–102.
[4] William H. Form et al., "The Compatibility of Alternative Approaches to the Delimitation of Urban Sub-Areas," *American Sociological Review*, 19, 1954.

each area were interviewed concerning how many people in the neighborhood they knew by name; whether they would continue to live in the neighborhood if they had a choice; and so on. Their answers were combined into a neighborhood intimacy scale, and each subarea was compared. The more homogeneous central city neighborhoods tended to score very low in intimacy. The generally disadvantaged people in the tenements of these areas did not associate with their neighbors, often did not even know their neighbors, and did not identify with their neighborhoods. At the periphery of the city, by contrast, the more homogeneous middle class areas displayed a high degree of neighborhood intimacy.

Similar results have been reported by Hawley and Zimmer from a sample that compared 6 metropolitan areas.[5] In terms of contact with persons in adjacent dwellings, they report more contact in suburban than in central city areas. Even in suburbs, however, only about one-third of the residents had relationships with their neighbors. Both studies also show a connection between neighborliness and the life cycle of residents. The greatest degree of neighborhood intimacy occurs among those with young children. As the children grow older, their parents' commitment to and contacts within the neighborhood decline. Among elderly persons and youngsters, the rate of neighborhood to extraneighborhood contacts is typically high because of limited opportunities for geographical mobility.

A degree of consensus in the studies indicates that neighborliness is generally somewhat higher in middle class and suburban areas. Central city neighborhoods are apparently characterized by extreme fluctuations in rates of interaction, from very low to very high. Neighborhood contacts within central cities are often minimal, but studies in the centers of Mexico City, East London, and Boston have also described the existence of "urban villages" in which relationships are quite extensive and personal. These communities are usually formed by relative newcomers to a city who "re-create" an intimate village-type community within the central city. In effect, the intimacy of their community prevents them from becoming "personally urbanized"; that is, from displaying the reserved and impersonal characteristics theoretically associated with an urban way of life.[6]

Efforts to define neighborhoods by patterns of interaction within areas have been complicated by an apparent trend toward declining neighborliness as a correlate of urbanism. There is substantial research to document the trend, but confusion has been generated by attempts to view reduced neighborhood contacts as indicative of increased social isolation. In cities, declining neighborliness seems to be replaced by increased social

[5] Amos H. Hawley and Basil Zimmer, *The Metropolitan Community* (Beverly Hills, Calif.: Sage Publications, 1970).
[6] The best known of these studies is Herbert Gans, *The Urban Villagers* (New York: Free Press, 1962). For a general review of many of these studies, see R. E. Pahl, "The Rural-Urban Continuum," in R. E. Pahl (ed.), *Readings in Urban Sociology* (New York: Pergamon, 1968).

relationships that stem from work places (interaction with fellow workers) and by relationships that are not confined to limited geographical areas.[7]

The distinction between feelings of isolation and neighborhood contacts is further clarified in a study of communities of various sizes reported by Fischer. He found a slight tendency for people in larger (metropolitan) communities to score higher in feelings of social isolation.[8] Subsequent analysis indicated a strong negative relationship between community size and knowing one's neighbors. This latter relationship was much stronger than the slight relationship between community size and social isolation. The difference in the magnitude is due, he states, to the fact that the pool of potential friends within a city is not confined to the immediate area. In villages, neighboring may be mandatory to avoid isolation, but in cities, social contacts can and do occur across great physical distances.

From the results of this research, it is understandably difficult to define urban neighborhoods or communities by the social contacts or sentiments of their residents. Within an urban context there is a geographically extended spatial structuring of social contacts. Within neighborhoods where there are symbolic identifications with a geographical area—places like Beacon Hill and Nairobi Village—the boundaries of such areas are often unclear. Further, within many geographically distinctive areas there appears to be little or no symbolic attachment to the area on the part of residents. I also have the feeling there is a growing difference between city and suburban identifications in cases where such identifications exist. Suburbanites seem more often to identify with a total community. City dwellers, by contrast, seem to identify with smaller and smaller geographical areas. For example, where a neighborhood was once an object of concern, many city dwellers' attentions are now confined to their own street. Parties, for example, are held only for "members" of a specific street; residents worry about maintaining racial balance only on their street and ignore adjacent streets, and so on.

How then are neighborhoods to be defined? How can the social characteristics of neighborhood residents be examined? One alternative is to accept arbitrary geographical delimitations of neighborhoods, such as census tracts, and then see what kinds of uniformities exist. The uniformities that may then emerge, however, are probably best viewed as the result of largely unplanned and unconscious social forces.[9] The next problem, a methodological one, is how concrete neighborhoods can geographically be

[7] William H. Key, "Urbanism and Neighboring," *Sociological Quarterly*, 6, 1965.

[8] Claude S. Fischer, "On Urban Alienations and Anomie," *American Sociological Review*, 38, 1973. In a cross-national investigation, Fischer also reports a slight tendency for feelings of malaise or unhappiness to be highest in the largest metropolitan areas. See "Urban Malaise," *Social Forces*, 52, 1973.

[9] A similar view of communities is presented by Norton E. Long, "The Local Community as an Ecology of Games," *American Journal of Sociology*, 64, 1958. For further discussion, see chapters one and two in Roland L. Warren, *The Community in America* (Chicago: Rand McNally, 1963).

delimited; that is, what are the boundaries of any given neighborhood? For many research purposes, neighborhoods have been equated with census tracts; thus, we begin by examining how census tracts are designated.

Around 1930, the Bureau of the Census began subdividing American cities into smaller units called census tracts. These were enumeration districts for the bureau, but efforts were also made to establish them in a manner that would facilitate social research. Therefore, it was sometimes assumed that creating socially homogeneous tracts would be useful for research purposes. In some ways, of course, the social scientists participating in these projects were engaged in a dangerous type of tautological exercise. They began with a belief that cities were composed of homogeneous "natural areas." They then located what homogeneous areas they could find and called them census tracts. Areas officially designated as census tracts were then left as data from which later generations were to study the degree to which cities are composed of natural areas.

A historical review of the establishment of census tracts shows that a number of different practices were actually used. In New York, the first city to be districted, the goal was to divide each borough into tracts of equal acreage. The city was subdivided into 3,400 census tracts, each containing about 40 acres. Because Calvin Schmid considered New York relatively evenly populated, he thought this procedure reasonable, but he did not follow it when he was asked to partition the three major cities of Minnesota. He took the by now familiar socioeconomic and land-use characteristics and superimposed them on street maps for each of the three cities. His objective was to delimit "the more significant and distinctive natural areas."[10]

Early designations of census tracts tried to balance actual and projected population sizes with natural area considerations and with topographical features such as mountains and lakes. The projections could not, of course, be perfect, and subsequent redistributions of population within cities have resulted in some remapping of tracts. Although such modifications have occurred, they have usually been resisted to permit unchanging units to remain for historical analysis. The most extensive research on census tracts was pioneered by Eshref Shevky and his associates in California. Their theoretical perspectives and corresponding statistical techniques are known as *social area analysis*.

SOCIAL AREA ANALYSIS

Shevky and Williams initially attempted to analyze and categorize the census tracts of Los Angeles according to three criteria: socioeconomic status of residents, family status (primarily birth rates and women's participation

[10] Calvin F. Schmid, "The Theory and Practice of Planning Census Tracts," *Sociology and Social Research,* 22, 1938; see also *Census Tract Manual* (Washington, D.C.: Bureau of the Census, January 1947).

in the labor force), and segregated ethnic groups.[11] Those census tracts with similar profiles on the three criteria were combined into larger units called social areas. Bell subsequently applied the same three indexes to San Francisco and found that similar social areas were formed by that city's census tracts.[12] Shortly afterward, Shevky and Bell reconsidered their data and presented a fuller (but still brief) theoretical justification for their findings.[13] This latter work has probably been the most influential one and has led to an association of social area analysis with Shevky and Bell.

In explaining the history of social area analysis, Shevky and Bell stated that Los Angeles was initially to be studied as a "community." The size and complexity of the city precluded going very far in this direction, however, and the researchers' orientation shifted dramatically to an examination of "the emerging characteristics of modern society." Large cities such as Los Angeles were then viewed as the best places to study these emerging characteristics. Each of the three criteria—socioeconomic, family, and ethnic status—were seen as indicators of major changes in industrial society. Their logic may be summarized as follows:

1. Industrially induced changes in the division of labor produce a modern system of occupations with socioeconomic status primarily determined by occupation. (Formal education and rent were also used as related indicators.)
2. Urbanization leads to a decline in the importance of the household as an economic unit. This is reflected by increased numbers of working women, a lowered birth rate, and more single-family dwelling units because of the declining importance of extended families.
3. Industrialization and urbanization are associated with greater amounts of migration. This results in greater population diversity and in more segregated racial and ethnic groups.

Material presented in earlier chapters makes some of these assumptions highly questionable. The decline in extended family living, for example, is a problematic assumption. And the segregation of industrial-urban populations could just as easily be viewed as *less* rigid. It must be remembered, however, that this theoretical presentation by Shevky and Bell was brief and sketchy and came after the fact; that is, after social areas had been inferred in the California cities. It was, according to Abu-

[11] Eshref Shevky and Marilyn Williams, *The Social Areas of Los Angeles* (Berkeley: University of California Press, 1949).
[12] Wendell Bell, "The Social Areas of the San Francisco Bay Region," *American Sociological Review,* 18, 1953.
[13] Eshref Shevky and Wendell Bell, *Social Area Analysis* (Stanford, Calif.: Stanford University Press, 1955).

Lughod, an "appended . . . 'rationalization' for Shevky's perspicacious and . . . 'happy' hunches."[14] Nevertheless, many of their hypotheses have been confirmed, as the following discussion will indicate.

To locate social areas in a city, Shevky and his associates began with a grid. Four levels of socioeconomic status were differentiated along the horizontal axis, and four levels of family status demarcated on the vertical axis. This results in 16 cells, each of which is labeled with a number (corresponding to its socioeconomic status) and a letter (corresponding to its family status). Then an S is added to the cell if most of the census tracts included in the cell have many low-status ethnic group members. (If the proportion is low, no S is added.) This entire procedure is illustrated in Figure 8–1 with portions of Bell's analysis of the San Francisco Bay Area.

The social area represented as cell 1D, for example, involves census tracts of low socioeconomic and low family status.[15] In 1950, (N = 0) indicates that there were no such census tracts in San Francisco. There was one similar tract, classified in cell 1C, and it also included a large number of traditionally segregated minorities. To illustrate further, social area 4A included seven census tracts in which residents were high in both family and socioeconomic status. The absence of an S in the cell indicates there were few minority residents.

This procedure for classifying social areas is based on the assumption that urban residential locations are determined by the three dimensions of socioeconomic, family, and minority status. No one dimension is considered sufficient to explain the total configuration of urban areas. In other words, although residential location is determined by socioeconomic status, for example, that is only one basis. Persons of like socioeconomic status

[14] Janet Abu-Lughod, "Testing the Theory of Social Area Analysis," *American Sociological Review, 34, 1969.*
[15] Low family status means few working women and high birth rates.

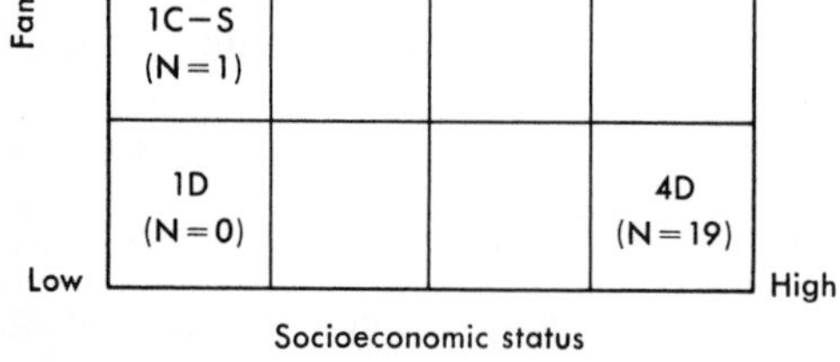

FIGURE 8–1 A sample of social areas in San Francisco.
Source: *Wendell Bell, "The Social Areas of the San Francisco Bay Region,"* American Sociological Review, *18, 1953.*

but different family status become "sorted" into different social areas. In the cities of any industrialized nation, Shevky and Bell propose, differentiation is multidimensional, and the dimensions are relatively independent of each other. Thus, social areas of low socioeconomic standing are expected to be equally likely to score high or low on family status, and the clustering of low-status ethnic groups in the area is also independent of socioeconomic and family status levels.

Factor analysis and social areas

Most studies, since Bell's of San Francisco, have used factor analysis as the major statistical technique. Factor analysis is actually a general category involving a number of specific types of techniques that differ somewhat from one another. However, there are similarities as well. An investigator begins with a large number of specific variables, ordinarily taken from census reports. Some of the most consistently utilized variables include percentage of women in the labor force, percentage of families with annual incomes over $10,000, percentage in the same residence 1965 to 1970. Correlations among all the variables tend to form a few clusters of strongly interrelated variables. These clusters are then assessed for the degree to which the included variables are all measures of the same construct.[16] If there is sufficient evidence that the clustered variables do measure the same thing, they are called a factor; and factor scores are derived by weighting each included variable.

Factor analysis is a method for reducing the number of variables. For example, an investigation may begin with separate measures of occupation, education, income, and monthly rent. All are generally found to be interrelated and to form a factor that is called socioeconomic status. Then census tracts (or cities, or whatever unit is being studied) are given a composite score on the socioeconomic status factor instead of the four separate variables. As long as the number of individual variables is significantly reduced, the analysis continues to generate additional factors.

The hypotheses of social area analysis would be most strongly confirmed if factor analysis of city areas such as census tracts produced the following results: (1) A reduction of variables into three factors: socioeconomic, family, and ethnic status; (2) smaller relationships among these three factors as the degree of industrialization increased. (This would indicate their increasing independence.)

Bell's findings in San Francisco were highly congruent with the first

[16] This description of factor analysis is necessarily simplified. The interested reader is advised to see R. J. Rummell, *Applied Factor Analysis* (Evanston, Ill.: Northwestern University Press, 1970).

expected result.[17] His factor analysis reduced the variables to the three expected dimensions and left very little variation between census tracts unexplained.[18] There was also a *relative* absence of relationships among the three factors that was consistent with the second hypothesis, namely, that the dimensions would be independent of each other in a highly industrial nation. Bell did, however, find an "uncomfortable" degree of relationship between socioeconomic status and ethnic segregation. (The higher an area's socioeconomic standing, the fewer the minority group members it contained.)

All the studies considered thus far were limited to California cities, so the generalizability of the technique had not yet been demonstrated. The results of a study subsequently reported by Van Arsdol and others that included ten large cities from across the country were therefore particularly important.[19] The investigators reported results that tended to support the Shevky et al. assertions. The variables did reduce to the three expected factors, and these three factors did provide a reasonably thorough summarization of census tract variation. However, all the factors were not completely independent of each other, and the data suggested different regional patterns of association. Particularly in the northern cities, there tended to be a moderate degree of relationship between socioeconomic status and ethnic segregation. In some of the southern cities, there was a moderately strong relationship between fertility (theoretically assumed to be a measure of family status) and socioeconomic status. Thus, ethnic segregation was partly linked to socioeconomic status in the North, whereas family size was related to socioeconomic status in the South.

In a study of the northern city of Toledo, Ohio, Anderson and Bean report a stronger degree of separation of ethnic segregation and socioeconomic status.[20] The family status factor, however, did not emerge clearly as a single dimension. In one area pattern, a low birth rate and a large number of working women were associated with a large number of single people and a highly transient neighborhood. In a second pattern, a high birth rate and a low number of working women was a more self-contained factor. In addition, some degree of interdependence among the family and segregation dimensions was also suggested by the weak tendency for the second family status pattern to involve black populations.

[17] Similar results were also simultaneously reported, in a San Francisco study, by Robert C. Tryon, *Identification of Social Areas by Cluster Analysis* (Berkeley: University of California Press, 1955).

[18] A good factor solution is one in which nearly all the possible variation of variables is accounted for by the derived factors.

[19] Maurice D. Van Arsdol, Jr. et al., "The Generality of Urban Social Area Indexes," *American Sociological Review,* 23, 1958.

[20] Theodore R. Anderson and L. L. Bean, "The Shevky-Bell Social Areas," *Social Forces,* 40, 1961.

In attempting to summarize the results of social area studies, we should differentiate between the two original Shevky-Bell hypotheses. Concerning the multidimensionality of areas, there is generally consistent support. That is, socioeconomic, family, and ethnic status appear to be the major bases on which urban social areas in the United States differ from one another. Their stature as independent dimensions, the second hypothesis, receives substantially less confirmation. Our ability to reach any conclusions with confidence, however, is hampered by methodological differences between various studies. In some cases, only central cities have been analyzed; in others, extended metropolitan areas. At this point we can only guess how much of the discrepancy in study findings is due to such differences in sampling units.[21] Another serious interpretive problem has been the fact that the various studies have not begun with uniform lists of variables. Obviously, this can result in somewhat different sets of factors with different patterns of interrelationships. Finally, an important component of the social area hypotheses requires comparison of cities that differ greatly in degree of industrialization. Up until now, only cities in the United States have been examined. An assessment of cross-national results is therefore necessary in order to clarify some of the issues. First, however, let us reconsider our initial questions about neighborhoods in the United States.

SOCIAL AREAS AS COMMUNITIES

At the beginning of this chapter we raised the question of whether it was possible to classify city neighborhoods according to the attitudes and behaviors of their residents. In actual practice, neighborhoods have been equated with census tracts, which have then been combined into social areas. To what degree are these geographical areas meaningful as social areas?

One dimension of social organization that has been widely studied is patterns of political and quasi-political participation. Voting preferences, for example, have been found to vary systematically by social area. More directly to the point, however, the nature of involvement in politically oriented voluntary associations displays markedly different patterns by social areas. In a study of metropolitan St. Louis, for example, Greer and Orleans examined differences among social areas.[22] As expected, how

---

[21] For a discussion of the methodology of social area studies, see Philip H. Rees, "Problems of Classifying Subareas Within Cities," in Brian J. L. Berry (ed.), *City Classification Handbook* (New York: Wiley-Interscience, 1972).

[22] Scott Greer and Peter Orleans, "The Mass Society and the Parapolitical Structure," *American Sociological Review*, 27, 1962.

people voted was related to their social area; but this relationship could be due solely to attitudinal differences resting on socioeconomic differences, and not to neighborhood characteristics per se. However, the investigators also indicate marked differences in political interest by social area and in the type and amount of local political participation. They conclude that social areas are informally structured so as to offer differing opportunities for participation. At least some of the differences between people are apparently due to the nature of social areas themselves.

Another common approach to studying social area differences is to examine the consequences of interarea differences on one of the three dimensions (socioeconomic, family, and ethnic status). Although many of the specifics vary, the studies are highly consistent in showing the strong effects of the individual dimensions. In Portland, for example, Polk reports a generally inverse relationship between juvenile delinquency and the socioeconomic status of neighborhoods: the higher the status, the lower the delinquency. But among neighborhoods that are all low in family status, delinquency increases positively with socioeconomic status.[23] It is not clear why this pattern occurs, but the results indicate the importance of isolating specific social area dimensions. Of paramount importance is the clear relationship between behavior and the dimensions of social areas.

A similar approach was followed by Greer in comparing two census tracts in the Los Angeles area nearly identical in socioeconomic standing and in ethnicity. (Both scored about average on the former, and both were predominantly composed of native whites.) However, one scored moderately high on family status (particularly as indicated by a low rate of fertility); the other scored moderately low. Greer then asked to what degree types of social participation varied in the two areas, which differed from each other only in family status. Some of his findings are summarized in Table 8–1.[24]

In interpreting the results, Greer proposes that local areas of a city attract populations on the basis of different life styles. The low family-status community attracts those who want to raise their children in a community in which they actively participate. This style, he observes, resembles the traditional American community in many respects. The high family-status community has fewer children and little interest in the local community. It resembles the extreme type of urban area described by Wirth (in Chapter 1). Notice also in Table 8–1 that kinship patterns do not vary significantly by type of community; neither does familiarity with leadership of the city. Thus, differences in local community participation and

---

[23] Kenneth Polk, "Juvenile Delinquency and Social Areas," *Social Problems,* 5, 1957. See also Charles V. Willie, "The Relative Contribution of Family Status and Economic Status to Juvenile Delinquency," *Social Problems,* 15, 1967.
[24] Scott Greer, "Urbanism Reconsidered," *American Sociological Review,* 21, 1956.

TABLE 8-1 Social participation and urban areas.

	Family Status	
Type of Participation	Low	High
Have friends in the area	50%	29%
Attend local cultural events	45	18
In organizations meeting in the area	62	26
Could name a local leader	32	21
Could name a Los Angeles leader	38	37
Visit kin at least monthly	63	67

interest do not appear to be related to differences in broader types of participation.

Greer's study deliberately focuses on only one of the three social area dimensions. The ethnic composition and the socioeconomic characteristics of a neighborhood also exert differential degrees of attraction to a heterogeneous urban population. In most cases it may be assumed that people sort themselves into neighborhoods (consciously or otherwise) on the basis of all three dimensions. How each dimension is weighted vis-à-vis the others is not entirely clear. From the patterns of extreme ethnic segregation in most cities it appears that ethnicity is an overriding consideration for persons of low ethnic standing. (Of course, this does not imply that the segregation is totally voluntary.) Where ethnicity is not a factor, there is some evidence to suggest that purely economic considerations are of less importance than general life style considerations in the selection of a

Area differences in family status are associated with marked differences in community involvement and neighborhood friendships (Toronto, Ontario, Canada).

neighborhood.[25] It is not clear, though, whether differences in the overall life styles of neighborhoods are due more to socioeconomic or to family status variables.

In summarizing the results of several decades of research into the differences between geographically defined social areas, Bell emphasizes how consistently behavioral and attitudinal differences have been observed.[26] The studies show, he states, that cities have many and diverse ways of life that differ by neighborhood, and that the social area typology manages to capture many of the varieties of urban life. This increases our confidence that the geographically designated areas are in fact social areas as well, but we must keep in mind that one important aspect of social area theory also relates to presumed cross-national differences as a result of varying degrees of industrialization.

SOCIAL AREAS: A COMPARATIVE VIEW

One of the first attempts to apply the Shevky-Bell scheme outside the United States was reported by McElrath in a study of Rome.[27] He divided the Italian city into *gruppi,* districts that in terms of population size were very much like American census tracts. Measures of family and socioeconomic status, extremely similar to measures used in the U.S. Census, were also available. No measure of ethnic segregation was available, so the analysis was two rather than three dimensional.

The degree of commonality, or shared variation, between these two dimensions in Rome was found to be about 25 times greater than in San Francisco, and about 10 times greater than that reported for any of the 10 American cities studied by Van Arsdol and others. Findings of this type are exactly what Shevky-Bell predicted, because the overall degree of industrialization (and urbanization) is substantially higher in American cities than in Rome. Therefore, the independence of the dimensions in the United States would be expected to exceed their degree of independence in Rome.

Further support for this hypothesis is obtained when still less industrialized nations are examined. In Cairo, for example, Abu-Lughod found that socioeconomic and family status were part of the same factor.[28] This factor involved measures of occupation, fertility, and so on. In Cairo not

---

[25] Charles Tilly, "Occupational Rank and Grade of Residence in a Metropolis," *American Journal of Sociology,* 67, 1961.

[26] Wendell Bell, "Urban Neighborhoods and Individual Behavior," in Paul Meadows and Ephraim H. Mizruchi (eds.), *Urbanism, Urbanization, and Change* (Reading, Mass.: Addison-Wesley, 1969).

[27] Dennis McElrath, "The Social Areas of Rome," *American Sociological Review,* 27, 1962.

[28] Abu-Lughod, *op. cit.*

only were they not independent of each other, but they were tightly inter-woven, as indicated by their presence in a common factor.

Madrid represents a level of industrialization between Cairo and Rome. In an analysis of social areas in Madrid, family and socioeconomic status were again found to be part of a common factor—in other words, highly interrelated.[29] When this common factor was further dissected by rotation, however, elements of the two dimensions sorted into separate (rotated) factors. Thus, Madrid appears to represent a level of industriali-zation at which family and socioeconomic status begin to become separable.

From Cairo to Rome to American cities, then, the independence of the socioeconomic and family status dimensions consistently increases. The ethnic segregation dimension has not been considered because of the unavailability of such data for Rome. McElrath views its omission as "not too serious" because, following Van Arsdol et al., ethnic segrega-tion is the least independent dimension in the United States. Nevertheless, we would like some indication of its generalizability as a dimension out-side the United States. Fortunately, relevant data are available in a study comparing Helsinki and Boston.

In this study, Sweetser controlled most of the methodological prob-lems that have often made comparisons difficult. The sampling from both cities included metropolitan areas, the data from both cities were analyzed in exactly the same way, and the original lists of variables were almost identical in both cities.[30] A socioeconomic factor composed of similar variables was obtained in both cities. A family factor was also obtained, but it involved two separate dimensions in Helsinki, fertility and women's careers. Their separation may be due to the relatively high percentage of Finnish women who work (58 percent), or because of the relatively unique pattern of fertility rates in Finland over the past quarter-century.

Of most direct relevance to us here was the absence of any ethnicity factor in Helsinki. This dimension was obtained in Boston, involving Irish, Italians, and blacks. On the socioeconomic factor in Helsinki, speaking Swedish was associated with higher status than speaking Finnish. This hint of a relationship between ethnicity and socioeconomic status is con-gruent with findings in northern American cities as reported by Van Arsdol et al. But the absence of any direct ethnicity dimension in Helsinki is difficult to explain. There is some evidence to suggest that ethnicity is often not an important dimension outside the United States. Its stature as a social area dimension in British towns, for example, is questionable.[31] Similarly, in Cairo, no ethnic dimension could be obtained despite a de-

[29] Mark Abrahamson and Paul Johnson, "The Social Ecology of Madrid," *De-mography,* 11, 1974.
[30] Frank L. Sweetser, "Factor Structure as Ecological Structure in Helsinki and Bos-ton," *Acta Sociologica,* 8, 1965.
[31] See Rees, *op. cit.,* p. 293.

liberate attempt to include both religious and nationality variables.[32] In Calcutta, by contrast, ethnicity was involved in two factors. The first was the residential concentration of Muslims, and the other, the commercial concentration of Bengalis.[33] Finally, in a social area analysis of two smaller African cities, ethnicity emerged as an independent dimension along with socioeconomic status and an additional dimension dealing with migration to the city.[34] There were also some indications of a family status factor, but it was rather strongly related to ethnicity.

The role of ethnicity as a dimension of residential stratification varies greatly from country to country, reflecting unique traditions of ethnic segregation that probably originate in historical patterns of immigration. The United States, for example, has been the destination point for international streams of migrants, whereas some Scandinavian countries have remained relatively homogeneous. Immigration histories thus present very different opportunities for ethnic segregation. In this respect, modern Israel is very much like the United States. Its three major cities—Jerusalem, Haifa, and Tel Aviv—are all composed of large numbers of international migrants.

Klaff divided each of these Israeli cities into geographical units called subquarters (SQ). His subsequent analysis indicates that there were substantial differences between SQs in socioeconomic status, as indicated by formal education, crowding in dwelling units, and so on.[35] In each city there tended to be a central section composed of SQs high in socioeconomic status and with a large percentage of Western-born immigrants. Sections outside the center in all the cities that had moderate socioeconomic status also tended to have a moderate number of Western immigrants; those that were low on one were also low on the other. Thus, socioeconomic and ethnic status are highly correlated in Israeli cities, in a pattern similar to that observed in northern American cities. The magnitude of the relationship appears to be greater in the Israeli cities, though, as would be expected by differences in industrialization.

In Israeli cities it is also possible to see the relationship independent of any individual ethnic group. The countries of origin of urban Israelis vary greatly from city to city. As of 1961, for example, one-fourth of the population of Tel Aviv and Haifa had emigrated from Poland, compared with only about 10 percent in Jerusalem; nearly one-fifth of Haifa's population emigrated from Rumania, compared with only about 5 percent in the other two cities; and one-fourth of Jerusalem's population is from Iraq or Morocco, compared with about 10 percent in the other cities. Who

---

[32] Abu-Lughod, *op. cit.*

[33] Brian J. L. Berry and Philip H. Rees, "Factorial Ecology of Calcutta," *American Journal of Sociology,* 74, 1969.

[34] Remi Clignet and Joyce Sween, "Accra and Abidjan," *Urban Affairs Quarterly,* 14, 1969.

[35] Vivian Z. Klaff, "Ethnic Segregation in Urban Israel," *Demography,* 10, 1973.

constitutes the non-Western population is markedly different in each Israeli city, although in each there is the same relationship between ethnicity and socioeconomic status.

The data, then, generally support the social area hypothesis with respect to socioeconomic and family status. With industrialization they become increasingly salient dimensions of residential stratification, and increasingly independent of each other as dimensions. In cities such as Madrid and Cairo, where degrees of industrialization are moderately low, a general "life style" dimension has been obtained. It contains items such as age differences between husbands and wives, servants in the home, and other indications of a bourgeois life style. Until a moderately high degree of industrialization is attained, there are apparently too few differences in socioeconomic and fertility-related considerations for them to be major dimensions. Ethnic segregation, the third dimension, does not appear to follow a consistent cross-cultural pattern. Perhaps there are simply too many traditions unique to each country.

THE SPATIAL DISTRIBUTION OF SUBAREAS

If the dimensions of social areas are examined spatially, their distribution in many cities is found to resemble the concentric zone pattern described by Park and Burgess. As circular areas become more distant from the center of a city, the socioeconomic status of residents tends to increase and the number of ethnic minorities tends to decrease. Family status, however, is often distributed in a manner inconsistent with concentric zones. As a result, entire social areas composed of all three dimensions display less of a concentric zone pattern than do the first two dimensions examined separately.

The accuracy of the Park-Burgess model is also lessened by the return flow of high socioeconomic status residents. As these people have moved into luxury highrise apartments in center cities, the inner zones of cities have become more heterogeneous. Outside the United States, many cities are in fact characterized by uniformly high socioeconomic status in the center, with status correlating negatively with distance from the center. A concentric zone *model* is still partially applicable, but the specific pattern is the opposite of the one described by Park and Burgess.

Even more fundamental restrictions on the concentric zone model are produced by the fact that ecological distributions in many cities also correspond fairly closely to Hoyt's sector theory. To review briefly, the sector theory views patterns of land use and residents' status as emanating radially out from the center. Instead of resembling the rings of a tree (as in concentric zone theory), the geographical distribution of a city is expected to resemble the slices of a pie.

In American cities there recently has been a return of persons of high socioeconomic status to high-rise apartments in the city center (Philadelphia, Pennsylvania).

Rome, Chicago, Tel Aviv

In order to examine these spatial distribution issues in more detail, let us begin by returning to Rome and McElrath's analysis of this city's tracts, or *gruppi*.[36] He established three sectors by examining all the subareas contiguous to the three major transportation arteries that run from the outer edge of the city into its center. Then three concentric zones encompassing the city were developed in accordance with the city's established administrative boundaries. Rome was simultaneously divided into both sectors and zones, roughly as illustrated in Figure 8–2.

On family status, areas adjacent to sector two scored highest, followed closely by sector one, with sector three far behind. Socioeconomic status followed the same ranking, but the greatest differences were between sectors two and one. By zone, McElrath reports almost identically high socioeconomic status in zones one and two, and sharply lower average scores in zone three. (At this point it may simply be noted that American cities typically have markedly lower socioeconomic status in the innermost zones.) With respect to family status, the zones display the same ranking: one highest, two intermediate, and three markedly lower.

Examination of zones within sectors followed a comparable pattern, but the differences between zones by sectors were much less significant.

[36] McElrath, *op. cit.*

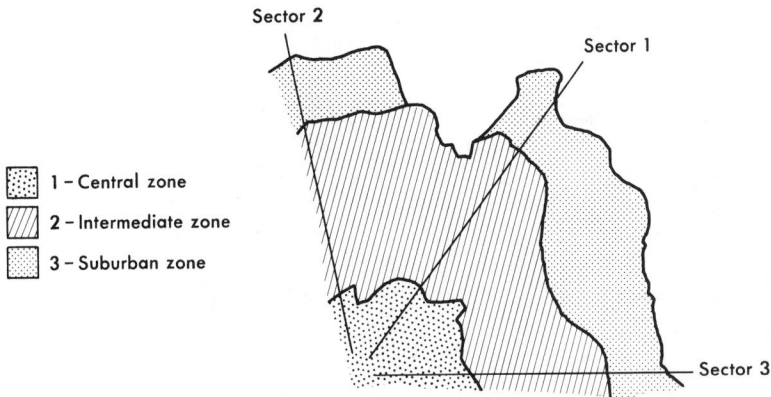

FIGURE 8–2   Sectors and zones in northern Rome.

To a degree, sectors containing areas scoring high on either status dimension tended also to score high on the other dimension. In short, zones and sectors did not operate completely independently of each other. Family and socioeconomic status in Rome, therefore, are distributed according to both sectors and zones.

Rees's reexamination of Chicago, originally analyzed only in terms of concentric zones by Park and Burgess, shows a similar combination of zone and sector influences.[37] He classified social areas in the city according to a combination of two factors, socioeconomic status and family age (or life cycle). His results, illustrated in Figure 8–3, shows an ecological distribution that clearly reflects the influence of both sectors and zones. The disproportionate number of blacks in the lowest socioeconomic tracts further supports our previous observation of a relationship between socioeconomic status and ethnic segregation (especially in northern American cities).

With respect to the central issue of zones and sectors, the data from Rome and from Chicago are highly compatible. In both cities, the ecological structure displays a combination of both zones and sectors. Another type of combined pattern has been observed in a study of four middle-sized northern American cities where zones and sectors have each been reported to exert more specialized influences.[38] These cities' socioeconomic distribution varied by sector, but not by zone. In contrast, family status varied by zone, but socioeconomic status did not.

[37] Philip H. Rees, "The Factorial Ecology of Metropolitan Chicago," in Brian J. L. Berry and Frank E. Horton (eds.), *Geographic Perspectives on Urban Systems* (Englewood Cliffs, N.J.: Prentice-Hall, 1970).
[38] Theodore R. Anderson and Janice A. Egeland, "Spatial Aspects of Social Area Analysis," *American Sociological Review*, 26, 1961. The four cities are Akron, Dayton, Indianapolis, and Syracuse.

Socioeconomic status and family age:

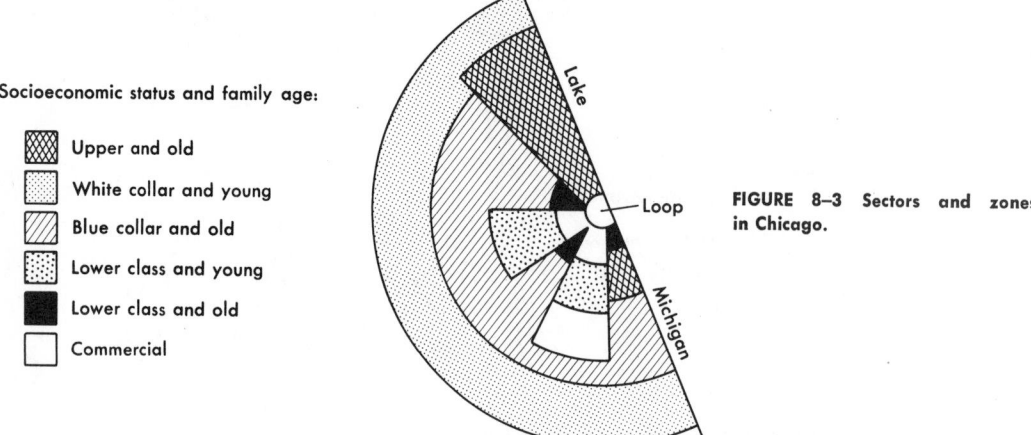

▨ Upper and old

▦ White collar and young

▧ Blue collar and old

▨ Lower class and young

■ Lower class and old

☐ Commercial

FIGURE 8–3 Sectors and zones in Chicago.

Still another type of interesting pattern is provided by contemporary cities in Israel. In Tel Aviv, socioeconomic status and immigrants' countries of origin are distributed largely according to concentric zones, with the highest status groups in the center.[39] In Jerusalem, the highest status groups are in the center zone, but the overall ecological distribution conforms more to sectors than to zones. A medium status sector runs to the north of the city, and there is a low status sector to the south. Thus, even within the same country the ecological configuration of cities can vary.

If we recognize these variations in findings among the studies, it seems reasonable to conclude generally that urban areas are ecologically arranged both by zones and sectors, though one or the other can predominate. The debate between the proponents of each theory, like so many others in sociology, is resolved by a split verdict: they are both correct, in part.

Madrid and San Juan: The Spanish colonial pattern

In the preceding discussion, we saw that central city areas in Rome score higher than peripheral areas in socioeconomic status, the opposite of the American pattern. There is a great deal of evidence showing the generality of this pattern, especially in cities where the degree of industrialization is not very high. We will begin with Madrid, Spain, for two reasons. First, a widespread "inversion" of socioeconomic status and ecological location throughout Latin America is attributed to Spanish colonial influence. The same pattern should therefore be evident in Madrid. Second, relatively few published studies of social areas in Madrid are available in the literature, making it a relatively "unknown" city and therefore interesting. For-

[39] Klaff, *op. cit.*

tunately there are some data available thanks to a Madrid metropolitan area census conducted during 1965 and 1966.[40]

Metropolitan Madrid is divided into three historical regions further subdivided into a total of twelve areas, as illustrated in Figure 8–4. In the

[40] Figures in the following section are taken from "Estudios de Cáritas Diocesena de Madrid—Alcalá," *Informe Sociologico Sobre la Situaciòn Social de Madrid,* Madrid, 1967.

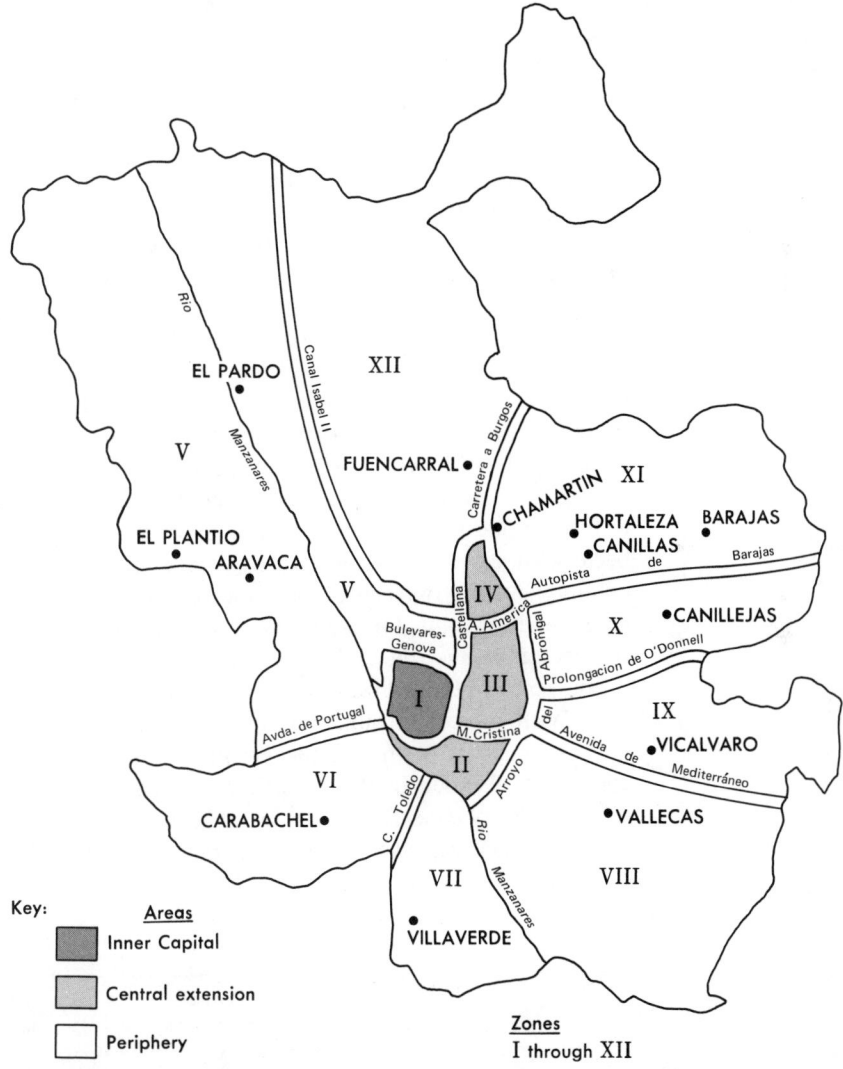

FIGURE 8–4. Areas and zones of Madrid.
Source: *Euramérica, S. A. Madrid,* informe sociológico sobre la situación social de MADRID, *1967, p. 33.*

TABLE 8-2 Socioeconomic status in Madrid.

Status	Inner Capital	Central Extension	Periphery
High status occupations*	41%	49%	24%
Low status occupations†	33	29	32
No formal education (husbands)	12	4	14
Post primary education (husbands)	23	50	18

High status occupations include professionals, managers, and general white collar employees (males only).
† *Low status occupations include unskilled workers and unskilled personal servants (males only).*

center is the capital district, the oldest part, containing government office buildings and small shops, major boulevards and narrow, winding streets. The second region partially surrounds the capital and contains three areas. Here are the major retail and commercial centers as well as private dwellings. The third region extends to the edge of the metropolitan area in all directions and is divided into seven areas by major highways and rivers.

Among the three regions there are substantial differences in socioeconomic standing, as indicated in Table 8–2. From the figures it seems clear that the highest socioeconomic status is in the three central areas surrounding the old capital. The periphery, which would be most comparable ecologically to suburban areas in the United States, is lowest in socioeconomic status. The inner capital averages in the middle of the three because it contains extremes. High-status professionals and government officials live in the center because of its proximity to their places of employment. Their domestic help also lives in the inner capital. Living in the center means old and crowded housing if you are poor, but it also means greatly reduced transportation costs.

With respect to indicators of family status, Table 8–3 describes the three regions. It is only in the periphery that family status variables are consistent. Women in the periphery are least likely to be employed and most likely to have large families. The inner capital and the central extension reverse relative family status positions, and this reversal raises two

TABLE 8-3 Family status in Madrid.

Status	Inner Capital	Central Extension	Periphery
Women as % of labor force	28%	34%	18%
% with no children	23	17	12
% with four or more children	15	19	21

interesting questions: what accounts for the differences, and how are large families reconciled with working women?

With respect to family size differences, there is a high correlation by region between family size and length of time in Madrid. Over half the inner capital residents were born in Madrid, and only 10 percent have lived in Madrid for less than ten years. In both the central extension and the periphery, permanence of residence in Madrid is much lower. Only about one-fourth of the population in each of these areas are natives, and over 20 percent have resided in Madrid for less than ten years. The regions are thus associated with differing degrees of urban acculturation, which in turn reflect differing family size norms. In other words, the inner capital has a more established (urban) tradition of smaller families. This is also indicated in Figure 8–5, which compares two generations of women according to the current generation's location in Madrid.

Part of the intergenerational differences are spuriously great because some of the mothers will continue to have children; their average family size will increase. The mothers' mothers, by contrast, are typically past child-bearing ages, so their average families are no longer subject to much of an increase. Therefore, although family size is probably decreasing in Madrid, it is not decreasing by as much as Figure 8–5 would indicate. But the difference between regions gives further evidence of the longer standing urban-related pattern of smaller families in the inner capital. Finally, ages of women decline with distance from the center. Thus, it may be projected that family size differences between regions will be further increased by the end of the current mothers' child-bearing cycles.

Each of the three regions, then, is associated with a distinct family and socioeconomic status pattern. The inner capital is inhabited by residents of both high and low socioeconomic status. Specifically, this includes government officials and professionals, who live close to their places of

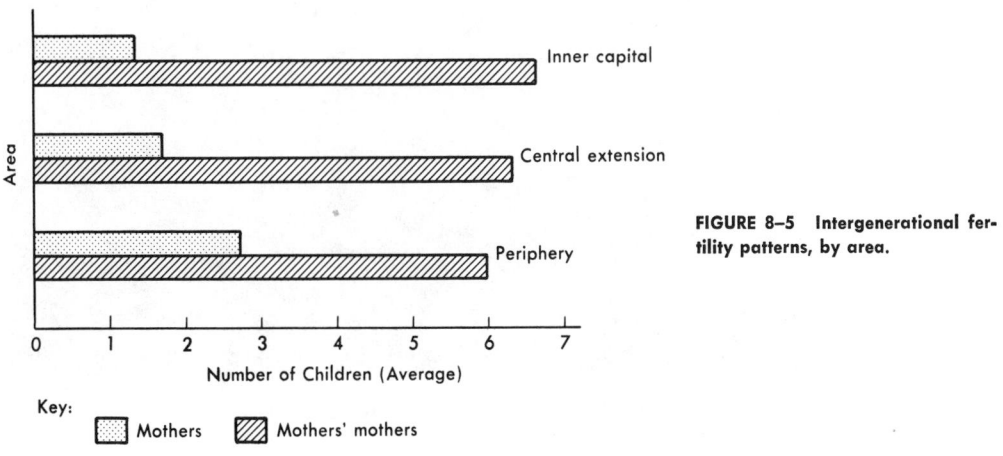

FIGURE 8–5 Intergenerational fertility patterns, by area.

employment. It also includes their domestic help—persons of low standing—who also live close to their places of employment. Despite these socioeconomic extremes, birth rates are uniformly relatively low, which is attributable to the long urban residence of both socioeconomic groups.

The central extension has the largest percentage of high socioeconomic status residents and the smallest percentage of low status residents. By comparison with inner capital residents, however, they are relative newcomers to Madrid. Many of the married couples who live in this area migrated to Madrid and worked and saved prior to marriage. This is often necessary because most of the modern apartments in the central extension must be purchased rather than rented, and they are expensive. A large percentage of the women who worked prior to marriage continue to do so after marriage, despite having moderately large families. They are able to do both because of the relative availability of domestic help to care for preschoolers. Work also need not interfere with a mother's desire to spend time with her children because of the widespread opportunities for women to work only until about two o'clock in the afternoon. (They simply do not return to work after the siesta.)

The periphery is characterized by large numbers of recent migrants (half of them have been in Madrid for less than twenty years), by relatively large families,[41] and by low socioeconomic standing. Thus, they re-

[41] The greatest average discrepancy between actual family size and the number of children a woman would consider ideal is in the periphery. This suggests that low degrees of acculturation are associated with low use of contraceptive techniques, due either to ignorance or "morality." This relationship is reported on Taiwan by Ronald Friedman et al., "Fertility and Family Planning in Taiwan," *American Journal of Sociology,* 70, 1964.

With increased industrialization, the outskirts of Mexico City have been turned into modern suburbs for employees of large factories.

semble the urban poor of most nations. Unlike American cities, though, the Madrid poor live in the "suburbs" rather than in the inner city.

Viewed comparatively, where the high status areas of a city are located tends to be related to industrialization. In more highly industrialized cities, the concentration of commercial and industrial activities near the center makes outlying areas more desirable for residential use. In addition, central cities tend to be older and their physical deterioration and crowding are additional incentives for people to seek outlying areas. The simultaneous development of transportation facilities makes suburban living more practical for a growing middle class.

This general pattern is illustrated by the ecological differences between traditional Spanish cities in Latin America. Due to Spanish regulations dating from the seventeenth century, Latin American cities have traditionally involved a clustering of high status groups near the center, or *plaza mayor*. Located in this plaza are the main church and the government and administrative buildings. For those who wanted to be close to the heart of Spanish colonial life, a central location was highly desirable; but the price of admission to the center was high status.

In order to assess the subsequent effects of industrialization, Schwirian and Rico-Velasco examined three Puerto Rican cities.[42] San Juan was the largest, with the most educated population and the lowest percentage of agricultural workers. Ponce and Mayaguez followed in that order. Each of the cities was divided into a number of concentric zones, moving out from a central point. Then within each area, the occupational, educational, and income status of residents was assessed. The results in San Juan showed strong positive correlations between distance from the center and scores on all three status variables. Thus, San Juan displayed an industrial pattern in which increasing socioeconomic status was positively associated with distance from the center. The relationships were very strong, but they were not perfect, especially with respect to distance and income. There was a group of wealthy persons living along the beachfront near the center. Waterfronts, it appears, are desirable locations, regardless of industrialization. (High status groups are also found near the center of cities in locales overlooking bodies of water in Chicago, Calcutta, and elsewhere.)

In Ponce and Mayaguez, by contrast, occupation, education, and income were inversely related to distance from the center. These cities displayed a classic Latin pattern in which high status (especially with respect to education) is associated with a central location. This classic Latin pattern is not confined to Latin countries. The same pattern characterizes many cities that are low in industrialization, and even a few that are highly industrialized, such as Haifa in Israel.

[42] Kent P. Schwirian and Jesus Rico-Velasco, "The Residential Distribution of Status Groups in Puerto Rico's Metropolitan Areas," *Demography*, 8, 1971.

San Diego, California.

9 The Social Integration of Urban Life

LIFE IN RUSSIA DURING THE REVOLUTION was a nightmare of unpredictability. The regulation that is normally provided by any political system was temporarily rendered ineffective while factions struggled to legitimate their own authority. It is probably terrifying enough just to dread a knock on your door late at night; but it is probably worse still not to be able to anticipate which side is knocking. The uncertainty was further multiplied because traditional values, sex-role norms, and vested class privileges were being overthrown along with a political regime.

Except in the most totalitarian society, social life is governed more by social norms than legal imperatives, although social norms and legal rules are generally mutually reinforcing. In our own society, for example, research indicates that there is enormous consensus concerning the seriousness of crimes. Persons of differing race, sex, and educational attainment all agree on a seriousness ordering of premeditated murder, forcible rape, armed robbery, prostitution, public loitering, and so on.[1] The formal legal penalties associated with these acts tend to follow the same ranking. Examination of other aspects of life indicates that at some point legal rules cease to be effective or even relevant, and regulation is almost completely by social norms. For example, almost everyone in a middle class sample agrees that the best age for a woman to marry is between 19 and 24; that the best age for people to finish school and go to work is between 20 and

[1] Peter H. Rossi et al., "The Seriousness of Crimes," *American Sociological Review,* 39, 1974.

22, and so on.[2] Of course there is not complete compliance with any social norm, but norms do provide common points of reference to which most people accommodate their behavior. Thus, between 1950 and 1970 in the United States the median age of a woman at first marriage hovered around 23 years.

In order to prevent the chaos of everyone marching to a different drummer, there must be some degree of normative integration; that is, compatibility or congruence among the norms. Suppose, for example, the best age for a woman to marry were considered between 19 and 24 years, but the best age for a man was between 45 and 50 years. If this became the norm it would be inconsistent with a number of other family and socialization norms currently held in our society. For example, paternal grandfathers could not stand in the same relationship to grandchildren as maternal grandfathers (the current norm) because they would be dead before grandchildren were born.

Just how much support norms must receive, and how integrated they must be, we do not know. However, the complex social organization associated with an urban society historically has been considered to involve potentially insufficient amounts of both consensus and integration. The more complex the society, the higher the risk that norms will not effectively bind individuals and groups to the larger social order. As a result, the capacity of such societies to regulate individual and group behavior becomes more problematic.

Sociologists have been joined by playwrights, novelists and filmmakers in studying changes in the social bonds that link people to the social order. The changes have been extensively analyzed in relation to urbanism and urbanization using concepts such as alienation, anomie, and isolation. These "master concepts" have been related to a wide assortment of problems. Rates of crime, suicide, divorce, and so on have all been examined in relation to normative integration and regulation. Similarly, various types of social movements and collective behaviors, such as the prohibition movement, strikes, and lynchings, have all been viewed as attempts to reintegrate the social order.

From this introduction it should be clear that in this chapter we will focus on norms. This requires an examination of individuals, because it is only individuals who are carriers of norms, who join social movements, and who commit suicide. As a result, it is often difficult to distinguish conceptually between individual acts and social norms. One way to maintain this distinction between levels of analysis is to focus on an admittedly hypothetical "average man." The social forces affecting this typical person are assumed to be indicated by the rates with which suicides or social

[2] Bernice L. Neugarten et al., "Age Norms, Age Constraints, and Adult Socialization," *American Journal of Sociology,* 71, 1965

movements or the like occur. Variations in the rates can be viewed as properties of the social system and correspondingly as indicators of social integration and regulation.

Failure to distinguish between the personal and the social levels of analysis creates a number of theoretical confusions and empirical mis-applications. For example, looking at individual cases, Robinson has re-ported a small positive correlation between nativity and illiteracy; persons who are foreign-born tend to be illiterate slightly *more* than the native-born. However, when the relationship between nativity and illiteracy is examined by region of the country, a moderately strong negative relation-ship is obtained. Those regions of the country with high proportions of foreign-born tend to have *low* rates of illiteracy.[3] The relationship between the same variables reverses because of the different units of analysis in-volved. What is true for individuals is not necessarily true for ecological or social aggregates.

REGULATION IN COMPLEX SOCIETIES

Thomas and Durkheim

One of the most perceptive and interesting analyses of urban-related changes in social organization was offered by W. I. Thomas. He viewed all people as motivated by four basic "wishes" that were partly learned and partly instinctual.[4] How these wishes would be expressed and satisfied —that is, the form they would take—was seen as a product of both cultural and social class influences. Thus, hunting for food or for sport might satisfy the same desire for exciting experiences as would shooting craps. In human society, he continued, the basic regulation of the wishes is "internal," determined by individuals in their "definitions of situations." By this Thomas meant that people must interpret any given social situation in a way that is meaningful to them. From their interpretation, an appro-priate way of responding will be suggested. Lower animals, by contrast, have their decisions imposed on them physiologically, biochemically, and so on. Durkheim had previously made this same point, arguing that the

---

[3] W. S. Robinson, "Ecological Correlations and the Behavior of Individuals," *American Sociological Review*, 15, 1950. This level of analysis problem described by Rob-inson has subsequently been called the ecological fallacy. A similar but more com-plex problem arises when relationships are examined in aggregates of different sizes. See Michael T. Hannan, "Problems of Aggregation," in Hubert M. Blalock, Jr. (ed.), *Causal Models in the Social Sciences* (New York: Aldine-Atherton, 1971).
[4] The wishes include the desires for new experiences, security, response, and recogni-tion. This discussion of Thomas is based primarily on his book, *The Unadjusted Girl* (New York: Harper & Row, 1967). Originally published in 1923.

social, or normative, control of behavior was a distinctive characteristic of human society.

What was especially problematic for Thomas and for Durkheim was how effectively a complex society could normatively control human desires. There is nothing in man's organic nature, Durkheim pointed out, to limit his desires. Therefore, how could anyone determine "the quality of well-being, comfort or luxury legitimately to be craved by a human being?"[5] Only society could, he thought. As the supraindividual, external force, only society has the moral power to "set the point beyond which the passions must not go." From Thomas's perspective, if unchecked, individuals tend to be hedonistic, seeking "pleasure first." For society, however, it is "safety first," a cautious orientation embodied in moral codes. These codes, or norms, are the generally accepted definitions of situations and they produce uniform ways of responding.

When a complex society is integrated, according to Durkheim, each of the specialized parts has its own place, and the arrangement of the parts is known to everyone.[6] He termed the nonintegrated condition *anomie,* and in various writings pursued two somewhat different views of anomie. The first entails a disjunction among the parts of a society; for example, its norms and its goals. Thus, institutionally emphasized means of attaining success, such as formal education, may not in fact result in attainment of socially valued goals, such as financial wealth.[7] A second view of anomie involves a weakening of external restraints that "unleashes" aspirations, resulting in the despair of unattainable desires.[8] Periods of great affluence, for example, particularly if they follow rapidly on the heels of depression, may lead people to seek increasingly more "bizarre" kicks. Their strivings are in vain, though, because unlimited desires cannot, by definition, be satisfied.

For Durkheim, as for Thomas, the risks of deregulation are most acute in contemporary urban societies. In peasant societies, by contrast, Thomas noted that the community is an important regulating and defining agent. The community reaches, he quotes a Polish peasant, "as far as a man is talked about." In contemporary societies, however, the community is viewed as having become "weak and vague," no longer able to validate moral codes. As a result, individuals become increasingly likely to redefine

---

[5] Emile Durkheim, *Suicide* (New York: Free Press, 1951), p. 247. Originally published in 1897.

[6] The spatial metaphor, each in its own place, was presented by Durkheim in *The Elementary Forms of the Religious Life* (London: Allen and Unwin, 1915), especially pp. 442–444.

[7] This type of anomie is emphasized by Robert K. Merton, "Social Structure and Anomie," in Merton's *Social Theory and Social Structure* (New York: Free Press, 1957).

[8] For a discussion of the two types of anomie, see Ephraim H. Mizruchi, "Aspirations and Poverty," *Sociological Quarterly,* 8, 1967.

Thomas considered community norms in modern cities too weak to regulate behavior uniformly in the face of multiple temptations (Manhattan, New York).

situations in new and unique ways, continuously introducing change and disorganization. Thus, he says, the invention of the bank check was followed by forgery; the sulphur match, by arson; the automobile, by seduction. Thomas described this process as "the individualization of behavior," and saw its consequences very much like Durkheim viewed those of anomie. In the small community of the past, repression of wishes, "was demanded of all, the arrangement was equitable, and . . . pleasure [was] not countenanced as an end in itself."[9] In modern cities, however, everyone feels that "too much is being missed in life." This feeling expresses itself in despair, depression, and sometimes "in breaking all bounds."

Both Durkheim and Thomas were sensitive to a tension between the community or society, on the one hand, and individuals on the other. In both theories, social change weakened the normative integration (Durkheim) or moral codes (Thomas), and individuals suffered the consequences. In his analysis of the antecedents of anomie, however, Durkheim appeared to be more interested than Thomas in examining integration at a purely social level of analysis. In other words, even though individuals suffered the consequences, anomie was viewed as a nonpersonal, "normative pathology." Strictly speaking, therefore, it is society and not individuals that are most appropriately characterized as high or low in anomie. To measure the individual corollaries of anomie, an *anomia* scale was later developed.

[9] Thomas, *op. cit.,* pp. 71–72.

Durkheim focused on changes in the division of labor as an antecedent to anomie and on changes in the suicide rate as a consequence. His theory of the division of labor has been discussed in an earlier chapter (see Chapter 3), so a brief review at this point will suffice. Population growth, technological developments, and increased rates of interaction within a more densely populated society were associated by Durkheim with the development of a more complex division of labor. As the division of labor became more complex, social integration became more problematic and the rate of suicide increased as a result. Note that social malintegration (or anomie) was utilized by Durkheim as an intervening or explanatory variable; that is, it was inferred to account for the relationship between the division of labor and the rate of suicide.

As an imprecisely defined intervening variable, social integration presented later generations of sociologists with a number of serious methodological problems. Given no direct measure of either integration or anomie, some investigators used changes in the division of labor, or related phenomena, as indicators. They then related these changes to rates of suicide, alcoholism, and so on. This procedure, however, precludes direct testing of a possible relationship between the division of labor and social integration, because the former is used as the indicator of the latter. Other studies moved in the opposite direction, inferring a degree of anomie from rates of illegitimate births, suicide, or juvenile delinquency.[10] However, using these rates to indicate the degree of integration obviously precludes testing the hypothesis that the high rates are produced by anomie.

Given the theoretical importance of the concept of social integration and the problems that ensue when it can be only indirectly inferred, sociologists have made several efforts to construct direct measures, but none have been completely adequate. One ambitious early attempt was made by Angell to measure the "moral integration" of American cities. His indicator of integration emphasized rates of crime and city expenditures on public welfare. Some of Angell's findings were of theoretical interest; for example, lower integration was found in cities with high rates of mobility and relatively large foreign-born populations.[11] But there were few subsequent efforts to utilize Angell's measure. It involved too much emphasis on the moral, or value, dimension of integration; and the inclusion of a composite crime index as one of the indicators precluded studying integration in relation to a number of potentially important consequences.

A more widely used measure, called "status integration," was later

[10] For an inventory of measurement practices, see the appendix by Stephen Cole and Harriet Zuckerman in Marshall B. Clinard (ed.), *Anomie and Deviant Behavior* (New York: Free Press, 1964).
[11] Robert C. Angell, "The Moral Integration of American Cities," *American Journal of Sociology*, 57, 1951.

developed by Gibbs and Martin. They assumed that the strength of individuals' ties to a larger society was determined by their opportunities for engaging in stable and long-term social relationships. For relationships to be stable, the participants must be able to adjust to each other's expectations. The degree to which an individual can conform to these expectations depends, in turn, on the degree to which he faces conflicts in the various roles he plays; that is, occupies positions that lead him to behave in ways incompatible with one another. Therefore, status integration is indicated by the proportion of a population that occupies incongruent statuses.[12]

In applying this measure, Gibbs and Martin examined the degree to which various types of statuses formed stable configurations. For example, they observed that a large percentage of persons in the occupational status of bartender were also in the marital status of divorced. This suggested some status incompatibility between being married and being a bartender —perhaps due to working odd hours or developing a cynical view of people. To be a young male parent and also a widower would similarly entail incompatible statuses.

Following Durkheim, they hypothesized that the greater the degree of status integration, the lower the rate of suicide. Their own analysis, using data from both the United States and Ceylon, provided moderately strong confirmation. Other research has replicated the finding of a negative relationship between status integration and suicide. However, the question that persists is: Does status compatibility really measure social integration? Turner has argued that logically inconsistent values associated with different norms do not actually conflict with each other in practice, and so do not produce low integration. For example, in order to capture a person who fails to stop at a stop sign, a policeman may pursue him in a high-speed chase on a crowded highway. Both the policeman and the general public would agree that public safety is more important than ticketing a minor traffic offender. Yet, Turner notes, most people do not regard the public dangers of the chase as inconsistent with their values. The weighing of alternative values, he concludes, simply does not occur in most concrete situations. People act, and they feel little sense of conflict or guilt. Thus, from Turner's perspective, people can handle incompatible statuses without disrupting relationships, so the proportion of such positions would not indicate the degree of social malintegration.[13]

If Turner's argument is accepted, the question that remains is why then does status integration correlate, as expected, with suicide rates? One obvious answer is that many variables correlate with suicide—socio-

[12] Jack P. Gibbs and Walter T. Martin, *Status Integration and Suicide* (Eugene: University of Oregon, 1964).
[13] Turner's view was actually expressed before the Gibbs-Martin theory. His comments were directed at Angell's moral integration, but are even more applicable to the Gibbs-Martin measure. Ralph H. Turner, "Value Conflict in Social Disorganization," *Sociology and Social Research,* 38, 1954.

economic standing, marital status, and so on. There is no necessary reason
to view any variable that correlates with suicide as a measure of social
integration just because it does correlate with suicide.[14] It is a highly complex problem to "validate" any indicator; that is, to demonstrate that it
actually measures what it purports to measure. In the case of a theoretically
complex concept such as social integration, one simple correlation is inadequate. Remember that Durkheim used anomie or malintegration as an
intervening variable; that is, as an explanatory concept to account for the
relationship between the division of labor and suicide. To assess its role as
an intervening variable, it is minimally necessary to show that integration
correlates not only with the presumed consequence (suicide), but with the
presumed antecedent (changes in division of labor) as well. This is the
essence of the "diagnostic procedure" described by Lazarsfeld. It does not
prove the reality of the intervening concepts, nor does it totally validate
their measure, but it does provide strong logical support.[15]

The type of data we need have been reported by Miley and Micklin
from a cross-national study of status integration and suicide rates in 24
nations. They utilized the Gibbs-Martin measure and obtained data on
suicide rates from United Nations publications. In addition, they also
measured several other variables in Durkheim's causal chain: population
growth, technological development, and the division of labor.[16] An over-
view of their findings is presented in the following schematic form:

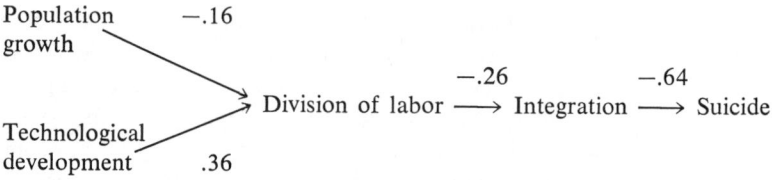

Beginning at the right end of the chain, we note that the reported
relationship between integration and suicide replicates the earlier Gibbs-
Martin finding. (Even the magnitude of the reported relationship is simi-

[14] Note too that the examples (socioeconomic and marital statuses) are also variables
used by Gibbs and Martin in constructing the status integration measure. Thus, the
compatibility index may correlate with suicide because of the independent effects of
the variables included.

[15] For a remarkably simple and thoughtful discussion of how to infer intervening
variables, see Paul F. Lazarsfeld, "Concept Formation and Measurement in the Behavioral Sciences," in Gordon J. Direnzo (ed.), *Concepts, Theory, and Explanation
in the Behavioral Sciences* (New York: Random House, 1966).

[16] Most of their indicators followed those used by Gibbs and Martin in their 1962
study of urbanization. See Chapter 3 for a review. James D. Miley and Michael
Micklin, "Structural Change and the Durkeimian Legacy," *American Journal of
Sociology,* 78, 1972.

lar.) Thus, the higher the integration, the lower the suicide rate, and the relationship is moderately strong. Moving farther to the left, the reported correlation between the division of labor and integration is in the expected direction; that is, the greater the changes in the complexity of the division of labor, the lower the degree of integration. However, the magnitude of the relationship $(-.26)$ is probably much lower than we would expect according to Durkheim. Moving still farther to the left, technological development predicts to changes in the division of labor about as expected, but population growth does not. The latter relationship is surprisingly small, and in a direction opposite that specified by Durkheim. The magnitude of the relationship, however, is too small to take much note of its direction.

In defense of Durkheim's theory, it should be pointed out that many of the sampled nations are rather highly industrialized. The effects of changes their population growth and technological development might have produced between 1950 and 1960 were not what Durkheim had in mind three-quarters of a century earlier. He was talking more about their initial effects on the division of labor. Of most concern to us here, however, are the last three variables in the diagram, because they indicate the role of status integration as an intervening variable between changes in the division of labor and rates of suicide. Here the results are equivocal: The status integration measure does predict to suicide, but changes in the division of labor are only weakly reflected in decreasing degrees of integration.

In reaching a conclusion, it is difficult to assess the significance of the weak relationship between the division of labor and status integration. Although Durkheim viewed integration as more problematic in societies with complex divisions of labor, their complexity per se was not viewed as a cause of anomie under normal conditions. Therefore, how strong a relaship between integration and the division of labor should be expected, following Durkheim?[17]

Srole's anomia

Social integration remains a theoretically interesting concept, but one that continues to defy unequivocal direct measurement at the social level of analysis. In part because of this measurement problem, and in part because of an interest in the psychological corollaries of anomie, the concept of anomia has been widely utilized. As presented by Srole, anomia reflects the "internalized counterparts" of strain at the social structural level.[18] Srole's anomia scale focuses on an individual's feelings that:

[17] For a discussion of the difficulties in measuring social integration and an inventory of other Durkheimian studies, see Robert M. Marsh, *Comparative Sociology* (New York: Harcourt, Brace, 1967).
[18] Leo Srole, "Social Integration and Certain Corollaries," *American Sociological Review,* 21, 1956.

Anomia entails feelings of being alone in a meaningless world (Manhattan, New York).

1. Community leaders are detached and indifferent to his needs.
2. Society is without order; that is, fickle, capricious, unpredictable.
3. The outcomes in life of people like himself are getting worse, not better.
4. Life is meaningless.
5. Personal relationships can no longer be counted upon.

Following publication of the Srole anomia scale, a number of studies attempted, often with positive results, to relate anomia to other personal attributes, such as authoritarianism and prejudice.[19] Like anomie, anomia has also been useful as an explanatory concept, particularly in reference to large-scale patterns of behavior that would otherwise be difficult to explain. In the spring and early summer of 1974, for example, near riots occurred in the baseball parks of many American cities. In Cleveland, during a ten-cent beer night, fans rushed onto the field and attacked a visiting team's outfielder. Many columnists attributed the incident to too much beer consumption. In New York, fans cursed at Cincinnati's out-fielder, Pete Rose, and then threw bottles and ice cubes at him. In this case the outburst was attributed to a fight between Rose and a New York player in the previous year's playoffs.

What made these events dramatic was the stature of baseball as the traditional American game. Unlike European soccer riots, there was no precedent in baseball for such collective disturbances. In addition, although

[19] See the appendix in Clinard, *op. cit.*

explanations specific to each situation were offered (too much beer, continuation of a feud), the widespread magnitude of the events suggested the need for a more general explanation. One manager may have been close when he attributed the lower inhibition of fans to changes in their views of ballplayers. "In the past," he stated, "kids didn't look at athletes as just ordinary humans. They held them in awe." But now, he concluded, they are regarded simply "as people."[20]

Breakdowns in traditional norms were stressed by Durkheim as part of the malintegration process in which individual and group behavior becomes deregulated. Thomas emphasized the same factors, most likely to occur in urban contexts, as leading to new and deviant definitions of appropriate behavior. In terms of Srole's anomia, several indicators suggest that it was increasing rapidly during the spring of 1974 and may have been an antecedent of the disorders. For example, Gallup polls at the time showed record low public confidence in then President Nixon, as well as generally declining confidence in other branches of government and in other institutions. The percentage of the population satisfied with the future facing them and their families had also been declining along with the percentage who were satisfied with the honesty and standards of people in the country.[21] The disturbances in the baseball stadiums may have been one concrete expression of widespread feelings that traditional norms were no longer applicable in a variety of situations.

Seeman's types of alienation

Several years after Srole's contribution, Seeman presented an influential classification of the sociological uses of the concept of *alienation*. In several respects it resembled Srole's anomia scale, and in subsequent research it became the more widely used of the two measures. Seeman's paper was a deliberate attempt to view breakdowns in the social bond from the standpoint of the individual. Working from the theories of Durkheim, Marx, and others, Seeman proposed five types of alienation. Briefly defined, the five types are these:[22]

    1. *Powerlessness*. The perceived inability of the individual personally to control his outcomes. (Not considered is whether the individual actually can influence his attainments, or even would like to be able to do so.)

[20] "The Ugly Sports Fan," *Newsweek,* June 17, 1974, pp. 93–94.
[21] Gallup Opinion Index, *Report 101* (Princeton, N.J., November 1973).
[22] Melvin Seeman, "On the Meaning of Alienation," *American Sociological Review,* 24, 1959. Seeman subsequently added a sixth dimension by dividing estrangement into cultural and work types.

2. *Meaninglessness.* Individuals perceive situations as being so ambiguous and unintelligible they do not know how to interpret them.

3. *Normlessness.* A perceived inability to predict the consequences of one's action and/or low confidence in the efficacy of society's institutions.

4. *Isolation.* An individual's sense of detachment; a low regard for dominant or widely shared values.

5. *Self-estrangement.* A separation of the individual from some model of what individuals might ideally be like. Also included is a sense of estrangement from one's own acts, such that people numbly conform with no sense of purpose and no intrinsic satisfaction.

Several of these dimensions of alienation are similar to other concepts discussed in this chapter. Both meaninglessness and isolation, as described by Seeman, strongly resemble the process of individualization described by Thomas. Both normlessness and meaninglessness have rather direct counterparts in Srole's anomia scale. And normlessness and isolation seem, at the individual level, to correspond with the two aspects of Durkheim's anomie. The more unique dimensions, powerlessness and self-estrangement, evolved out of a somewhat different Marxian tradition. Marx's concept of alienation was more sensitive to inequalities in power and to the tendencies of industrialized divisions of labor to estrange individuals from the work process, and ultimately from themselves as well.[23]

The fact that many aspects of anomie, anomia, and alienation overlap is not surprising because all three concepts deal with the way in which individuals are integrated into society. And to some degree, the dimensions of all three concepts view integration as based on the normative framework of a society.

Although Seeman's original presentation did not consider the social conditions associated with alienation, subsequent research has focused on dimensions of alienation in relation to collective disturbances in much the same manner as studies of anomia. Seeman's own study of alienation in Paris prior to the French workers rebellion in 1968 is illustrative. During 1966 and 1967, Seeman gave questionnaires to a large sample of persons in Paris and Los Angeles. He was not trying to predict crises such as the French rebellion, but from a later comparison of workers in the two countries he was able to attempt a reconstruction of the events preceding the widespread disturbance.[24]

From the questionnaires Seeman found that French workers, in general, tended to score somewhat higher on alienation and anomia than their American counterparts. The greatest differences between the samples were

[23] Karl Marx, *Capital* (New York: Modern Library, 1936).
[24] Melvin Seeman, "The Signals of '68," *American Sociological Review,* 37, 1972.

on powerlessness and normlessness on the alienation measure, and on the "detachment of public officials" aspect of the anomia scale. From these differences he concluded that French workers were not very much more alienated in general, but did feel considerably less able to influence their fates. Correspondingly, the French workers were less likely to vote in elections, less interested in political affairs, and scapegoated their discontents with more hostility toward Jews, blacks, and other ethnic groups. The lower the education of respondents and the lower their occupational status, the greater their feelings of powerlessness in both France and the United States. Differences between samples were quite consistent, however, even when these class-related variables were taken into account; that is, French powerlessness exceeded American powerlessness by about the same amount regardless of the educational or occupational levels of the respondents compared.

In reconstructing the work strikes and campus disorders that constituted the 1968 French crisis, Seeman also found that many of the early leaders belonged to organizations such as unions which gave them a feeling they could influence collective decisions. In order to reconcile this pattern of participation with the generally high powerlessness believed to have promoted the disorder, Seeman differentiated between two different types of perceived powerlessness: personal and social. The early activists, he argues, have a high sense of personal efficacy but feel blocked and estranged from social power. Studies of black community protests and campus disorders in the United States also show an initial leadership composed of those who feel a sense of personal mastery. Such people are required to get a movement going. Whether it will then become widespread may depend on the existence of large numbers of persons who feel personally *and* socially powerless who will join the movement.

This analysis of the Paris "revolution" did not really demonstrate that increasing alienation (or powerlessness) was the causal variable. Similarly, our discussion of collective disturbances in American baseball stadiums did not prove that anomia (or alienation) was the causal antecedent. These studies do, however, illustrate the usefulness of such theoretical concepts. It is also not by accident that our examples tend to be drawn from events that occurred in cities. Urban centers have historically been viewed as the context within which the various types of alienation and anomia arise. Thus, as Durkheim noted, modern (i.e., urban) civilization is the "cradle" of suicide.

The association between cities and actions that may indicate estrangement, however, does not necessarily mean that urban populations score higher than rural ones on these dimensions. Particularly with respect to powerlessness, for example, a number of studies indicate more alienation in small towns. In their analysis of a small community in upstate New York,

Alienation often is high in small towns because of people's tacit recognition that certain attainments are not possible there (Galeton, Pennsylvania).

for example, Vidich and Bensman reported widespread feelings that deci-sion-making was concentrated in Albany and Washington. Residents per-ceived themselves as having little influence. In addition, many people seemed simultaneously to recognize and deny the fact that real achieve-ments were not attainable in rural America. Thus, they were forced to use self-deception in order to maintain their small-town values in an urban society.[25]

In an analysis of three communities also in upstate New York, Mizruchi reports similar findings. Utilizing Srole's anomia scale, he found that high anomia was slightly less prevalent in the most urban community, a suburb of Syracuse. A village near Cortland, viewed as the most rural community, we found to have somewhat higher proportions of persons scoring high in anomia. In light of community studies such as these, Mizruchi suggests that anomia may be higher in contemporary rural com-munities now that the entire society is highly urban. However, he suggests, anomia may formerly have been higher in urban areas when the society was predominantly rural.[26] Anomia, in other words, is a consequence of being out of step with the social structure.

[25] Arthur Vidich and Joseph Bensman, *Small Town in Mass Society* (Princeton, N.J.: Princeton University Press, 1958).
[26] Ephraim H. Mizruchi, "Romanticism, Urbanism and Small Town in Mass Society," in Paul Meadows and Ephraim H. Mizruchi (eds.), *Urbanism, Urbanization and Change* (Reading, Mass.: Addison-Wesley, 1969).

Cities have historically been associated with life styles that are considered deviant by conventional standards. Examples of "deviant" social roles that have flourished in urban contexts include the prostitute, the revolutionary, and the poolroom hustler. The term life style may require some elaboration before proceeding further. Many women may occasionally engage in prostitution in order to obtain some quick money in a pinch; many men may occasionally try to hustle a pool game with the same motive. In both these cases, however, the deviant (or "marginal") activity is sporadic. Unless these people are caught and labeled, the deviance is not a major part of their own self-concept or the way they are viewed by others. In talking about deviant life styles, by contrast, we are talking about those whose daily lives are organized about the deviant activity, for whom the routine performance of the behavior is a career, whose self-concepts entail being a prostitute or a pool hustler.

The prevalence of such life styles in cities is related by Merton to the "anomic" quality of urban social organization. Cities, he argues, have historically been associated with "great expectations." They attract people who believe they can attain fame, fortune, and power. And in a society such as ours, these things probably can be attained only in major cities. Obviously, however, only a few will capture the brass rings, and most people will tone down their aspirations to modest, and attainable, proportions. But some may cling to their hopes, only to experience blocked opportunity structures. "The unchosen provide," Merton states, "a reservoir from which are drawn some of the anomics of society . . . (their) bitter disappointment . . . leads to despairing retreat or aberrant ritualism or . . . open rebellion."[27] It also leads to new roles, or new uses of old roles, as people "improvise" to find the route to success.

The poolroom hustler, as described by Polsky, is an interesting example of a life style geared to "making it" in a conventionally deviant manner. Hustlers come from all parts of the country, but most move to a big city in order to ply their trade. The essence of good hustling is finding a victim (formerly called a "fish") who can be led to underestimate the hustler's true ability. A high turnover of people who do not know each other intimately is therefore required and it cannot normally be obtained outside of major cities.[28]

The overriding similarity in hustlers' backgrounds is their lower class origin, where the poolroom is a more common neighborhood institution. Almost none of them attend college and about half do not finish high school. The common class background is due mostly to the fact that

[27] Robert K. Merton, "Anomie, Anomia and Social Interaction," in Clinard, *op. cit.*, pp. 223, 224.
[28] Ned Polsky, *Hustlers, Beats and Others* (Chicago: Aldine, 1967).

hustling—unlike many other occupations—does not present barriers to entry for lower class persons. In addition, the attributes required to be successful at hustling—playing it cool, "heart," self-reliance—are more accessible to lower class youths. Finally, connections count for nothing. As in the traditional Horatio Alger myth, rewards are the result solely of hard work, practice, and individual ability.

Most of the hustlers Polsky talked with just seemed to drift into it as an occupation. Many skipped high school frequently and spent their days in the poolroom. With practice they soon exceeded their peers in ability and found hustling a good way to make money. As one hustler recounted his gradual transition into the career: "I was better at hustlin' pool than anything else, so I figured I would keep on doin' it" (p. 81). Despite an obvious dislike of the economic roller-coaster aspect of their lives, hustlers usually remarked that "It beats working." In addition, the nature of the life itself, with its emphasis on excitement, toughness, "conning," and so on, is highly congruent with the lower class subculture of their origins. Seen from Merton's perspective, the pool hustler is an innovator, following conventional success goals of wealth and fame. The means utilized, however, violate conventional middle class standards because they involve gambling, nonsteady employment, no legitimate credentials, and a scene of operations that has traditionally lacked respectability.

The careers of many "radicals" are a tightrope act between innovation and rebellion. An interesting example is provided by Howard's description of Robert Williams, who moved from chairman of a North Carolina NAACP chapter to urban guerrilla warfare advocate in exile in Red China. In 1959, Howard begins, Williams was struck by the discrepancy between black and white justice in North Carolina and issued a statement that blacks should arm themselves for purposes of self-defense. He was regarded as radical, as a result, even though his positions on integrated housing and education were only conventionally liberal. Subsequently suspended from his NAACP position, Williams formed a "rifle club" to promote self-defense in the black community. Early in the 1960s, amid growing local tension, Williams was accused of kidnapping a white couple. He denied the charge, but feared the consequences and fled to Cuba and then Red China.[29]

By the mid-1960s, Williams's newsletters from Peking showed a marked change in orientation. Gone was the former emphasis on changing the institutional means—through educational programs, for example—in order to achieve cultural goals of equality and integration. In its place was a rejection of the capitalist system, which was perceived as inherently racist. The new tactic was urban warfare; a black guerrilla army that

---

[29] John Howard, "The Revolutionary," in William McCord et al. (eds.), *Life Styles in the Black Ghetto* (New York: Norton, 1969).

would attack the enemy "at his weakest point." Despite such statements, however, the emphasis was on defensive "warfare" and this same emphasis carried over to the Black Panthers. Many of the Panthers' goals, Howard states, are "distinctly nonrevolutionary." They want homes, jobs, and cars; "what they got up in [the suburb of] Piedmont." Whether their goals will change, Howard concludes, depends on the larger community's response to their demands for equality and justice.

In sum, Merton argues that cultural goals and institutional means are most likely to be vague, internally inconsistent, or incongruent within cities. All these states, following Durkheim, are symptomatic of anomie, and they produce deviant life styles. But, according to Merton, the great expectations and freedom from traditional controls that make cities anomic are not "an epitaph of the city." These same conditions underlie the greatest human accomplishments. Business leaders, intellectuals, and Supreme Court Justices have also been historically concentrated in cities. "The free-ranging intellect," he concludes, "thrives in an atmosphere of relative autonomy in the midst of plenty of people, just as . . . roving muggers and thugs thrive in an atmosphere that provides room for individual movement, not easily subjected to social control."[30]

The final consequence of social integration we will consider is rates of mental illness. This line of research in sociology began with an ecological emphasis, then moved to a normative emphasis in which rates of mental illness were viewed as a function of the normative integration of subareas.

MENTAL ILLNESS IN THE CITY

The ecological explanation

The most influential pioneering study of rates of mental illness within cities was reported by Faris and Dunham from an analysis of hospital patients' records in Chicago. They examined the rates of first admissions to public and private hospitals and nursing homes, then related these rates to patients' former ecological locations. They assumed, following Park and Burgess, that Chicago could be divided into a series of concentric zones. In their initial calculations, all types of mental disorder—using the hospitals' classifications—were lumped together. They found that overall rates of illness were highest by far in the innermost Loop and the immediately adjacent zone of transition. By zone three the rates had dropped markedly, and they continued to decline gradually and consistently with succeeding zones' distance out from the center. In the very center the overall rates were more than five times higher than in the peripheral zones.[31]

[30] Merton, *op. cit.,* p. 224.
[31] Robert E. L. Faris and H. Warren Dunham, *Mental Disorders in Urban Areas* (Chicago: University of Chicago Press, 1939).

In further analyzing their data, Faris and Dunham found that this ecological pattern was due mainly to the distribution of various types of schizophrenia, the most commonly diagnosed psychosis of first admissions. The second most commonly diagnosed disorder, manic-depressive psychosis, appeared not to follow any ecological pattern. In explaining their findings, Faris and Dunham emphasized an ecological interpretation that utilized previous Chicago studies of delinquency and crime, family disorganization, and so on. In all these studies, a concentric zone pattern was reported. Therefore, they argued, the zones are natural areas; each possesses its own climate, which determines the rate with which any type of phenomenon, including psychosis, will occur. Within this ecological context they emphasized the causal importance of social isolation in influencing the rate of mental disorder. For example, the rooming houses and transient hotels of the central zones were viewed as not conducive to enduring relationships. Occupancy was generally so transitory that even a long-term resident could not establish stable relationships.

Subsequent studies in Chicago and in other American cities such as Seattle reported similar ecological patterns of mental disorder. Studies conducted in Paris and Bordeaux on psychologically disturbed children also showed high rates to be concentrated in certain geographical areas. One such place was described as a melting pot and rooming house area. To a degree, the concentric zone pattern was indicated, with the highest

Ecologists attribute high rates of mental illness to areas where transitory life precludes the establishment of enduring relationships (Chicago, Illinois).

rates in the center. But some central areas were also characterized by very low rates, and some peripheral areas had very high rates.[32]

The finding of high rates in both center and periphery was also reported in a study of Austin, Texas. Here, however, the different occupational and cultural compositions of similar geographical areas were associated with very different rates of disorder. Professional persons, for example, tended to have very high rates, a result attributed to the marginality of their social role. The Spanish-American community, by contrast, was characterized by very low rates, a result attributed to its cohesiveness.[33]

Some of the discrepancies among studies are probably more apparent than real. For example, in the preceding chapter we saw that the concentric zone model does not fully fit the ecological pattern of many cities. Many of the early studies were influenced by the Park-Burgess formulation, however, and explicitly sought a statistical relationship between concentric zones and rates of disorder. Not finding such a relationship does not necessarily negate all ecological hypotheses; it may merely suggest the limitations of one particular ecological model.

A more serious theoretical problem involves how a relationship between rates of mental disorder and any ecological configuration can be explained. Dunham and others have continued to insist that the social, cultural, or personal factors which lead to mental illness must be spatially distributed. If medical research had been better able to isolate the factors that produce schizophrenia, then it would be possible to identify more precisely the specific causal agent(s) in ecological areas. Other sociologists, such as John Clausen and Melvin Kohn, recognize the contributions made by ecological studies while pointing out the inherent inadequacies of ecological explanations. If, for example, a high rate of mental illness area is characterized by low socioeconomic status, high mobility, and many foreign-born, how is it possible to identify which of these characteristics are responsible for the high rates? They also question the representativeness of the individuals who do become ill. Even small areas, they point out, may not be homogeneous with regard to race, income, and so on. Do the individuals who become ill adequately represent the area? These and other issues, in their view, place serious limitations on all ecological studies.[34] Consider also our previous discussion of heterogeneous

[32] For a discussion of the French studies, in English, see chapter 4 in Roger Bastide, *The Sociology of Mental Disorder,* trans. Jean McNeil (New York: McKay, 1972).

[33] E. Gartley Jaco, "Social Factors in Mental Disorders in Texas," *Social Problems,* 4, 1957.

[34] Further clarification of the ecological arguments is presented in the debates between Clausen, Kohn, and Dunham that originally appeared between 1954 and 1957. They are reprinted in Neil J. and William T. Smelser (eds.), *Personality and Social Systems* (New York: Wiley, 1970), pp. 125–149.

residential areas such as midtown Manhattan. Clearly, very different life styles and very different rates of mental illness would have to be expected even within a concentrated geographical area such as midtown.[35]

The social class explanation

To judge from the nature of later studies, most sociologists seem to have agreed with the criticisms of the ecological approach. During the past twenty years, most studies have focused on social class differences, using ecological considerations only in the construction of social class indicators. But although these studies have been highly predictive, they too have been unable to resolve many of the same theoretical ambiguities.

One of the landmark studies of social class and mental illness was jointly conducted by Hollingshead (a sociologist) and Redlich (a psychiatrist). Their investigation, in New Haven, Connecticut, was impressive because of its methodological thoroughness. They obtained not only city hospital records, but also information from clinics and private practitioners in Connecticut and nearby states, including metropolitan New York. Thus, they were able to conclude that they had data on at least 98 percent of all New Haven residents who were receiving psychiatric care at the time of the survey. The survey was later supplemented by a sample of nonpatients from the community used as a comparison population.[36]

Based on three factors (ecological area of residence, occupation, and education), people in New Haven were assigned to one of five social class positions. The five classes ranged from a very small "upper-upper" class through a larger "lower and working" class. In analyzing the relationship between class and illness, Hollingshead and Redlich also differentiated between two degrees of maladjustment: neuroses and psychoses.

Looking first at neuroses, the New Haven study reported markedly higher prevalence in classes one and two than in class three, and markedly higher prevalence in class three than in classes four or five. There were more male than female neurotic patients, and in every class except five, the prevalence of neuroses was lowest among youngsters (under age 15) and the elderly (over age 55). The marked differences between classes remained, however, even when rates were examined by age and sex. Among both males and females the rates of the more serious psychoses were found to increase with advancing age. Thus, greatest prevalence was among the elderly. The rates of psychoses by social class were also dramatically different from those of neuroses. Psychotic disorders were most prevalent

[35] Highly relevant is Gans's view that urban ways of life are due to social class positions and to stages in the life cycle, and not to "settlement types." Herbert Gans, "Urbanism and Suburbanism as Ways of Life," in Arnold M. Rose (ed.), *Human Behavior and Social Processes* (London: Routledge and Kegan Paul, 1962).
[36] August B. Hollingshead and Frederick C. Redlich, *Social Class and Mental Illness* (New York: Wiley, 1958).

in class five, followed by the other classes in inverse order. Prevalence in class five was more than twice as high as in class four, whereas the other interclass differences were small but consistent.

In the earlier ecological studies, such as Faris and Dunham's in Chicago, it was explicitly concluded that wealth-related factors were not associated with rates of mental disorder. Ecological areas were viewed as the causal variables. In defense of this conclusion it was argued that if the poverty of residents in innermost zones was the cause of the high rates, then the same high rates should be expected for all types of mental disorders. In the Faris and Dunham study, it will be recalled, manic-depressive psychoses were unrelated to zones. However, their approach does not seem adequate to explain why subsequent studies found intra-zone differences related to occupation, ethnicity, and so on. The Hollingshead and Redlich focus on social class, with ecological location considered only in relation to social class, does seem better able to explain such variations. In addition, by differentiating between neuroses and psychoses, Hollingshead and Redlich also present a possible explanation for why later ecological studies have reported high rates of mental disorder in both innermost and peripheral zones. The former are presumably psychoses; the latter, neuroses.

In defense of their view, Faris and Dunham stated that they included admissions to private nursing homes as well as public hospitals, so that both rich and poor potential patients had an opportunity to be included in the survey. But this earlier study does not compare in thoroughness to the Hollingshead-Redlich study. The latter was more exhaustive; it included a range of possible treatment types and covered a wide geographical area. Persons of different classes were most likely to be included in the true proportions with which they were seeking psychiatric help. A final, and very important, basis for difference in the two studies is the type of rate they examined. Faris and Dunham focused exclusively on the *incidence* of new cases during the study period. By contrast, Hollingshead and Redlich looked mostly at *prevalence;* that is, all cases being treated during the study period. If there are differences by social class in the typical length of psychiatric treatment, then measures of prevalence and incidence will yield quite different results. And this is exactly what Hollingshead and Redlich found when they examined both types of rates.

In New Haven, the upper class average length of treatment for neuroses was substantially longer than the lower class. On the other hand, length of treatment for psychoses was reversed. Once a class five patient is diagnosed as psychotic and committed, he tends to remain in treatment an average of over twelve years, nearly twice as long as class one and two patients. Because of these differences in average length of treatment, there is always a backlog of upper class neurotic and lower class psychotic patients. This produces marked class differences in studies of the *prevalence* of mental disorders. Examination of the number of all types of new cases in New Haven shows the social classes to be much more alike. The *incidence* rate is still higher in class five, but the other classes are not very different from each other.

What is the "true" rate?

The observed relationship between social class and rates of mental illness raises a number of questions. Among the most important of them is this: Does social class correlate with "true" rates of mental illness, as opposed to hospitalization records? Needless to say, the state of the art in psychiatry precludes our determining a "true" rate that will be acceptably defined for everyone. An admirable attempt to answer this question, however, was made in the previously discussed study of midtown Manhattan.[37] In this investigation, almost 1,700 randomly selected residents between the ages of 20 and 59 were interviewed in their homes. Most had never been treated for a mental disorder. Included in the several-hours-long interview was a psychiatric evaluation that dealt with immaturity, depression, psychosomatic illness, and so on. Based on the severity of the symptoms indicated, each person was placed in one of four mental health categories: well, mild, moderate, and impaired. In terms of the distribution of midtown's residents, the mild symptoms category was largest, containing about 40 percent of the classified sample. The remainder of the subjects were about equally divided among the other three categories. According to the psychiatrists in the project, about 40 percent of this noninstitutionalized population was moderately or severely incapacitated by psychological problems; 40 percent was mildly impaired, and only about 20 percent was free of any symptoms.

Social class was measured by occupation and education and assessed at two different points: father's standing while the respondent was growing up and respondent's present (adult) status. Increasing percentages of impairment as social class declined were observed using both the parental and present measures, but differences relating to the latter were most marked. For example, in the highest (present) socioeconomic level about 12 percent were judged impaired, compared with almost 50 percent in the lowest group. A number of other social variables were found to be weakly or moderately correlated with the mental health ratings. Impairment increased with age, especially after age 50; the divorced and separated had higher rates than the married. However, there were no independent relationships between mental health and immigrant generation, nationality origin, religion, or rural-urban origins. Of all the variables, social class was by far the best predictor.

[37] The following discussion is taken primarily from volume 2 of the Mid-town Manhattan Study. Thomas S. Langer and Stanley T. Michael, *Life Stress and Mental Health* (New York: Free Press, 1963).

In order to explain further the reasons for the relationship between class and illness, the investigators hypothesized that class might be related to the experience of stress in life. By stress they meant the environmental forces impinging upon an individual that make adjustments difficult. A number of stress factors were isolated, including such experiences as parents who quarreled often, poor physical health, and childhood economic deprivation. The more of these stress factors that were present, the greater was the mental health risk. Most stress factors, however, were *not* related to socioeconomic status. In addition, the lowest status respondents showed more frequent rates of impairment regardless of the number of stressful situations they had experienced.

One rather pronounced difference between social classes involved the adaptive devices employed in response to stress. Low status persons more frequently became excessively suspicious or alcoholic. Their adaptive responses were less effective and often produced other impairments, such as those related to drinking problems. They were also the kind of adaptive devices that put these people in legal difficulties, making their disorders more conspicuous. In the higher status groups, by contrast, greater inhibition apparently prevented their adaptive responses from further exacerbating their difficulties. These people often became anxious, for example, and developed obsessive worries about their jobs. Such a reaction does not increase emotional satisfaction in life, but it may prevent loss of job and attendant economic problems from compounding the situation.

Class differences in adaptive responses to stress have contributed to the development of two types of theories to explain the relationship between social class and mental hospitalization rates. One of these theories, emphasizing societal reactions to illness, argues that the "true" class differences are exaggerated. Evidence for this perspective stems from the observation that lower class symptoms may be more flagrantly observable to police, social workers, and other community agents who are also more involved in the "monitoring" of lower class life. High status people, on the other hand, can better hide their illnesses. And if they are observed, they have the contacts and the resources to fight successfully against being committed. It may also be that in our society the label "crazy" is reserved more for the low status person; those of high status who behave in the same way are considered merely eccentric. Perhaps psychiatrists, who are also products of their society, are not immune to making invidious class-related diagnoses.[38] A second model of mental illness emphasizes class differences in "sophistication." Upper status persons, it is argued, are more likely to recognize when they need help and to have the resources and knowledge to obtain it. Because of these predispositions, it is contended that hospitalization rates actually understate class differences.

It seems probable that both perspectives have a degree of validity. To

[38] For further discussion of this perspective, see Thomas J. Scheff, *Being Mentally Ill* (Chicago: Aldine, 1966).

see which provided the best explanation, Gove and Howell deduced a number of specific hypotheses from each theory and tested them on a sample of state hospital admissions. First, they proposed, higher status persons should more often be self-admitted or have their admission initiated by a close relative. This is what they found, with lower status persons' hospitalization more frequently initiated by more distant agents.[39] Correspondingly, the denial of illness by lower status persons and their immediate families should result in longer periods of illness prior to hospitalization and more severe disturbances at the time of hospitalization. The data support both of these expectations. In other words, because of the class differences in the paths to hospitalization, lower status persons are mentally ill longer and more seriously before they are committed. Thus, the results indicate that hospitalization rates probably tend to underestimate the lower class excess of mental disturbances more than they overstate them.

The drift theory

The research reviewed here has indicated that rates of mental disorder are related more to social class differences than to sheer ecological location within a city. The rates of serious mental impairment have consistently been found to be higher in lower than in upper strata, regardless of whether they are based on community surveys or assessments of hospitalization records. But it remains unclear why the relationship is so consistent. That is, is the relationship between social class and mental illness spurious, or does social class cause differential rates of mental illness in cities?[40] And if the relationship is causal, what is the "causal agent" of social class? Most relevant to these questions and to our preceding concern with urban-induced aspirations is the well-known *drift* theory.

The basic argument of the drift theory is that low social class positions are a consequence rather than a cause of mental illness. It is argued that mental disorders make it impossible for an individual to cope with life and work and result in downward mobility. The impaired individual is skidding downward and reaches a low status position prior to hospitalization.

One of the first statements of this possibility was made in an ecological framework. Burgess, in the preface to the Faris and Dunham study, raised the question of whether people who were previously disturbed moved ultimately to the zone of transition in order to escape into its

---

[39] Walter R. Gove and Patrick Howell, "Individual Resources and Mental Hospitalization," *American Sociological Review,* 39, 1974. See also William A. Rushing, "Individual Resources," *American Journal of Sociology,* 77, 1971.

[40] The relationship between social class and psychological impairment is less clear in rural areas. See, for example, Dorothea C. Leighton et al., *The Character of Danger* (New York: Basic Books, 1963). This is volume 3 of the Stirling County Studies.

anonymity and isolation. Faris and Dunham, of course, argued the reverse causal sequence. The young age of the patient population in the zone to them seemed inconsistent with the pattern suggested by Burgess. Ensuing research on drift in relation to socioeconomic status has produced inconsistent results, due in large part to methodological differences between studies. Several studies, for example, have examined intergenerational mobility, comparing sons' occupational levels with their fathers'. In this framework, the midtown Manhattan study found the highest degree of impairment among downwardly mobile sons.[41] Similarly, in an analysis of schizophrenics, Turner reported that downward intergenerational occupational movement occurred very frequently.[42]

In contrast, Hollingshead and Redlich found that over 90 percent of the schizophrenic patients in their sample were in the same class as their parents.[43] Unlike the other studies, however, they used a multiple-item measure of class, rather than solely occupation. When intergenerational studies focus on occupation, there is apparently more support for the drift hypothesis.

Still other studies, such as Rushing's, have examined drift as an intragenerational process; that is, as downward occupational mobility in the person's own lifetime. To control for drift, at least partially, he classified hospital patients according to their prior "major job," rather than their status immediately prior to hospitalization. The data nevertheless indicated an inverse relationship between status and hospitalization rates.[44]

Looking at the variety of results suggests that although a drift phenomenon, however measured, may be operating to inflate the potentially causal relationship between social class and mental illness, it does not totally negate it. That is, something related to social class seems to produce mental illness in cities, even though the reverse sequence is also indicated. Even the studies that contradict the drift hypothesis do not generally show much upward mobility in their samples. Hollingshead and Redlich, for example, emphasize the absence of any mobility in their sample of schizophrenics.[45] This raises the possibility that blocked mobility aspirations are the correlate of social class that "explain" the relationship between class and mental illness. Theoretically, this conclusion is congruent with our preceding discussion of anomie, role innovation, and so on, all of which showed urban-induced aspirations to threaten the social integration of urban life.

---

[41] Langer and Michael, *op. cit.*

[42] R. Jay Turner, "Social Mobility and Schizophrenia," *Journal of Health and Social Behavior*, 9, 1968.

[43] Hollingshead and Redlich, *op. cit.*

[44] William A. Rushing, "Two Patterns in the Relationship Between Social Class and Mental Hospitalization," *American Sociological Review*, 34, 1969.

[45] Similar findings are reported by H. Warren Dunham et al., "A Research Note on Diagnosed Mental Illness and Social Class," *American Sociological Review*, 31, 1966.

Houston, Texas.

10

Metropolitanization

AT THE TURN of the twentieth century, most American cities were relatively compact. Population densities were high in the center and then declined rapidly. Population immediately outside city boundaries in areas that were to experience rapid suburbanization after 1920 was particularly sparse. The subsequent growth of urban areas involved a great deal of expansion, a continual movement of the population out toward the city boundaries and beyond. By the middle 1960s there were actually more people in the suburbs of cities than in the cities themselves.

DEFINING METROPOLITAN AREAS

This population redistribution stimulated a need for a label that would include the areas extending beyond the political boundaries of the city. The city proper—a political denotation—was becoming increasingly less adequate for certain types of demographic and ecological considerations. One such designation, initially presented in 1949, is called a *standard metropolitan statistical area,* abbreviated as SMSA. A number of criteria must be met before a community is given SMSA status. The most important are that it contain (1) one central city with 50,000 persons, or (2) contiguous ("twin") cities with combined populations of 50,000.

Each SMSA includes the *entire* county in which the central city (or cities) are located. It also includes those adjacent counties (in their entirety) that are deemed to be economically and socially integrated with the central city's county. This means at least 15 percent of the adjoining county's labor force commuting to work in the central city's county, or at least 25 percent of the central city county's labor force commuting to the adjacent county. In addition, at least 75 percent of any included county's labor force must be in nonagricultural occupations. These are the major criteria, but official designation of an SMSA also involves a number of other specific considerations.[1]

By counting only entire counties, SMSAs typically include some rural or farm populations within a county that probably should not be considered part of the metropolitan area. Thus, SMSAs "overinclude" people and places, but they generally overinclude less than about 10 percent of a total SMSA. Therefore, they overbound a metropolitan area to a much lesser degree than focusing only on a politically incorporated central city would underbound it.

In 1950 the classification "urbanized area" was developed. It includes a central city (or cities) and the more densely populated area immediately around it. This is the "built-up area," according to the Census Bureau, "that would be identified from an aerial view." In effect, urbanized areas attempt to exclude those parts of a county that may be incorrectly classified by SMSAs. They also exclude certain distant populations who do rely on the city for shopping, daily newspapers, and so on. There is therefore no absolute criterion for preferring one measure over the other. And as would be expected, different ways of defining and measuring metropolitan areas produce results that correlate *very* highly with one another.[2]

Although the *rate* of urbanization declined after 1950 in most parts of the country, the rate of metropolitanization increased. The percentage of the population living in a metropolitan area (defined by SMSAs) increased more between 1960 and 1970 (17 percent) than it did between 1950 and 1960 (6 percent). By 1970, slightly over 70 percent of the United States population lived in a SMSA.[3] This increase occurred for two reasons: (1) The number of communities able to qualify for SMSA designation increased from 160 (in 1950) to 212 (in 1960) to 243 (in 1970); and (2) the areas previously designated as SMSAs were continuing to grow and expand.

Simultaneous with the overall growth of SMSAs was a redistribution of the population within them. This primarily involved the growth of suburban areas in relation to central cities. Particularly in the Northeast, and

[1] See U.S. Department of Commerce, *The Methods and Materials of Demography* (Washington, D.C.: GPO, 1971), pp. 127–130.
[2] See the appendix to Jeffrey K. Hadden and Edgar F. Borgatta, *American Cities* (Chicago: Rand McNally, 1965).
[3] U.S. Department of Commerce, *Metropolitan Area Statistics* (Washington, D.C.: GPO, November 1971).

to a lesser degree in the Midwest, the absolute size of many central cities actually declined while the SMSAs were growing. In the West, both cities and suburban areas have grown, but the most dramatic increases have been in central cities. In the South, SMSAs vary substantially, individually resembling those in the East or West.

The redistribution of populations within SMSAs has been due in part to the often-described "flight to suburbia." White, middle class families, particularly those with young children, have moved outside their central cities to avoid integrated schools, crime, crowded housing, and a variety of other problems perceived to be worse in the city. In very large part, however, the redistribution is also due to selective patterns of migration between SMSAs.[4] Consider, for example, a white family living in the city of Cleveland preparing to make a job-related move to Pittsburgh. They are substantially more likely to move to suburban than to inner-city Pittsburgh. The result is a move from city (of Cleveland) to suburb (of Pittsburgh). If the same family moves to a newer, growing area out West, such as Phoenix, they are much less likely to choose a suburb. Thus, inter-SMSA movement redistributes the population of western SMSAs differently from those in the East or Midwest.

More than just geographical region is involved in residential preferences. The age (and deterioration) of cities, the percentage of minority group residents, and so on are all involved. Thus, if our hypothetical family were moving to Los Angeles they would be less likely to move within the city limits than they would in Phoenix. Relevant variables like age of city, however, are associated with overall regional differences that account for the regional patterns. A sample of SMSAs is presented in Table 10–1 to illustrate these trends. Examination of this table indicates how the central population of SMSAs in the East and Midwest generally declined from 1950 to 1970. Note the large relative growth of central cities in the West and the intermediate pattern in the South after 1960. Some of the effects of migration are indicated in the last two columns. They clearly show part of the reason why many cities are increasingly inhabited by non-white populations, an issue that will be discussed in detail in later chapters.

TWO KINDS OF SUBURBS

The growth of SMSAs has been the result of two types of suburbanization. One involves city populations moving into newly developed residential areas outside the city limits, regardless of whether their move is within or between SMSAs. A second type involves an "invasion" of older, formerly

---

[4] Alan B. Kirschenbaum, "A Flight from Suburbia," in Paul Meadows and Ephraim H. Mizruchi (eds.), *Urbanism, Urbanization and Change* (Reading, Mass.: Addison-Wesley, 1969).

TABLE 10-1   SMSA population redistribution, by region.

SMSA	Population in Central Cities			Net Migration to Central Cities (%)	
	% SMSA in 1970	% Change 1960-1970	% Change 1950-1960	White (1970)	Non White (1970)
East					
Baltimore	43.7	− 3.5	− 1.1	−150	32
Buffalo	34.3	−13.1	− 8.2	−111	9
New York	68.2	1.1	− 1.4	−956	436
Philadelphia	40.4	− 2.7	− 3.3	−246	40
South					
Atlanta	35.7	2.0	47.1	− 83	33
Memphis	81.0	25.3	25.6	35	23
Mobile	50.4	− 5.4	10.0	− 92	− 11
New Orleans	56.7	− 6.3	57.2	− 31	− 11
Midwest					
Chicago	48.2	− 5.2	− 1.9	−646	113
Cleveland	36.4	−14.3	− 4.2	−206	− 3
Detroit	36.0	− 9.5	− 9.7	−387	98
Kansas City	40.4	6.6	4.1	− 29	13
West					
Dallas	54.3	24.2	56.4	8	47
Los Angeles	45.1	12.5	27.1	− 78	7
Phoenix	60.1	32.4	311.1	72	6
San Diego	51.3	21.6	71.4	28	17

Source: *U.S. Department of Commerce,* Metropolitan Area Statistics (*Washington, D.C.: GPO, November 1971*).

autonomous communities usually located farther away from the city. These may have been fishing villages, farm communities, or small industrial areas prior to being joined to the metropolitan area by suburbanization.

The first type has been called a *residential,* or *dormitory,* suburb. Its primary characteristic is the high percentage of residents who commute daily to work outside of the suburb. Communities of this type tend to be relatively newer and have a high percentage of private family homes rather than multiple-dwelling apartment units. Those who live in residential suburbs tend to be well educated, in professional or executive occupations, and in upper income brackets.[5] The second·type has been called an *employing* suburb, and it is characterized by smaller percentages of residents commuting out of the suburb to work. This is, of course, related to the historical difference in the nature of their settlement. There also tend to be consistent socioeconomic differences between the two types of suburb,

[5] Leo F. Schnore, "The Social and Economic Characteristics of American Suburbs," *Sociological Quarterly,* 4, 1963.

with the residents of employing suburbs having less education, less prestigious occupations, and so on.

As metropolitan areas expanded, engulfing formerly autonomous communities, many suburban areas have also become mixed types, involving what may almost be termed two subcommunities. The strains and tensions this can produce have been examined by Dobriner in a case study of the community fictitiously called Old Harbor.[6] A New England community whose history goes back to the seventeenth century, Old Harbor's "morals committee" traditionally examined the respectability of potential new residents. For several hundred years it remained a conservative Yankee village. After 1867 the railroad periodically brought a few outsiders into the village, but their presence was highly visible. Dobriner quotes the letter of a native villager to a relative in 1872: "There has been a very curious thing this summer, I must have seen 15 or 20 strangers in town."

Automobiles brought transient strangers into Old Harbor in larger numbers, and at first they came only during the summer to enjoy the village's beaches. But the city, some 35 miles away, kept expanding and inching closer. During the 1940s and 1950s, new housing developments kept springing up in and around Old Harbor. In the center of town the "old village" remains: some long-established stores and tree-lined streets. You cannot find room to park a car on Main Street any more, though. In sharp contrast to the quiet shade of the old village are the lawnmowers and hedge trimmers of the suburbanites, while in the background tree cutters and bulldozers are busy making more suburbs.

Few communities outside New England can trace their histories back three hundred years. Throughout the United States, however, hundreds of more recently settled communities have since World War II been invaded by metropolitan expansion. Conflicts between natives and suburbanites typically ensue because of the different life styles of each. In Old Harbor, the old settlers tend to be small businessmen whose stores or factories are in the town. They feel they have roots in the village. The suburbanites are salaried professionals and executives, most of whom work outside the village. To them and to their families, Old Harbor is a school, a beach, a cocktail party. The village is not an end in itself as it is to the old settlers. Many of these differences find political expression in such issues as school bonds. The old settlers are traditional and conservative and equate education with the three Rs and a little red schoolhouse. The suburbanites want expensive, modern education for their children and a school curriculum that seems radical to the old settlers.

Although there is inevitable conflict between the two groups, there is also a symbiosis. The old villagers dislike the traffic on Main Street, but it

[6] William Dobriner, "The National History of a Reluctant Suburb," *The Yale Review,* spring 1960.

also means more customers for local retailers. The future of Main Street? To the south of the village Dobriner describes shopping centers that will accommodate thousands of cars and offer a wider variety of merchandise, and discount stores that offer a better price. In general, as suburban residential areas have expanded, commercial activities have followed closely behind. Main Street in Old Harbor may ultimately lose customers, but the losses are insignificant when compared with the losses of Main Street in the city's central business district (CBD). This issue will be discussed in detail in Chapter 11; here we will briefly outline the process of retail store concentration and expansion.

Casparis illustrates this process by dividing retail shopping clusters into three locations: city CBD ("downtown"); major retail centers (MRCs) located in the city, but not the CBD; and MRCs located in the suburban ring. Following Census Bureau designations, MRCs are concentrations of retail stores that usually include a department store. In the suburban ring, MRCs tend to be planned shopping centers. In cities outside the CBD, they may be either shopping centers or neighborhood developments.

When the CBD has a sales volume of about \$50 million, Casparis reports that it begins to "spin off" MRCs.[7] This happens with an SMSA of several hundred thousand persons. Additional increments in population size or CBD sales results in a proliferation of MRCs. When the SMSA population is over about 2.5 million persons, there is an average of nearly 45 MRCs, and seven MRCs with sales of over \$50 million. SMSAs with less than half a million population have an average of only about three MRCs, none of whose sales reach \$50 million.

As would be expected, the larger the SMSA population, the smaller the percentage of total SMSA shopping sales that occurs in the CBD. In the smallest SMSAs, CBDs account for nearly 50 percent of SMSA shopping sales; they account for only about 25 percent in the largest SMSAs. The percentage losses of CBDs are almost completely gained by MRCs (opposed to "dispersed shopping"), and the suburban MRCs gain in relation to city MRCs.

The decentralization of retail shopping, as a function of increasing SMSA size, is consistent with the *multiple nuclei* theory of urban development.[8] As described in Chapter 1, this theory views the metropolitan area as possessing several nuclei, in contrast to the Park-Burgess concentric zone theory, in which the CBD is viewed as the nucleus. Thus, MRCs become more specialized types of centers, their distinguishing characteristics corresponding with the socioeconomic characteristics of nearby residential areas.

[7] John Casparis, "Shopping Center Location and Retail Store Mix," *Demography*. 6, 1969.
[8] Edward L. Ullman, "The Nature of Cities Reconsidered," *Papers and Proceedings of the Regional Science Association,* 9, 1966.

The development of metropolitan areas depends largely on efficient, short-distance transportation facilities. The automobile, of course, is the best example of a means of transportation that permits extensive population diffusion. With expansion, however, comes the problem of integrating and coordinating activities within a distending area. Communication, which tends to expand along with transportation, provides one means of integration. The wireless was associated with the horse and buggy, the telephone and radio with the automobile. An expansion of government services, however, is the most visible type of coordination. The settlement of the frontier in the nineteenth century and the ensuing subdivisions of states into counties through the first decades of the twentieth century provide an interesting illustration of the expansion-integration process.

For a government at any level effectively to regulate activity within its jurisdictional area, it must be able to enforce its regulations.[9] The government's "threat capability" declines as a function of its distance from an area, and distance is in turn determined by the available means of transportation. In other words, "how far five miles are" depends on how one

[9] Arthur L. Stinchcombe, *Constructing Social Theories* (New York: Harcourt, Brace, 1968), pp. 216–231; and Kenneth E. Boulding, "The City as an Element in the Intranational System," *Daedalus,* 97, 1968.

Expansion into new frontiers in the nineteenth century limited government enforcement capacities and led to the creation of new jurisdictional areas.

TABLE 10-2 Number of new counties.

State	Prior to 1850	1850-1890	1890-1930	After 1930
Illinois	99	3	0	0
New York	59	1	2	0
Oregon	8	23	5	0
South Carolina	29	6	11	0

is going to get there. As a population pushes into frontier areas, a government's threat capability declines, assuming the time costs of transportation remain unchanged. To move the seat of government to a new site equally close to all areas under its jurisdiction has rarely been attempted. The more common solution is to create a new jurisdictional area, with a new seat of government located close to the new center. At the county level, within states, this is exactly what happened between 1790 and 1930, according to Stephan.[10] Table 10–2 presents some representative states.

Variation in when there was a rapid proliferation of counties is related to time of settlement, time of admission to the Union, and so on. The uniform pattern in growth, according to Stephan, is "segmental"; that is, the addition of homogeneous territorial units. Visually, such a growth pattern might look something like the scheme shown in Figure 10–1. Each + indicates a county seat. Thus, at time 1 there are two small and two large counties. At each succeeding time, there are more counties and the size of the largest counties is reduced.

After 1925, Stephan reports, only one new county was created in the entire United States. The absence of further segmental growth is due to the spread of the automobile after this time. Motor vehicle registration in the United States increased from 1 in 10,000 persons in 1900, to 1 in 5 persons by 1930. Thus, the increasing dispersal of population leads to segmental growth when systems of transportation remain constant. With

[10] G. Edward Stephan, "Variation in County Size," *American Sociological Review*, 36, 1971.

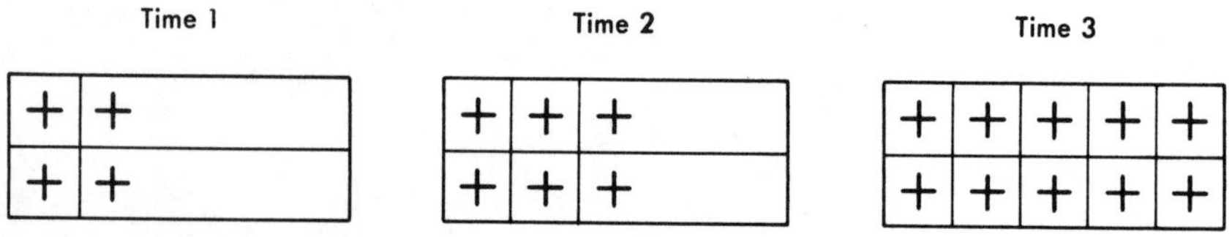

FIGURE 10–1
Adapted from G. Edward Stephan, "Variation in County Size," American Sociological Review, *36, 1971.*

the widespread use of the automobile, the time costs of geographical distance decline, and government regulations can be effectively monitored over longer distances. There is no need for additional segmentation.

The bicycle

In the nineteenth century, the populations of American cities became more dense. Suburban areas were not developed, and outlying towns remained autonomous. Long-distance transportation facilities such as railroads were more efficient during this period than short-distance facilities such as horse-drawn streetcars. The constraints of transportation can be more precisely stated if we make two assumptions: (1) People want to return home from work every day, and (2) one hour is as long as most people are willing to spend commuting.[11] With a horse-drawn streetcar, the "zone of daily interchange," or one hour's travel, was 5 miles. The bicycle, after its innovation in the 1880s had stimulated further road improvements, better than doubled this distance. The bicycle also put "average" city families in contact with neighboring towns on Sunday afternoon outings. (The horse and carriage, by the 1890s, was owned only by more well-to-do families.) Urban electric trains extended the zone of daily interchange to nearly 20 miles—and a substantially more comfortable 20 miles. Contact between cities and outlying towns was further increased by these trains, and then still further increased by the automobile, with its hourly distance of up to 50 miles. Recent commuter rail lines have extended an hour's journey to 80 miles, in some cases.

These transportation innovations were not unique to the United States. The modern bicycle, for example, was developed in England and introduced here in 1879 after two unsuccessful importing attempts in 1819 and 1869. Automobile manufacturing crossed the Atlantic, largely through Ford and Ford Ltd. The extension of urban areas as a consequence of improved transportation was also not unique to the United States. Between 1950 and 1960, for example, the number of daily commuters into London from outside the "green belt" more than doubled.[12]

The history of all innovations, however, is simultaneously one of opposing forces and resistance. We met these forces in the discussion of the innovation of birth-control techniques. Given our current attitudes toward bicycles, automobiles, and so on, resistance is difficult to imagine now, but it was once quite strong. The innovation of the bicycle, as described by Aronson, is illustrative.[13] Prior to 1879, two previous attempts at in-

---

[11] Amos Hawley, *Human Ecology* (New York: Ronald, 1950).
[12] Peter Hall, *The World Cities* (New York: McGraw-Hill, 1966). The green belt is a circular area of open countryside encircling London about 15 miles out from the center.
[13] Sidney Aronson, "The Sociology of the Bicycle," *Social Forces,* 30, 1952.

novation were unsuccessful, largely because of mechanical defects in the wheels, brakes (they had none!), cranks, and so on. By 1890, though, the United States "bicycle boom" was on: mass production lowered the price from about $150 to $18, and bicycle ownership was estimated at almost 1 in 7 persons.

Resistance to the bicycle, however, took many forms, foreshadowing much of the later opposition to automobiles. One source was based on competition for roadways. Walking pedestrians lobbied against the bikes, and horsemen resented their intrusion and often took to "running down" the cyclists. There was also a medical controversy. Cyclists claimed riding was a panacea capable of curing rheumatism, gout, indigestion, and alcoholism, among other ills. Medical associations, however, catalogued a new group of afflictions that would befall bike riders: "kyphosis bicyclistorum," or bicycle stoop, from bending over while pedaling, and "cyclist's sore throat," from the dusty roads.

Moral and religious debate was also intense. The determined look on the face of cyclists was labeled a disease ("bicycle face") and attributed

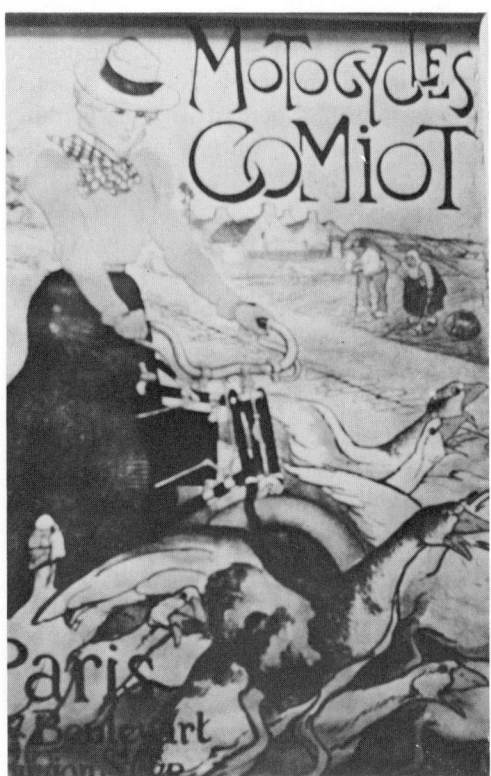

Bicycles made rural areas more accessible to city dwellers, but the bikes were condemned as corrupters of women.

to cycling on the Sabbath. Bikes were also blamed for the corruption of women: bicycles built for two had no room for a chaperone, and women cyclists often boldly exposed their ankles. The Woman's Rescue League of Washington, D.C., is quoted by Aronson as claiming that bicycle riding led to immorality and more than anything else helped to "swell the ranks of reckless girls . . . the army of outcast women."

The bicycle won out in most cases, and its victories paved the way for the automobile. Its specific contributions, according to Aronson, were these:

1. The standardized, assembly-line manufacture of bicycles was directly applied to automobiles. In 1900, for example, 56 automobiles were manufactured in bicycle factories, and the census classified automobiles under the heading of bicycles.
2. The bicycle repair shops (over 6,000 in 1900) became automobile repair shops and training grounds for automobile repairmen.
3. Political lobbies of the cyclists (for example, the League of American Wheelmen) led to dramatic road and highway building without which automobiles could not have functioned. In addition, the league successfully backed legislation to erect street signs at intersections, light streets, and post a variety of travel signs.

The bicycle also put many middle class city families in contact with the countryside on Sunday afternoon outings. Where climates permitted, some moved to the outskirts permanently and commuted to the city by bicycle. Moving was then economically feasible because bicycles were inexpensive to operate and low demand for suburban lands made their rental as cheap as that of tenements.

The automobile

Although the bicycle paved the way for the automobile, literally and figuratively, and the automobile may be viewed as extending changes introduced by the bicycle, the effects of the automobile were still dramatic. One of the best descriptions of its effects is provided by the Lynds in their classic study of Muncie, Indiana, fictitiously called Middletown. During the 1920s, the Lynds described how the automobile impinged on all aspects of life in Middletown. People were no longer as likely to sit on their front porches and talk with their neighbors, for example. Instead, they went for rides. As these neighborly chats declined, people spent less time decorating their yards. Status was now determined not by front yards, but by automobile ownership.

The moral battles previously fought over the bicycle were also re-kindled. Buggy-riding during the 1890s, the Lynds point out, was not permitted after 8:30 P.M. without a chaperone. With automobiles, how-ever, dating couples were going to parties farther away from home. They were staying out later, and there were no chaperones at all. All this led the judge of Middletown's juvenile court to claim: "The automobile has become a house of prostitution on wheels."[14]

An increasing distance between work and residence was another major consequence of the automobile. During the 1890s, everyone in Middletown lived very near where he worked because most people had to walk. Even during the early 1920s, over half of Middletown lived within a mile of work. The Depression that began in 1929 slowed the rate of new car purchases, but the automobile had so changed patterns of residence, courtship, and life in general that it was almost "Depression proof," ac-cording to the Lynds. People postponed marriages, delayed having chil-dren, and gave up new clothes. Between 1929 and 1933 all retail sales in Middletown fell dramatically *except* the receipts of gasoline stations. And the number of cars registered in Middletown increased every year, even though there was a greater number of used cars during the Depression.

In Middletown, all sections of the community were in increased contact because of the automobile. In other parts of the country, formerly separate communities were "joined" by the automobile. For example, Linden and Flint, Michigan, were several hours of travel apart prior to the automobile. In 1900, no one in Linden's labor force was employed in Flint. By 1950, however, Flint employed nearly half of Linden's labor force.[15]

From aerial photographs, urban population expansion appears to flow *smoothly* outward along with improved means of transportation. Down on the ground, though, transportation innovations (like all innova-tions) typically are resisted at first because they disrupt established pat-terns of life. In Middletown, the automobile—in conjunction with other innovations—was described as changing all the ways in which people had become accustomed to "experience" their world. It contributed to enor-mous cultural lags, in Ogburn's terms, and to a general resistance to any further changes. "It may be that most people are incapable of tolerating change and uncertainty in all sectors of life at once," the Lynds surmised; "and . . . they may . . . welcome the security of extreme fixity and changelessness."[16]

---

[14] Robert S. and Helen M. Lynd, *Middletown* (New York: Harcourt, Brace, 1929), p. 114.
[15] Amos H. Hawley, *Urban Society* (New York: Ronald, 1971).
[16] Robert S. and Helen M. Lynd, *Middletown in Transition* (New York: Harcourt, Brace, 1937), p. 315.

The private automobile largely replaced all prior modes of intraurban transportation, and use of more recent mass transportation systems has been hampered by the automobile's role in shaping the ecology of many cities. For example, highly dispersed cities such as Los Angeles developed into major population centers in conjunction with the increased use of private automobiles. They are "expressway cities."

The energy crisis of the 1970s has stimulated a search for more economical alternatives to the private automobile. Elevated rail lines, for example, involve about one-tenth the per-passenger cost of private automobiles. The search for alternatives has ranged from billion-dollar computerized systems such as BART in San Francisco to attempts to bring back the old-fashioned trolley car in Portland, Philadelphia, and Dayton. (The first urban trolley in the United States began running in Portland in 1893.)[17] In most cities these efforts have met with limited success. In some cases complex systems such as BART have been victimized by the publicity given accidents. They have also often turned out to be extremely expensive to build and operate, thereby requiring extensive financial subsidies. In general, however, mass transit systems have been underutilized not because of financial costs, but because of time costs.

In an analysis of Boston, for example, the use of mass transit (subways) in comparison with private automobiles was found to be virtually unaffected by the amount of fare charged working commuters. Even free mass transit would not attract significantly greater numbers of commuters because of the differences in time involved.[18] Reduced fares would bring more shoppers into the central business district, but it would not affect total automobile use; that is, reduced fares attract subway shoppers who would otherwise not travel downtown. It is only when population distributions are such that automobiles are both slower and more expensive (as in New York) that sizable numbers of people will commute to work by mass transit.

An additional deterrent is personal fear. Despite efforts in many cities to overpublicize security and to underpublicize robberies and rapes, public awareness of these problems discourages substantial numbers of potential mass transit users. In Chicago, for example, a "confidential" survey for the city by the Transportation Institute of Carnegie Mellon University showed that 20 percent of nonriders cited fear as a reason for not using the bus; 25 percent cited fear in connection with nonuse of the rail system.

[17] Robert Lindsey, "Urban America," *The New York Times,* September 8, 1974.
[18] Gerald Kraft and Thomas Domencich, "Free Transit," in Matthew Edel and J. Rothenberg (eds.), *Readings in Urban Economics* (New York: Macmillan, 1972).

These differences in apprehension were supported by differences in crime rates, which were about 10 times higher on the rapid transit system (platforms or trains) than on the bus lines.[19]

The Chicago survey also indicated that platforms and stations with the highest crime rates tended to be concentrated in black ghetto areas, even though most victims were white. From descriptions of assailants and from arrests, it appears that most of the offenders were under 30 (80 percent), black (92 percent), and male (97 percent). Police apprehension rates were about the same as those for all types of robberies in the city, about 38 percent arrested. Finally, approximately half of all bus and train robbery victims required hospitalization, usually as the result of beatings. (Weapons were shown in most robberies, but were infrequently used.)

It is paradoxical, in a way, that fear of crime—and racial crime in particular—prevents further use of mass transit because the same type of fear has also contributed to the suburbanization that so dictates the rational use of mass transit. Data indicating the precise contribution of fear of crime to moves from city to suburb are lacking, and there are also relatively little trustworthy data to indicate the actual amount of difference between city and suburban crime rates. But there are survey results showing substantially less feeling of being threatened in suburbs than in central cities. In a survey of four metropolitan areas in Missouri, for example, Boggs reports that central city residents perceive both personal and property crimes as 3 to 10 times more likely to occur than do suburban residents.[20]

Quite apart from time costs, monetary expense, and physical danger, more extensive use of mass transit facilities is also impeded by emerging commuter patterns. Efficient mass transit systems are generally based on the principle of moving large numbers of dispersed suburban residents into a compact central city location. This requires suburbanites to use private automobiles (or buses) to get from their homes to train stations. Available land around the train station is then converted to parking facilities and/or bus terminals.

Census data for metropolitan areas in 1970 indicate two commuting trends that run counter to traditional mass transit principles. First, although approximately 50 percent of the suburban labor force commutes daily into the central city, only a very small percentage work in the central business district. Most people therefore require an additional mode of transporta-

[19] Harry Golden, Jr., "CTA Train Crime," *Chicago Sun-Times,* June 30, 1974, pp. 3, 28.
[20] The four metropolitan areas are St. Louis, Kansas City, Springfield, and Columbia. Sarah L. Boggs, "Formal and Informal Crime Control," *The Sociological Quarterly,* 12, 1971.

Expressway cities are large cities whose ecologies are intimately related to private automobile use. Even if funds were available for mass transit, it would be of limited utility (Los Angeles, California).

tion from the transit station to their work site. Second, as employment sites such as factories have moved outward to suburban locations, an increasing percentage of central city labor forces are commuting "in reverse."[21] In 1970, about 20 percent of central city residents commuted daily to work outside the city. Because they are traveling to highly dispersed work sites, an additional mode of transportation from transit stations is particularly necessary. Often there is also the problem of no available land around city stations to accommodate parking lots or bus depots.

When there is need for extensive use of additional modes of transportation, the efficiency of mass transit systems can be severely limited. In Paris, for example, about 40 percent of the million persons employed in the center of the city commute daily from suburban areas, mostly via the Metro, the urban railway network. (Over a quarter of a million people commute daily through one terminal station alone.) But the worst rush-hour congestion in Paris is on the boulevards outside the terminals as

[21] The suburbanization of employment sites is discussed in Chapter 11. Figures on commuting patterns and mass transit use are presented in the Appendix.

commuters scramble for cabs and buses to take them from the terminals to their offices and shops.[22] Extensive reliance on mass transit does not necessarily end commuter transportation problems; it may merely push them from suburban expressways to city boulevards.

How much continuing suburbanization will further exacerbate the transportation problems of metropolitan areas is difficult to predict. As this book is being written, in 1974, energy shortages, scarcities in certain raw materials (such as plumbing fixtures), and very tight mortgage money are producing a marked decline in housing starts. From a record of over 2.5 million starts in mid-1972, private housing starts were approximately cut in half by late 1974.[23] How temporary this decline will be is difficult to predict, but even if suburbanization and related commuting problems become no worse, the current situation is essentially intolerable because of the health risks being generated in the form of air pollution. Motor vehicles emit over 90 percent of the carbon monoxide in the air, over 60 percent of the hydrocarbons, and almost 50 percent of the nitrogen oxides.[24] They contribute about 50 percent more total pollutants than industry, power plants, space heating, and refuse disposal combined.

METROPOLITAN INTEGRATION

As the automobile carried people farther and farther out from the central city, communications followed. The radio signals and daily newspapers that also moved out to "fringe" areas helped to integrate them into a single diffuse community. Theoretically, it is expected that there will be a general development in the central city's organization to integrate and coordinate the enlarged community. This is known as the theory of *ecological expansion,* which states that there will be a balancing of centrifugal (expanding) and centripetal (integrating) forces.[25]

To test this theory, Kasarda examined expansion measured by the percentage of a metropolitan area (SMSA) population that resides in the suburban ring. The suburban components of 157 SMSAs were classified as small (less than 30 percent of the SMSA population), medium (30 to 70 percent), or large (over 70 percent). Centripetal forces were measured by the percentage of central city residents employed in integrating or coordinating occupations such as transportation, real estate, and so on.[26] The

---

[22] Hall, *op. cit.*

[23] *U.S. News and World Report,* September 2, 1974, pp. 33–36.

[24] Mathew Edel, *Economics and the Environment* (Englewood Cliffs, N.J.: Prentice-Hall, 1973).

[25] Hawley, *Human Ecology, op. cit.*

[26] John D. Kasarda, "The Theory of Ecological Expansion," *Social Forces,* 51, 1972.

TABLE 10-3 Central city employees per 1,000 residents.

Occupational Categories	Size of Suburban Ring		
	Small	Medium	Large
Transportation, communication	29	36	43
Finance, insurance, real estate	20	25	33
Public administration	20	24	36

results show that expansion is strongly associated with increased coordinative functions in the central city. Some of the results are presented in Table 10–3.

A horizontal scan of the rows of Table 10–3 indicates that as the suburban component of SMSAs increases (expansion), there is a corresponding increase in the proportion of people in integrating and coordinating activities in central cities. Absolute increases in the size of the suburban ring have the same effect. Kasarda also reports that suburban expansion leads to an increase in centripetal employment in the suburbs as well, but this increase occurs later and is much smaller than the central city increase. Thus, although suburban growth leads to increased integrative activity within suburban areas, the major response is in the central city.

Influence of cities

The influence of cities on metropolitan areas and on extended geographical regions is a widely studied phenomenon. It was initially presented in Chapter 2 in the discussion of how primate cities affect an entire country. In more modern countries, extensive influence tends to be limited to a more discrete geographical area. Beyond a certain distance, the influence of other cities becomes more pronounced, although certain cities (such as New York and Chicago) continue to operate as super-regional integrators. For example, about one-third of all national associations (business, education, health, and so on) have their headquarters in New York.[27]

From a variety of perspectives, New York can be viewed as a major coordinator of national activities. It is a major headquarters for national organizations. It is still the point of origin for many wholesale items (for example, clothing, furs) distributed throughout the United States. It is also the most important center of national communications in the country, a major locus of national and international politics, and a major financial

[27] Stanley Lieberson and Irving L. Allen, Jr., "Location of National Headquarters of Voluntary Associations," *Administrative Science Quarterly*, 8, 1963.

All cities exert influence over extended geographical areas, though their range of influence varies (western New York–Pennsylvania state line).

center. In some respects, New York is in a class by itself. Among American cities, it stands unparalleled as an international city as do Paris, London, and Tokyo.[28]

Other American cities also stand out as national integrators, and internationally to a lesser degree. Chicago and Atlanta, for example, score highly on most of the same dimensions as New York. But they are to extended geographical regions what New York is to the entire country. They can all be classified in the "super" metropolis category, or New York could be separated out, according to the goals of any given classification scheme.

In terms of integration and coordination most cities are probably average, by definition. Culturally and economically they dominate a metropolitan area and beyond, but their outward reach is more confined than that of the "super cities." Still other cities can be classified as somewhat above and somewhat below average. One such classification is presented in Table 10–4.

In order to better understand how this hierarchy is constructed, consider your own place of residence for a moment. When you file your federal income tax return, do you send it outside your metropolitan area? If not, give your city a point as an integrator. If you do send it out, give that point to the city to which it is sent. Does your city contain one of the twelve

[28] Hall, *op. cit.*, esp. chap. 1.

Federal Reserve Banks that regulate the activities of all banks in their districts? If so, give your city a point as an integrator. Now let us consider your city only in relation to its extended metropolitan area. Give it a point whenever you can answer affirmatively any of the following questions: Do people from the area go into the city for medical specialists? high fashion clothing stores? dog licenses? Is the area served by the city's newspapers and television stations? airports? At least some of the answers inevitably will be yes, because all cities provide some degree of integration or coordination.

A number of studies have attempted to classify cities according to their degree of local (SMSA), regional, or national integration. The categories used and the placement of specific cities into categories has varied somewhat from study to study, but there is a sizable degree of consensus.[29] A summary of results is presented in Table 10–4, using the following categories:

1. National metropolis: Cities that integrate activities in the entire country (New York) or else serve as the major city in a region (Atlanta), connecting that entire region to a national network. (They have also been given labels such as super metropolis, national centers, and first order cities.)

2. Regional metropolis: Cities that provide extensive coordination in more limited regions and can be major points of connection for

[29] The major studies considered in this classification are Mark Abrahamson, "The Social Dimensions of Urbanism," *Social Forces,* 53, 1974; Robert L. Carroll, "The Metropolitan Influence of the 168 Standard Metropolitan Area Central Cities," *Social Forces,* 42, 1963; Otis D. Duncan et al., *Metropolis and Region* (Baltimore: Johns Hopkins, 1960); Rupert B. Vance and S. Smith, "Metropolitan Dominance and Integration," in Rupert B. Vance and Nicholas J. Demerath (eds.), *The Urban South* (New York: Van Rus, 1954). Comparison of the findings is also made difficult by a twenty-year time span in the figures utilized.

TABLE 10-4   Influence of SMSA central cities.

National Metropolis	Regional Metropolis		Average City		Nonintegrator
Atlanta	Cincinnati	Los Angeles	Akron	Milwaukee	Baltimore
Chicago	Columbia (S.C.)	Nashville	Columbus	Philadelphia	Baton Rouge
Dallas	Denver	Phoenix	El Paso	Rochester	Binghamton
New York	Detroit	St. Louis	Indianapolis	Spokane	Erie
	Kansas City	San Francisco	Jacksonville	Syracuse	Flint
	Little Rock	Seattle	Louisville	Tulsa	Johnstown
					San Diego
					Scranton

such a region to the national metropolis. (They have also been termed mature, limited, or regional metropolises; and second order cities.)

3. Average cities: Cities that provide goods and services to their own metropolitan areas, at an "average" level, but influence extended activities primarily as satellites of the regional centers. (They have also been called lesser metropolitan areas, third order cities, and local service centers.)

4. Nonintegrators: Central cities that provide relatively little coordination over metropolitan activities; portions of the metropolitan area may actually be more dependent on the central city in a different (but not too distant) metropolitan area. (They have also been called subdominant and satellite cities.)

The classification in Table 10–4 is not a complete listing of all SMSAs; rather, it includes a sample of those for which different studies are more or less in agreement concerning their relative placement. Excluded are many cities that score very differently depending on which characteristics are emphasized in the classification.

All cities provide a degree of integration, even the nonintegrators whose influence is low. Variations in influence cannot be totally explained, but two characteristics are related to differences. The first is city size. There is a weak to modest relationship between size and influence. This can be seen by examination of the table: the less influential cities tend to be smaller, though there are obvious exceptions even in this limited sample. Second, there appears to be some relationship between influence and proximity to other metropolitan areas. In the more urbanized Northeast, cities tend to score lower on influence than in the South or West. Exceptions are again apparent, though, indicating that this type of influence is not tied predominantly to geographical location on a national or extended regional basis. Within states, however, some vestiges of the relationship remain. For example, within states having two major metropolitan areas (population over 1 million), there is a marked tendency for the metropolitan areas to be at opposite ends of the state. As illustrations, consider New York (Buffalo and New York City), Ohio (Cleveland and Cincinnati) Missouri (St. Louis and Kansas City), Pennsylvania (Pittsburgh and Philadelphia). There are exceptions (notably Houston and Dallas in Texas), but the general within-state pattern seems to hold more often than not.

This discussion of influence suggests additional meanings for the terms "urban" and "metropolitan" with which Chapter 6 began. At that point, urbanization was viewed as the percentage of a population living in an urban area. Metropolitanization was viewed according to the distribution of a population in an urban area and its environs. These are still useful definitions from a demographic perspective. From an organizational perspective, however, a metropolitan or an urban society is one in which the integration of major social activities is accomplished through a hierarchical pattern of relationships between and among cities or metropolitan areas. As this process has occurred in the United States, city dominance has become more evenly distributed and separated from geographical location.

San Diego, California.

11 Fiscal Aspects of City-Suburban Relations

IN RECENT YEARS the mayors of most big cities have had an uphill struggle to find enough revenues to keep their cities going. Taxes have been raised on residences and industries to the point where further increases might actually reduce revenues by encouraging more movement to the suburbs. The mayors have lobbied in Washington and in state legislatures to increase the amount of funding allocated to cities. Nothing they have done, however, has yet been able to make up the growing deficits in city budgets.

Simply because they are older, central cities have had larger expenditures for renewal and redevelopment than their suburban areas. Poor, minority-group ghettos have also grown faster in central cities than in their suburbs. This subpopulation has required more in the way of city services while simultaneously giving the city a smaller tax base from which to raise revenues. Finally, there is a "spillover exploitation" that has been costly to central cities: the cost of educating people (an investment) who later migrate to the suburbs (providing a return on the investment to a different locale); the cost of rush-hour traffic control for commuters who pay taxes to suburbs; the cost of parks, zoos, and other recreational facilities that are also used by suburbanites who frequently do not contribute to their maintenance.

In this chapter we will examine the economic effects of changing city populations and the nature of the suburban drain on city resources. Let us begin, however, with the current budgetary situation of central cities.

The basic fact of life for most cities recently is that expenditures have increased more rapidly than revenues. Deficits are the obvious result, with a growing percentage of each succeeding year's expenditures being allocated to interest on previously assumed debts. Thus the red ink accumulates. This general trend is illustrated in Tabel 11–1, which contains a summary of figures for all cities with populations of 50,000 and over.

Looking first at expenditures, it is apparent that all operations of city governments were increasing in costliness. The fastest rising expenses, however, were related to minority-group residents and were for welfare, health, and police protection. The revenue part of the budget shows the largest increases to be allocations from states and from the federal government. Such intergovernmental transfers increased even more substantially in the 1970s as evidenced by recent legislation. The Revenue Sharing Act of 1972 provided an average of $6 billion a year, with two-thirds going to local governments according to their population size and density. The

TABLE 11-1 Revenue, expenditure and debt, 1966 to 1971.

Item	1966-67 (in millions)	1970-71 (in millions)	% increase 1966-67 to 1970-71
Total Revenue	$24,096	$37,367	55
Total Expenditure	24,375	39,061	60
Major sources of revenue			
Property tax	7,351	10,041	37
Sales tax	1,645	2,780	69
State govts.	4,001	7,401	85
Federal govt.	803	1,861	132
City charges	3,695	5,788	57
Utility	4,043	5,578	38
All others	2,558	3,918	53
Major expenditures by function			
Utility	4,206	5,803	38
Education	3,194	5,242	64
Police	2,046	3,471	70
Highways	2,025	2,664	32
Sanitation	1,911	3,010	58
Health	1,302	3,324	79
Fire	1,302	1,996	53
Welfare	1,265	2,688	113
Housing and renewal	815	1,442	77
Debt interest	745	1,308	76
All others	5,634	9,247	64

Adapted from: Stanley M. Wolfson, "Economic Characteristics and Trends in Municipal Finances," The Municipal Yearbook (Washington, D.C., 1973).

Mass Transit Act of 1974 provided an average of almost $2 billion a year for urban mass transit, again on the basis of city size and density. Most of this federal legislation, however, has had explicit exclusions that have limited its helpfulness. Revenue sharing, for example, specifically prohibits spending any of the funds for education, and as we shall see later, this is one area in which intergovernmental transfers have traditionally discriminated against big cities. To illustrate further, funds from the Mass Transit Act can be used only for building transit systems and purchasing buses, not for reducing operating costs to avoid further fare increases.

The basic problem is that recent urban-oriented legislation has not provided sufficient funding to offset what has been a historic bias against cities, and in some cases also against suburbs. In 1965, for example, the population of the United States was divided into almost equal thirds in central cities, suburbs, and the rest of the nation. State and federal aid, however, was distributed quite differently, as shown in Table 11–2.

Educational financing is one area in which state and federal aid has particularly displayed an anticity bias. (It will be recalled from Table 11–1 that education is among the largest of city expenditures.) In the six major metropolitan areas of New York State, for example, per-pupil state aid in the 1966–1967 fiscal year averaged over $100 more in the suburbs than in the central cities.[1] (And revenue sharing, it will be recalled, specifically excludes educational expenditures.) A recent example of the continuing bias against aid to big cities was the dramatic difference in the press coverage given to a special New York State task force on school financing. On Saturday, February 2, 1974, this task force proposed new ways to calculate funds for each district in the state. It was widely assumed that the governor would recommend the plan, though its acceptance by the state legislature was another matter. In their Sunday editions, newspapers covered the task force report in very different ways. The *New York Times* coverage was on page 26, and it reported that the task force did not

[1] Committee for Economic Development, *Reshaping Government in Metropolitan Areas* (New York: CED, 1970).

TABLE 11-2 Anticity bias in intergovernmental transfers.

Destination of Support	State and Federal Aid, as % of:	
	Local Taxes	Total Local Expenditures
Central cities	44%	27%
Suburbs	53	29
Rest of nation	74	37

Source: *Committee for Economic Development,* Reshaping Government in Metropolitan Areas *(New York: CED, 1970).*

recommend any new state money for education. The *Times* also reported that the proposed plan would eliminate "categorical urban aid" and replace it with 25 percent more aid for each pupil scoring low on state evaluation tests, a criterion that would be "of particular benefit" to big city school districts.[2]

One of upstate New York's most politically influential newspapers, the *Syracuse Herald American* (Sunday circulation, 250,000) also reported on the task force in its Sunday edition. Its story was on the front page, under the subheadline "Plenty for Big Cities, Condolences for Small." The Syracuse paper emphasized how small rural districts might be hurt by the new formula, despite the fact that Syracuse was counted as one of the state's "big five" cities and would receive a portion of any funds specifically designated for big city districts. The proposed plan, it said, would do little for poor and small districts such as Salmon River. "But most of the reporters at the capital session," the paper's correspondent noted, "represented places like New York City and Buffalo."[3]

Despite the anticity bias, the amount of intergovernmental transfers to cities has clearly been increasing. It has simply failed to increase rapidly enough to offset rising city expenditures on health, welfare, renewal, and so on. Table 11–1 indicates that growing debt has characterized all cities, but that the magnitude of debt—even on a per capita basis—has not been equal in all cities. The largest have experienced the most serious financial problems, as indicated in Figure 11–1. The largest cities have accumulated the largest deficits because all the factors that increase expenditures and reduce revenues have been most pronounced in the largest cities. One

[2] The *New York Times,* February 3, 1974, p. 26.
[3] The *Syracuse Herald American,* February 3, 1974, p. 1.

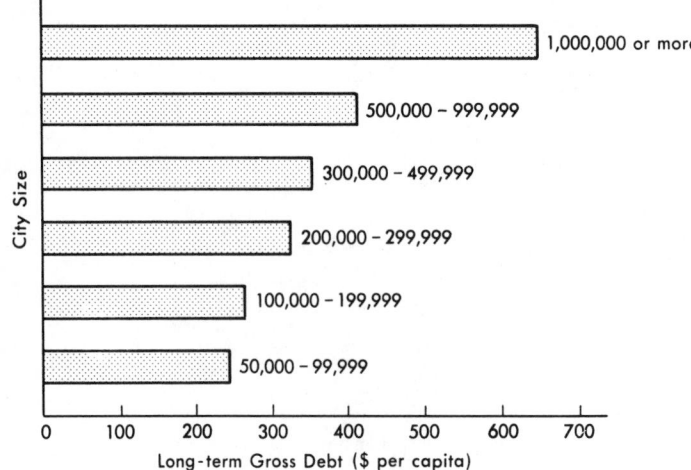

FIGURE 11–1 Per capita debt by city size, 1970–1971.
Data from Stanley M. Wolfson, "Economic Characteristics and Trends in Municipal Finances," The Municipal Yearbook (*Washington, D.C., 1973*).

Part of the reason that central city debts have increased is the growth of elderly and minority populations (Jacksonville, Florida).

such factor involves the relative growth of poor populations in central cities—the elderly, minority groups, and blacks in particular.

THE BLACK POPULATION AND CITY BUDGETS

There is perhaps no issue subject to more controversial explanations than fiscal policies involving nonwhite minority groups. It can be demonstrated that such minority groups put special pressures on city budgets, but it is often easy to overlook the fact that this "price tag" is a product of systematic historic discrimination, some of whose costs are coming home to roost. It is also easy to overlook many other social benefits, such as social security, that disproportionately favor the longer-living white population. Part of the difference lies in the fact that benefits associated with nonwhite populations tend to come from financially besieged cities, whereas benefits associated with white populations accrue from the relatively affluent federal government. We will have more to say about these issues in the conclusion of this section. Here, let us begin with the distribution and wealth of the nonwhite population.[4]

[4] The terms "nonwhite" and "black" may be read interchangeably in this section. Over 92% of the nonwhite population is black, and some of the studies included here focus solely on blacks.

The rapid suburbanization that has characterized post-World War II United States has largely been a movement of whites. The suburban populations of metropolitan areas were 4.5 percent black in 1950, and were still less than 5 percent by 1970. Projections to 1980 estimate that suburbs will then be only about 6 percent black.[5] The more recent suburbanization by blacks, however, has come to resemble more closely that of whites. Before 1960, suburban blacks were of lower socioeconomic status than their black central city counterparts. This suggests, of course, that suburban blacks were living in the least desirable suburban communities, communities that happened to be outside the city but lacked all the other amenities connoted by the term suburban. After 1960, the socioeconomic status of city and suburban blacks was reversed due to the selective suburban migration of higher status blacks.[6]

Despite the overwhelmingly white character of suburbanization, there was some rapid suburbanization by blacks during the 1960s. One investigation of this process is reported by Connolly, who examined only suburbs in which the black population doubled or more than doubled between 1960 and 1970 and reached at least 10 percent of that suburb's total population by 1970.[7] Growth of this type occurred in two different ways. In one case, inner-city ghettos expanded into contiguous parts of the metropolitan area. In Cleveland, for example, the black population expanded eastward across city lines into predominantly white suburbs. In the second type of growth, a small, previously existing black suburban population began to grow and expand, as happened in a number of Chicago suburbs.

With either type of growth, high segregation remained typical. Blacks remained in predominantly black census tracts even when blacks outnumbered whites in the suburb. The major change was that there were more of the predominantly black tracts. Other tracts in the same suburb remained over 95 percent white. Central city patterns of racial segregation were reappearing in the suburbs. In 1970, although suburban blacks' socioeconomic positions were generally higher than those of central city blacks, they remained behind suburban whites. The gains of suburban blacks (who were previously behind central city blacks) were due largely to the high percentage of working black women in the suburbs.

Among women, the traditional discrimination against blacks seems to have declined markedly during the 1960s. In fact, among better educated women, some degree of "reverse discrimination" may even have occurred, as illustrated by the figures in Table 11–3. Because of affirma-

---

[5] Harold X. Connolly, "Black Movement into the Suburbs," *Urban Affairs Quarterly*, 9, 1973.
[6] Reynolds Farley, "The Changing Distribution of Negroes Within Metropolitan Areas," *American Journal of Sociology*, 75, 1970.
[7] Connolly, *op. cit.*

TABLE 11-3   Ratio of black to white female earnings.

Educational Level	Income Ratio, 1959	Income Ratio, 1969
Less than elementary school	85%	92%
High school graduate	78	101
College graduate	67	118

Source: *Reynolds Farley and Albert Hermalin, "The 1960's,"* Demography, *9, 1972.*

tive action programs, the demand for black women employees may have increased their market value, or black women may simply be more motivated than their white counterparts. Whatever the reason, by 1969 the better educated black women appeared to be earning more than similarly educated white women.[8]

With respect to total family income, however, it is unclear whether black families in general were gaining relative to white families. Relevant data are presented in Table 11–4. If the nonwhite families are compared to each other over the years involved, they appear to have fared increasingly better. The same result is indicated by examining changes in their income as a percentage of white family income (in the last column). Notice, however, that if the figures in column 2 are subtracted from column 1, the absolute differences in income do not indicate gains for the subordinated group. The absolute difference increased in magnitude between 1947 and 1959 and has remained about the same since then. Thus, what we conclude is strongly influenced by how our figures are arranged.[9]

[8] It must be noted, however, that Census data on nonwhite populations in particular are subject to a degree of error. In addition, the comparisons may be misleading if black and white females systematically differ in terms of seniority, hours of work, or some other noncontrolled variable.

[9] The time dimension itself can also influence conclusions. Specifically, one alternative is to compare persons of the same ages in different years; for example, persons aged 25 to 34 in 1960 and 1970. This obviously involves comparing different people who may have had different experiences due to being born a decade apart. This has

TABLE 11-4   Median family incomes.

Year	White Families	Nonwhite families	Ratio Nonwhite to White
1947	$5,194	$2,660	51%
1959	7,106	3,661	52
1965	8,424	4,666	55
1969	9,794	6,191	63

Source: *Reynolds Farley and Albert Hermalin, "The 1960's,"* Demography, *9, 1972.*

Our analysis indicates, then, that suburbanization has been, and continues to be, a predominantly white phenomenon. Among blacks, recent suburbanization has involved movement out of the city by the highest status blacks, with suburban life styles being maintained by a large percentage of working women. For the central cities, the migration patterns of both blacks and whites has meant a growing proportion of poor black residents.

In order to assess the impact of these patterns on central city budgets, Terrell has asked, "What if blacks' characteristics were the same as whites' with respect to income, welfare and educational needs, etc.?" His investigation included a sample of 46 large central cities, with population and financial data from 1960 to 1962.[10] The data are therefore somewhat old, but they probably still reflect a reasonably accurate estimation of current budgetary influences.

With respect to revenue collection, Terrell's findings indicate that the lower median incomes of nonwhite families resulted in per capita revenue losses varying from 38 cents in San Jose to nearly $30 in Miami. Because of differences in collection procedures, the revenue hypothetically lost because of lower black incomes varies somewhat independently of absolute per capita losses. Thus, Newark's per capita loss of about $13 reduced that city's total revenues by only about 6.5 percent. In contrast, a revenue loss of $11.65 per capita in Birmingham reduced that city's total revenue by almost 23 percent.

Some of Terrell's assumptions seem ideological. They are troubling to me and warrant a moment's reflection at this juncture. Although the incomes of black and white families are distributed around different averages, the distributions are also overlapping. That is, some black families earn more than most white families; some white families earn less than most black families. If the goal were solely to explain differences between cities' capacities to raise revenue, it would make more sense to analyze the effects of having poor residents, regardless of race. Then the analysis would examine the effects of families who earn incomes somewhere below the average, regardless of whether they are black or white. In addition, to call this analysis "The Fiscal Impact of Nonwhites" is accurate, but only one way of looking at the question. It strikes me as being equally appropriate to call this analysis "The Fiscal Impact of Discrimination." The

---

the advantage of vividly portraying whether the circumstances of any group are changing. On the other hand, it ignores changes that may occur at different points in different groups. For example, it would take more than a different decade to reflect changes that might be occurring among black 5-year-olds. It would, in fact, take 25 years for most of them to reach the age group being analyzed. (This would necessitate a comparison of 1960 with 1985.) Nathan Hare, "Recent Trends in the Occupational Mobility of Negroes," *Social Forces,* 43, 1965.
[10] Henry S. Terrell, "The Fiscal Impact of Nonwhites," in Werner Z. Hirsch et al., *Fiscal Pressures on the Central City* (New York: Praeger, 1971).

TABLE 11-5 Additional fiscal impact of nonwhites, by function.

City	Education	Police	Welfare	% Total Impact
Birmingham	15.43	−0.07	—	31
Chicago	13.23	3.23	0.33	22
Dallas	8.10	2.07	—	17
Detroit	15.74	4.35	1.10	18
Indianapolis	7.11	1.93	—	13
Louisville	5.62	0.78	—	20
New York	2.57	1.67	0.58	7
Omaha	3.33	0.72	—	8
Portland	2.31	0.71	—	3
San Antonio	1.30	−0.07	—	4
Toledo	6.17	1.50	0.23	10

Source: *Henry S. Terrell, "The Fiscal Impact of Nonwhites," in Werner Z. Hirsch et al.,* Fiscal Pressures on the Central City *(New York: Praeger, 1971)*.

figures would be the same, but they would be interpreted in a quite different context. With these concerns in mind, let us consider expenditures.

Terrell subsequently analyzed the effects of nonwhite populations on city expenditures such as education, police, and welfare.[11] His findings, in a sample of the cities, are presented in Table 11–5. In general, the impact of nonwhites on city budgets is greater in southern than in northern cities, because the former tend to have greater racial differences in incomes. The single largest impact occurred in the border cities of Baltimore, Richmond, and St. Louis. Impact here was probably greatest because of the migration patterns into border cities, which tend to be the destination of the poorest and least educated nonwhites moving from the rural South to the industrial North. In turn, there is a relatively large movement of more affluent and better educated nonwhites out of the border cities to other metropolitan areas.

Before pursuing our next topic, the movement of employment out of cities, let us look at the preceding discussion from a broad perspective. The data presented have indicated that black populations have the effect of lowering city revenues and increasing city expenditures for a number of functions. The education of blacks in predominantly ghetto schools is more expensive; the correlation between ghettos and crime results in higher police expenditures; and the black population receives relatively more welfare than the white population.

However, before we conclude that blacks, or any other predominantly poor group, are a fiscal burden, we must recognize that there are two types of welfare in the United States. Tussing describes the first of

[11] Welfare is "irrelevant" in many cities, where welfare payments are made by county rather than city governments.

these, social insurance, as welfare for the nonpoor. It is disguised so as "to protect the integrity and dignity of the people involved." Public charity, by contrast, is undisguised and connotes an illegitimate notion, dependency.[12] Benefits allocated to the poor are generally viewed in the latter category, and because they tend to be administered by local governments they are more visible. The social insurance benefits for the nonpoor are not only disguised but are administered in less visible state or federal governmental units. Similarly, federal payments to the nonpoor tend to be made directly to individuals and without restrictions (for example, Social Security benefits). Local payments to the poor are made through mediating agencies (such as welfare or employment agencies) with a great many restrictions on how payments are dispensed and used.

As an illustration, Tussing cites the deduction of interest for home mortgages on federal tax returns. This is a benefit for the nonpoor, of course. The cost of this deduction to the government was $2.5 billion in 1971. If recognized as a rent supplement, this would be the single most expensive federal housing program. Social Security benefits are another example Tussing gives of the psychological differences in types of welfare. It is not a separate insurance plan, he points out, but part of the overall government budget. (Surplus receipts are "lent" to the Treasury for all purposes—defense, agriculture, and so on.) In addition, it is financed through a clearly regressive tax that takes from the poor. Only the first $12,000 in income is taxed (as of 1974) and excluded from taxation are sources of income unique to the rich: interest and capital gains, for example. In conclusion, any analysis of the "black burden" on cities must also recognize that such arguments are insensitive both to the levels of government involved and the dual system of welfare practiced in the United States.

THE FLIGHT OF THE TAX BASE

As indicated in Table 11–1, about 30 percent of city revenues stem from property taxes assessed to residential and commercial (including industrial) properties. In most cities, between half and two-thirds of locally taxable real property is residential; the remainder is commercial (and industrial).[13] An additional 8 percent of revenue stems from sales taxes, which are wholly in the commercial sector. Thus, residential and commercial functions contribute about equally to city revenues.

Since the end of World War II, as more affluent residents have moved out of cities, they have been replaced by less affluent residents. The quality of private residences in the city has deteriorated both from tenant

[12] A. Dale Tussing, "The Dual Welfare System," *Society*, 11, 1974.
[13] Data for selected cities are in U.S. Department of Commerce, *Census of Governments*, Vol. 1 (Washington, D.C.: GPO, 1972).

As private housing in central cities has deteriorated, it generally has been demolished without replacement, rather than renovated (Syracuse, New York).

neglect and from owner reluctance to invest in improvements. When demand for city apartments is great, the professional landlord need not make improvements; when demand is weak, he is afraid to invest.[14] As a result, "marginal" residential neighborhoods in cities rapidly become slums, and the property tax base of city budgets is further eroded. Once set in motion, the deterioration of city neighborhoods stimulates still further movement to suburbs by those who are able to afford such moves. Since the late 1950s there has also been a movement of commerce and industry from cities to suburbs. In some cases, commerce has moved in response to residential shifts; for example, retail stores have moved to suburban shopping centers to be more accessible to markets. In other cases, firms have moved to suburban locations in order to have commuters find them more desirable as employers. Regardless of which initially stimulates the other, both trends mutually contribute to the long-term erosion of the central city's tax base.

During the first decade after World War II, central cities lost relatively little of the total metropolitan area employment despite the residential shift that was occurring. Beginning in the mid-1950s, though, the rate of loss in most employment categories began a rapid increase. In one sample of SMSAs, for example, the central city's share of SMSA employment in various service categories actually increased slightly between 1948 and 1956, from 81 percent to 84 percent of the total. By 1967, however, the cities' average share of SMSA employment in this service category had declined to 72 percent. Central city employment in manufactur-

[14] George Sternlieb, *The Tenement Landlord* (New Brunswick, N.J.: Rutgers University Press, 1969).

ing, retail, and wholesale trade also remained relatively unchanged until the mid-1950s and then also began to decline rapidly.[15]

During the late nineteenth and early twentieth centuries, a substantial concentration of industry in central cities was encouraged by the concentration of labor and transportation costs. In addition, because much industry was primary in nature, closeness to sources of raw materials was particularly important. During recent decades employment in primary industries has declined as an accelerated part of the overall decline in goods-producing employment (for example, manufacturing). The industries that have provided the most new jobs—electronics firms, aircraft manufacturers, and so on—have not usually been tied to a source of raw materials or constrained by proximity to final markets. Technological improvements have reduced all types of transportation costs. The result has been to make industries more "footloose," to increase the degree to which locational decisions can be based on "amenities" such as employee desires for proximity to higher quality school districts.[16]

The factors that have contributed to firms' abilities to be footloose and emphasize amenities have all tended to favor suburban relocations. (They have also contributed to relocation from larger to smaller SMSAs and between regions as well.) Thus, as we have seen, the central city's share of total SMSA employment, particularly in manufacturing categories, has generally become smaller. Birch's examination of these employment changes in more detail indicates a number of large differences among cities and metropolitan areas. The central cities of newer (post-1930) SMSAs have actually been able to attract employment, particularly in manufacturing. They have also been able to hold their own or improve in other major employment sectors. It is in the oldest (pre-1900) SMSAs that central cities have lost employment, particularly in manufacturing and retail trade. One important difference related to age is density. The newer cities, with about half the population density of the older ones, still have open room for new plants, office buildings, and stores. In addition, the newer cities have more often been built around road networks, making them better situated with respect to modern highway transportation. The older cities, by contrast, were more often built around railroad networks and harbors that no longer offer the most efficient transportation. But as Birch points out, the young cities of today will eventually become the old cities of tomorrow, and there is no reason to expect them to escape the perils of old age.[17]

The basic outline of a city's life cycle is first a young period in which

[15] David L. Birch, *The Economic Future of City and Suburb* (New York: Committee for Economic Development, 1970).

[16] Thomas M. Stanback, Jr., and Richard V. Knight, *The Metropolitan Economy* (New York: Columbia University Press, 1970).

[17] Birch, *op. cit.*

manufacturing, parking lots, and expressways expand across low-density land. With age comes increasing density and increasingly expensive central city land that leads to the decline (or stabilization) of all activities, with services the least affected. Law firms, banks, stockbrokers and a host of other services all benefit from a central location and from close proximity to one another. Thus, central cities become "elite service centers" with a greater percentage of all other types of employment moving to suburban locations.

In retail trade, the movement to the suburbs has been very pronounced, given the importance of proximity to consumer markets to the location of stores. The greatest loss in the percentage of total SMSA retail sales has occurred in the central business districts of cities. Their losses have been the gains of shopping centers located predominantly in the suburbs. Again, losses have been related to size. The larger the metropolitan area, the lower the percentage of total SMSA sales accounted for by the CBD, the greater the percentage accounted for by retail centers, and the greater the proportion of retail and shopping centers located far outside the city limits. These patterns are illustrated, with 1963 figures, in Table 11–6.

The strong positive association between retail centers and SMSA size, corresponding with the inverse relationship between size and CBD sales, is supportive of the multinuclei theory of urbanization discussed in preceding chapters. In other words, as the urban area grows and expands, retail stores continue to seek "nucleated" locations, but such nucleated locations, rather than being confined to the CBD, are disbursed throughout the city and suburbs.

From the middle 1950s through the early 1960s, most central business districts declined in importance as retail centers; that is, CBDs accounted for declining proportions of total SMSA retail sales. SMSAs were becoming increasingly multinucleated with respect to retail structures, and

TABLE 11-6   Retail sales and SMSA size.

SMSA Size (000)	% SMSA Retail Sales			% Shopping Centers ≥ 20 miles from CBD
	CBD (1963)	Central Cities	Retail Centers	
Less than 600	43%	67%	22%	42%
600 to 1,199	29	57	35	45
1,200 to 2,399	29	45	36	54
2,400 and over	25	40	39	65

Sources: *All data except central city figures are from John Casparis, "Shopping Center Location and Retail Mix in Metropolitan Areas,"* Demography, *6, 1969. Central city data are from the* U.S. Census of Business, *1967.*

Downtown Minneapolis, Minnesota, was lined with trees and closed to automobile use to attract more shoppers. These are before-and-after pictures.

it appeared that the original nucleus (the CBD) might virtually cease to function as a retail center. Because an increasing number of these dispersed centers were located in suburban areas, it meant further loss of sales tax revenues for the city and an ominous indication of future loss of commercial property taxes. In many communities, however, the "downtown" had attained symbolic value as a shopping center, and the trend ruffled civic pride. During the 1960s a number of cities, usually with the aid of inter-governmental transfers for urban renewal, again began to invest in their CBDs. The most common approach was to try to increase the attractive-ness of the downtown to potential shoppers, both city and suburban. Streets were closed to traffic to provide shoppers with convenient rights of way; parking facilities for commuter shoppers were enlarged; and in many Canadian and American cities with inclement winters, enclosed shopping was planned in order for the CBD to compete more effectively with suburban malls.

Between 1963 and 1967 (the last year for which relevant data are available) many of the largest cities were able to reverse, or at least slow, the retail shopping decline of their CBDs. In most of the smaller cities, however, the decline continued. Table 11–7 gives figures for a sample of SMSAs, showing changes in their retail sales patterns.

In the largest SMSAs, CBD sales generally increased between 1963 and 1967; there are also indications that this trend continued into the 1970s. In most of the larger SMSA's, however, CBDs did not make up all the ground lost prior to 1963: Note that most CBDs still remained lower in 1967 than in 1958. Among the smaller SMSAs there was not yet any indication of a comparable pattern, though losses also exceeded gains be-tween 1958 and 1967.

To review briefly, the data presented in this section have indicated a general trend in which the property tax and sales tax bases of central cities have been eroded by the suburban movement of the more affluent resi-dential sector, industrial employment, and retail trade. Against this back-ground, the fiscal problems of central cities have been further exacerbated by a direct suburban drain on city resources.

TABLE 11-7   SMSA size and CBD sales.

SMSA	Change in CBD % of Total Retail Center Sales in SMSA		1967, CBD % of Retail Center Sales in:	
	1963-67	1958-67	City	SMSA
Small				
Akron	−15%	−29%	17%	8%
Albany	−24	−34	18	4
Jacksonville	+ 8	+13	20	13
Scranton	+10	+ 2	34	19
Tacoma	−33	−29	16	10
Large				
Atlanta	+ 4	+ 5	24	14
Baltimore	+18	− 4	14	7
Cincinnati	+ 8	−11	24	11
Detroit	+ 7	− 7	12	4
St. Louis	+ 7	−12	18	6

Source: U.S. Census of Business, *1967*.

In most metropolitan areas central cities have traditionally provided a number of "free" services to suburban residents; that is, services paid for by revenues raised exclusively by the central city, from central city residents and businesses. In other cases there has been some city-suburban sharing of costs, but such arrangements have often been of questionable equity. Part of the problem, of course, stems from how to determine a fair assessment. Say, for example, the city library system is open to county residents. From the standpoint of the city, all library costs should be borne equally on a per capita or per user basis. From the perspective of suburban communities, however, the library is "already there." The city has already made the capital investment for city residents. The fair share for suburbanites, it is argued, should be only the marginal costs, or those that are added by noncity users. In most situations the added-on costs will be much less than the straight per capita costs. Which is considered fair depends mostly, as one might expect, on whether a city or suburban resident is being asked to judge.

This kind of situation, with its morally "gray" areas, is one of the knotty problems that have impeded the political integration of metropolitan areas (see Chapter 12). The history of most metropolitan areas, however, is replete with much less ambiguous examples of city exploitation. One interesting, if somewhat extreme, illustration is provided by the history of the Nashville–Davidson County relationship.

Throughout the 1950s, city residents paid for facilities that were shared with suburban residents and facilities that were exclusively or predominantly used by suburban residents. Examples of the latter were the Nashville Park system, three-fourths of which was located outside city limits. Another example was the high school tax. Nashville residents were taxed to support both a city and county high school system. County residents used only the latter, and were taxed only on the latter.[18] Metropolitan government, finally voted in 1962, readjusted some of the gross inequities in Nashville.[19] In virtually all metropolitan areas, however, continuing inequities are built into metropolitan life. For example, many suburban residents commute daily to work into the central city. In one study of the 43 largest cities, it was reported that vehicle use charges, city licenses, and intergovernmental transfers provided less than half the revenues necessary to equal the cities' expenditures on highways; and this did not include city expenditures for other traffic-related purposes, such as

[18] Daniel R. Grant, "Urban and Suburban Nashville," *Journal of Politics,* 17, 1955.
[19] Daniel R. Grant, "Metropolitics and Professional Political Leadership," *Annals of the American Academy of Political and Social Science,* 73, 1964.

police.[20] The deficits had to be made up out of general city revenues, and it is clear that cities incurred much of this deficit to facilitate city-suburban commuting.

On the plus side for cities, many commuter patterns contribute to city revenues. The most obvious example is suburban shoppers whose purchases contribute directly to city revenues via city sales taxes and indirectly by increasing commercial property values. Even as commuters to offices and jobs in the city, suburbanites contribute to city budgets through the utilization of city buses and subways. In fact, because of the suburban users it may be possible for city residents to use such services at reduced costs. In one study of 65 large cities it was found that *overall* commuter effects did not have a negative fiscal impact on cities.[21] Although workers' commuting did raise various city expenditures, they were also associated with increased city revenues, from increased state and federal funds, increased per capita income of city residents, and so on. The suburban shoppers also contributed to city revenues in the above-mentioned ways.

The issues involved are clearly quite complex. It may be shown that commuter-related revenues and costs are approximately offsetting, but this emphasis ignores whether commuter sharing of facilities lowers their value to city users by congesting streets, crowding buses, and so on. On the other hand, it also ignores the fact that if it were not for suburban users, transportation systems and retail shopping convenient to city users might not be there at all. Finally, there are complex issues involving patterns of exploitation within the entire metropolitan area. Most studies have looked only at central cities in relation to total suburban exploitation. They have overlooked the way in which a specific suburb, because of its metropolitan area location, may be "exploited" by other suburbs in their relationship to the central city.[22] If suburb X is between suburb Y and the central city, suburb X may incur nonreimbursed expenses in facilitating commuting between suburb Y and the central city.

Suburbanization, then, tends to demand exploitative central city expenditures, though they are partially offset by other revenues cities receive. The web of fiscal interrelationships in a metropolitan area is quite complex, however, and it is one basis for arguing for political integration of metropolitan areas. There are also many noneconomic advantages to political metropolitanization, and many objections as well, as we will see in the following chapter.

[20] William W. Vickrey, "General and Specific Financing of Urban Services," in Joseph E. Haring (ed.), *Urban and Regional Economics* (Boston: Houghton Mifflin, 1972).

[21] Phillip E. Vincent, "The Fiscal Impact of Commuters," in Hirsch et al., *Fiscal Pressures on the Central City* (New York: Praeger, 1971).

[22] Harvey E. Brazer, "Some Fiscal Implications of Metropolitanism," in Guthrie S. Birkhead (ed.), *Metropolitan Issues* (Syracuse, N.Y.: Syracuse University Press, 1962).

Winnipeg, Manitoba, Canada.

12 Political Integration of Metropolitan Areas

IN ROUND NUMBERS, approximately 40 percent of the contemporary United States population resides in the suburban areas of major cities. The remaining 60 percent is almost equally divided between central cities and small towns (including rural areas). Thus, suburbanization is a salient demographic reality. The functional integration of activities in cities and their suburbs has partly taken place through commuting and shopping patterns, newspapers and television stations, and a large number of other commercial activities. Despite some notable exceptions, though, the next step—political and administrative unification—has lagged far behind the demographic and ecological transformations.

PROLIFERATING LOCAL GOVERNMENTS

As the portion of the metropolitan area outside central cities has grown, there have been a variety of local responses to the new demographic and ecological realities. Cities such as Oklahoma City have expanded, annexing adjacent communities to the city proper. Cities such as Minneapolis and St. Paul have managed effectively to coordinate activities in the larger metropolitan area without changing city boundaries. In most cases, however, there has simply been a proliferation of local governments in new townships and municipalities. The majority of these new suburban governments have been at least semi-autonomous, providing their own services to residents and raising revenues through property taxes. An indi-

245

cation of how such local governments have continued to proliferate is provided in Table 12–1, which gives a representative sample of SMSAs, with local government data from 1962 and 1972.

Examination of the table indicates that the number of new townships, municipalities, and so on, generally increased between 1962 and 1972. The small decline in the percentage of local governments with property tax powers between 1962 and 1972 suggests a slight tendency toward consolidation of government services despite the continuing emergence of new governments. The number of independent school systems, for example, declined in a majority of these SMSAs. Although the trend continues to be toward the proliferation of local governments, many of the most pressing urban problems—such as mass transit and air pollution— are actually metropolitan area problems. That is, they require coordinated decision-making at the metropolitan level. Central cities, as the historical nucleus, might be logically expected to have played the major role in stimulating such coordination. However, fiscal considerations such as those previously described have been an obstacle; so too have a variety of political factors that will be described in this chapter.

State governments have limited ability to provide the impetus for metropolitan integration because metropolitanization has frequently disregarded state boundaries. Almost one-fourth of the metropolitan areas in the United States cut across state lines. Through its funding policies, the federal government has recently attempted to stimulate "multijurisdictional" agencies to confront metropolitan problems. Typically, however, the activities of such agencies have been placed under the control of local governments, permitting local dominance to subordinate area-wide policy.

TABLE 12-1   Local governments in metropolitan areas.

Area	No. of Local Governments		% with Property Taxes	
	1962	1972	1962	1972
Birmingham	44	92	84%	77%
Boston	125	147	67	61
Denver	205	272	96	96
Detroit	241	241	96	95
Hartford	48	68	88	74
Jacksonville	11	9	81	88
Los Angeles	234	232	99	97
Louisville	129	181	81	70
Minneapolis-St. Paul	261	218	97	95
Philadelphia	963	852	74	66
Phoenix	101	112	100	90
St. Louis	439	483	94	91

Source: *U.S. Department of Commerce,* Census of Governments, *Vol. 1, Government Organization* (*Washington, D.C.: GPO, 1962, 1972*).

In addition, federal programs, with their rural bias, have often forced too large a geographical area to be included in federally financed projects. The comprehensive health planning program of the Department of Health, Education, and Welfare, for example, combines metropolitan with rural areas. Instead of integrating metropolitan activities, such programs actually serve only to distribute urban resources across both urban and rural areas.[1]

Although the United States has been transformed, demographically and ecologically, into a metropolitan society, there is no political level corresponding to metropolitan areas; neither federal, state, nor local jurisdictional levels provide a congruent form. Metropolitan governments have been difficult to design and implement because they would almost necessarily have to possess fluid and flexible boundaries in order to keep pace with metropolitan area growth, in marked contrast to city or state governments, whose political boundaries are relatively fixed and unchanging. Part of the problem is that dynamic institutions are difficult to design; and when new arrangements are explicitly political, concerns over "whose ox would be gored" are only natural.

One of the most interesting examples of the kinds of problems that have plagued city-suburban relationships is provided by the decade-long conflict between the city of Milwaukee and the suburb of Wauwatosa.[2] The problem began in 1954 when the growing residential and industrial suburb just to the west of the city limits found itself unable to provide its residents with sufficient water. There was no organized suburban utility with which Wauwatosa could join. To drill additional wells of its own and develop storage facilities would have cost the suburb about $2 million. Consultants advised its officials to purchase the additional needed water from the city of Milwaukee. The city, however, did not want to sell. The Milwaukee City Council felt that by withholding water it could induce suburbs to become part of the city through annexation. Otherwise, suburbs would receive vital city services while escaping higher city taxes, encouraging further suburban migration of both industries and residents.

During the next five years, attorneys for the city and suburb argued in court and petitioned the state's Public Service Commission. One exchange between the lawyers cut to the core of the problem. The Wauwatosa attorney argued against forming an independent suburban water system. "It would be a duplication of Milwaukee's facilities," he said. The entire network of suburbs, countered the city's attorneys, was a "duplication of Milwaukee's facilities." In 1958, the state commission finally ordered the city to provide the water. To appeal further would create the

1 Melvin B. Mogulof, "Federally Encouraged Multijurisdictional Agencies," *Urban Affairs Quarterly*, 9, 1973.
2 David D. Gladfelter, "The Political Separation of City and Suburb," in Richard T. Frost (ed.), *Cases in State and Local Government* (Englewood Cliffs, N.J.: Prentice-Hall, 1961).

risk that the state legislature would create a metropolitan water authority, resulting in the city's complete loss of control. So Milwaukee's mayor complied, but months later there were still charges that the city was not delivering the fully mandated supply. The next round of conflict began in 1959 when a Democratic Milwaukee councilman, who had opposed sale of the water, was nominated to be head of the state Public Service Commission. The predominantly Republican legislators from the Milwaukee County suburbs opposed confirmation of this man, whom they saw as "an advocate of the suburbs' adversary—the city." The vote followed party lines. Because almost two-thirds of the state legislature was Republican, confirmation was denied—a victory for the suburban Republicans.

The Wauwatosa example illustrates what have historically been the major impediments to city-suburban unification: competing political and economic interests. In the following pages we will see how differences in party preferences and in political processes more generally prevent city-suburban unification. In the last section of this chapter we will examine cooperative ventures in specific activities, including mass transit and police services.

PARTY AFFILIATION

In the typical American city, the mayor is a Democrat and the city council is predominantly Democrat as well. In the typical suburban town surrounding the city, the elected leadership is predominantly Republican. To merge city and suburbs into a single political unit therefore creates immediate concern over loss of power for both parties. In the central city it is recognized that the total suburban vote is larger than that of the city. This creates apprehension that a "metro-mayor" would be a Republican. In individual suburban towns, unified voting by all the suburbs is less likely to be assumed. The central city is perceived as the single largest voting unit and so a Democratic takeover is feared in metro elections.

It is factually true that city residents tend to affiliate themselves more with the Democratic party and suburban residents more with the Republican party. Exactly how this situation comes about, however, has been the subject of numerous theories, only some of which have been empirically supported. The party affiliation differences do seem to be related to socioeconomic status, to migration patterns, and to racial and ethnic differences. They do not appear to be related, upon close inspection, to patterns of social mobility or to suburban life styles. Before considering these influences it must be pointed out that party affiliations are somewhat volatile, changing in response to the popularity of a current incumbent or to national and local events. (Following the Watergate disclosures, for example, Republican party identifications fell in the voting age population. Democratic identifications did too, but to a lesser extent.) Thus, the apparent strength of either party, and the bases of its support, will appear to vary somewhat according to events at the time of an investigation. Our goal as sociologists is to uncover the relatively enduring patterns, but it is often difficult to differentiate between such patterns and short-term trends. With this in mind, let us proceed.

One popular explanation for the Republicanism of suburbs ties it directly to suburban life styles: home ownership, a "culture of affluence," and so on, are all viewed as making suburbanites more conservative and therefore Republican.[3] This view, widespread among political analysts during the 1950s and 1960s, was probably the result of rapid suburbanization occurring simultaneously with the Eisenhower era (1952–1960). The coincidence apparently led to an exaggeration of the influence of suburban living, per se, on party affiliations, as indicated by subsequent elections.[4]

Another argument that was apparently based on a spurious historical association involved the effects of upward social mobility on party affiliation. The experience of social mobility is related to city-suburban movement, which in turn is related to Republicanism. Theoretically, it was assumed people who "made it" would be psychologically relieved, giving rise to a "cult of gratitude" that would express itself by "overconformity" with traditional middle class behavior, such as Republican voting.[5]

It is difficult, methodologically, to differentiate between the effects of high status, on the one hand, and social mobility on the other. The latter also includes high status (in relation to previous lower status). Both measures overlap, making it difficult to isolate their independent effects. However, reanalysis of the studies that led to the "overconformity" hypothesis relating mobility to Republicanism indicates that the middle class who have experienced upward mobility are no more Republican than the stable (nonmobile) middle class.[6] In other words, party affiliation is related more to current socioeconomic position than to recency of attainment.

One way in which socioeconomic differences in party preferences have become strongly linked to city-suburban differences is through differential patterns of migration. It is Republicans who are most likely to move to suburbs and also most likely to retain their party affiliations after moving.[7] Part of the reason for this pattern is indicated by Campbell's analyses

[3] It should also be recognized that it is precarious to generalize in this way. In different regions of the country, or in local politics, it may not be possible consistently to relate conservative-liberal dimensions to political parties.
[4] Timothy Schiltz and William Moffitt, "Inner City/Outer City Relationships in Metropolitan Areas," *Urban Affairs Quarterly,* 7, 1971.
[5] Joseph Lopreato, "Upward Social Mobility and Political Orientation," *American Sociological Review,* 32, 1967.
[6] Andrew Hopkins, "Political Overconformity by Upwardly Mobile American Men," *American Sociological Review,* 38, 1973.
[7] Charles G. Bell, "A New Suburban Politics," *Social Forces,* 47, 1969.

of differences between movers and nonmovers. Among Democrats, those who move out of the central city are somewhat better educated, slightly wealthier, and in slightly higher-status occupations than the Democrats who remain. Among Republicans, by contrast, all these socioeconomic differences between movers and nonmovers are substantially more pronounced.[8] Thus, not only have more Republicans than Democrats moved to suburbs, but the Republicans who have migrated—by virtue of their socioeconomic characteristics—have been the Republicans most likely to retain their party affiliations. Going one step further, there is evidence from national survey data to indicate that men's initial party preferences are determined more by their parents' preferences than by their socioeconomic position. Initial party preferences are, in turn, strongly correlated with later (that is, current) affiliations.[9] Therefore, although socioeconomic positions influence party preferences, such preferences are apparently still more strongly influenced by the political socialization provided by parents earlier in life.

Historically, a good deal of urban political socialization has been tied to ethnic groups; for example, the traditional commitment of the Irish community to the Democratic party in Boston. Ethnic politics today are in large part racial politics, with blacks replacing previous immigrant groups as the popular backing for Democratic candidates. Correspondingly, a number of studies have shown blacks to exceed whites in political activity even though blacks are more likely than whites to feel estranged or alienated from government.[10]

In order to investigate whether racial differences in participation and in attitudes were part of a political socialization process, Orum and Cohen selected a sample of several thousand school children in midwestern cities. About half the sample was drawn from predominantly black ghetto schools and most of the remainder from predominantly white middle class schools. There was sufficient overlap, however, that it was possible to make a variety of racial comparisons holding socioeconomic position constant. All the youngsters included were in grades 4 through 12.[11]

The results showed that the black children generally had more political knowledge than the white children, based on questions concerning past and present governmental incumbents. Also as expected, amount of information increased with age and with the social class of the respondent. Among youngsters from middle class (white collar) homes, there were

[8] Angus Campbell et al., *The American Voter* (New York: Wiley, 1964).

[9] David Knoke, "A Causal Model for the Political Party Preferences of American Men," *American Sociological Review,* 37, 1972.

[10] David O. Sears, "Black Attitudes Toward the Political System," *Midwest Journal of Political Science,* 12, 1969.

[11] Anthony M. Orum and Roberta S. Cohen, "The Development of Political Orientations Among Black and White Children," *American Sociological Review,* 38, 1973.

few racial differences in political participation; that is, in campaign activities, political demonstrations, and so on. However, among the children from blue collar backgrounds, black youths consistently scored higher than their white counterparts in political participation.

The greatest racial differences were on matters of partisanship. The older a black youngster, the more likely he or she was to see differences between the two parties in terms of which does more for rich people, poor people, the entire country, and so on. The older a white youngster, however, the less likely are the two parties to be seen as different. Thus, among children as young as eight years of age, differential perceptions and evaluations of political parties have already begun to appear. These views, developed early in life, act as "selective controls" that screen and filter later perceptions, leading to successively greater partisanship. The older black children were also asked a number of questions concerning their sense of identity with the black community—whether "Afro" hairstyles are "dignified," whether the police are trying to "wipe out" militant black organizations, whether the government must see to it that blacks and whites receive equal treatment, and so on. The results indicate, in general, that identification with the black community is positively related to political knowledge, cynicism, and so on.

In summary, both racial and socioeconomic differences are related to political affiliation. In addition, the studies surveyed suggest that there may be important differences in degrees of partisanship as well. As we will see in the following section, such differences are pronounced between

Greater identification with the black community today is associated with political knowledge and participation (Chicago, Illinois).

cities and suburbs and provide an additional impediment to the political integration of metropolitan areas.

ISSUES VS. PARTISANSHIP

Fundamental city-suburban differences in political orientations have a long-standing history. Many suburban municipalities, Greer points out, originally formed solely because incorporation prevented annexation by the central city. Other suburban governments initially had diverse, but equally specific, reasons for being: to circumvent city housing or pollution standards or to meet state laws for securing liquor licenses.[12]

As these communities have grown in size and become autonomous in the eyes of residents, part-time government officials have been replaced by full-time, professional city managers. These city managers tend to have highly professional administrative, and nonpartisan, orientations. In a study of city managers in the nine-county San Francisco Bay Area, for example, about half had completed postgraduate schooling (in law or public administration), and most felt it was inappropriate for them to be involved in city council elections.[13] (The average size population of a community represented by a city manager was 36,000 in the Bay Area, compared to about 10,000 nationally.)

The orientations and backgrounds of suburban city managers are probably an accurate reflection of the nonpartisan character of many suburban populations. Greer views the typical contemporary suburb as highly familial; that is, oriented to the community as a site for family living. This leads to a strong interest in school, church, and other youth-centered organizations. But these interests are not usually translated into political participation. Suburbanites are less likely than central city residents to vote in school board elections, for example. In addition to familial orientation, most suburbanites are concerned with their investment in their homes and, correspondingly, in the community. Problems associated with rapid population growth, the quality and cost of municipal services, and so on are therefore highly salient. Again, however, the problems do not ordinarily become translated into partisan politics. It is generally perceived, Greer states, "that there is no Republican or Democratic way of collecting garbage."

There are, of course, other cleavages within suburbs. The common conflict between old and new residents, for example, was described in the case of Old Harbor (Chapter 10). There may also be conflicts between groups of residents and the professional administrators who manage the

---

[12] Scott Greer, *Governing the Metropolis* (New York: Wiley, 1962).
[13] Ronald O. Loveridge, *City Managers in Legislative Politics* (Indianapolis: Bobbs-Merrill, 1971).

The quality of such municipal services as garbage collection is more likely to be viewed in partisan, party terms in cities than in suburbs (Chicago, Illinois).

town's services. Everyone may *not* agree on the best way to collect garbage. But the point is that none of these issues is likely to be defined in terms of partisan politics. Nonpartisanship, like familial orientation, is part of the typical suburban life style.[14]

The political history of central cities, by contrast, is the history of machines—highly partisan politics as a business. ("When a man works in politics he should get something out of it.") During the late nineteenth and early twentieth centuries—the heyday of city machines—the machines were tied to immigration and were avenues of mobility for immigrants or the sons of immigrants. Successful machine politicians reflected the ethnic groups of their cities. They themselves possessed little formal education and no prior family wealth. Tenure in office brought "payoffs" and an avenue of economic mobility for their supporters. Government as an instrument for idealized public service was foreign to the urban bosses.[15] From precinct official up, political influence was sold in the marketplace by these political entrepreneurs. Access to the machine meant victory for an aspiring officeholder because the machine's slate was consistently elected in the absence of real two-party contests. Party loyalty was therefore stressed as the price of admission. Meanwhile, the party faithful expected, and received, concrete rewards (jobs, government contracts) in return for their support.

During the first decades of this century urban bosses and their machines were the objects of "charter reform" efforts directed at changing the votes for dollars characteristic of municipal governments. Underlying

[14] An influential early statement of suburban "No-partyism" is presented by Robert C. Wood, *Suburbia* (Boston: Houghton Mifflin, 1958).
[15] Joel A. Tarr, "The Urban Politician as Entrepreneur," in Bruce M. Stave (ed.), *Urban Bosses, Machines, and Progressive Reformers* (Lexington, Mass.: Heath, 1972).

some of these idealistic notions, however, were ethnic considerations. Support for reform in many cities was concentrated in the periphery of the cities, in the more affluent white Protestant communities. The drive for a civil service system, for example, was simultaneously an attack on the qualifications and the ethics of ethnic political leaders.[16] At the same time, many businesses were expanding and becoming national in scope. As this occurred, they became less interested in purely local politics and the machine lost some of its support from an important ally.

At the same time that progressive reform movements were attacking the machines and business interests were shifting from local to national politics, there was also a decline in the number of immigrants moving into American cities. For most machines, ties to inner-city nationality groups were an important source of support. As the number of new immigrants declined, the children and grandchildren of the foreign-born were becoming assimilated, their ethnic identities becoming diluted. Thus, contemporary studies indicate that ethnic allegiances are less important influences on voters than party loyalties.[17] These party loyalties, however, in many cases have their origins in prior ethnic identifications; the party tie remains even after the ethnic tie is weakened. Second- and third-generation Germans in Cincinnati, for example, may be moved less by ethnic appeals at the polls than their newly arriving parents. Many continue to vote Republican, however, because of turn of the century ties between the German community of Cincinnati and the then Republican machine of Boss Cox. The degree to which ethnic loyalties can influence voting has also been reduced in many cities by a tendency for both parties to present ethnically balanced slates of candidates. Voters therefore have not had to choose between party and ethnic loyalties.

To what degree have reforms, assimilation, and so on, reduced the effects of ethnically linked party politics in municipal elections? To examine this question, Gordon has analyzed voter turnouts in a sample of about 200 major cities between 1940 and 1960. He focused on size of turnout because it is indicative of both competitiveness and perceived relevance. The more hard-fought an election and the more voters feel affected by the outcome, the larger will be the turnout on election day. The ethnic effect was examined by focusing on the percentage of foreign-born in a city. It correlates very highly with the percentage of subsequent generations in a city as well, thereby indicating the overall presence of nationality groups.[18]

[16] Richard C. Wade, "Urbanization," in C. Vann Woodward (ed.), *The Comparative Approach to American History* (New York: Basic Books, 1968).
[17] Gerald Pomper, "Ethnic Group Voting in Nonpartisan Municipal Elections," *Public Opinion Quarterly*, 30, 1966.
[18] Daniel N. Gordon, "Immigrants and Municipal Voting Turnout," *American Sociological Review*, 35, 1970.

In general, from 1940 to 1960 the correlation between the percentage of foreign-born and voter turnout in cities consistently declined; from a modest relationship of .40 in 1940 to a small, but still significant, relationship of .16 in 1960. In the East more than in any other region of the country the relationship has dropped the least. This may be because as the initial location of European immigrants, the East is historically most tied to ethnic politics.

Further examination of the results shows that foreign descent continues to influence voting turnout in nonpartisan cities where voters select a number of candidates of either party (for example, five of the ten councilmen on the ballot), but it no longer significantly affects turnout in partisan cities, where voters select either a Republican or a Democrat for each office. This absence of influence in partisan elections, which is even true in the East, is explained by Daniels as due to the campaign excitement generated by the parties in partisan elections. Voter enthusiasm is generated without ethnic appeals. It is also due, in part, to the tendency of both parties to present balanced slates. Therefore, the size of voter turnout is not related to the relative size of ethnic groups in cities where Republicans are pitted directly against Democrats. In nonpartisan elections, however, the intensity of competition and the degree of voter interest continue to be influenced by the size of nationality groups.

All the conditions that produced highly partisan political orientations within cities—ethnic competition, political machines, and so on—have tended to decline. Desires for "civic minded" government and professional politicians rather than political machines and bosses have correspondingly increased. In this respect cities and suburbs have become politically more alike. However, the salience of ethnicity has not completely vanished and neither have all remnants of big city machines. (Of course, all is not pure and holy in suburban politics either.) These remnants continue to produce differences between city politics (which are more partisan) and suburban politics (which are more nonparty, issue-oriented). And these differences continue to provide an obstacle to the political integration of metropolitan areas.

PATTERNS OF REFERENDUM VOTING

From analyses of a number of cities and counties that have held referenda on political consolidation, it is possible to identify different sectors within metropolitan areas that have consistently lined up either for or against consolidation. These uniformities, perhaps surprisingly, tend to persist whether the proposed plan would effectively create a new level of metropolitan government or simply better integrate somewhat duplicated services. Attitudes toward political unification appear to be based on positions in the socioeconomic structure that produce different perceived likelihoods of gain or loss from consolidation. In some cases they are also based on certain general convictions, or moral orientations. The influences of these convictions or differential positions appear sufficiently strong that variations in the nature of specific referenda have little impact. In the analysis that follows, we shall focus on three metropolitan areas: Nashville,[19] St. Louis,[20] and Miami.[21] Between 1948 and 1962 there were six different referenda in these three communities, four with negative outcomes.

In most instances, strong support for consolidation was expressed by civic and church organizations, who saw it as resulting in "better" government. In Miami this meant less corruption; in St. Louis, civic improvement; in Nashville, "beat the machine." In terms of a civic crusade, congruent support was frequently expressed by daily newspapers in the cities involved. Major business groups, such as local chambers of commerce or downtown merchants associations, also typically advocated consolidation. They viewed the administration of metropolitan government as more efficient and as creating more favorable conditions for business and industry. In Miami, for example, the more affluent county (Dade) had a better credit rating and was preferred over the city in business dealings by the airlines.

Diverse groups have usually lined up against consolidation. One group is composed of predominantly suburban Republicans who perceive metropolitanization, in any form, as part of a larger "conspiracy." In St. Louis, for example, a citizen's group of this type simultaneously opposed fluoridation, federal income taxes, and so on. In Nashville a group of this type was run by a prominent leader of the John Birch Society.

In suburban areas, vocal opposition has been regularly expressed by local weekly papers who may perceive metropolitanization as a threat and whose general editorial policy is anticity. Along with county Republicans they emphasize home rule issues, that whatever problems may exist in the community are best solved locally. County Republicans have agreed and have often also feared a political takeover by Democrats as well. County Democrats, generally a minority, have feared their own political futures might be hurt if they were aligned with the city's Democratic party. One of the issues most favored by all the county opposition groups has been school districts and the loss of local school board autonomy.

Within cities, organized labor has tended to oppose consolidation

[19] The following analysis of Nashville is based on David A. Booth, *Metropolitics* (East Lansing, Mich.: Institute for Community Development, 1963); and Daniel R. Grant, "Metropolitics and Professional Political Leadership," *Annals of the American Academy of Political and Social Science,* 353, 1964.
[20] The St. Louis analysis is based on Henry J. Schmandt et al., *Metropolitan Reform in St. Louis* (New York: Holt, 1961).
[21] The Miami analysis is based on Edward Sofen, *The Miami Metropolitan Experiment* (Bloomington: Indiana University Press, 1963).

because it would dilute labor's influence over city administrations. Minorities, and especially blacks, have held the same position. From the standpoint of blacks, just when their size in central cities could produce black control, along comes metropolitanization to "change the rules of the game."[22] Central city mayors often have tended to oppose consolidation, presumably because they questioned their chances of becoming "metro mayors." However, their opposition has ordinarily been expressed in paradoxical terms; they claim the specific proposal, whatever its content, does not go far enough. In this way, mayors can discretely protect their vested political interests without publicly appearing to be opposed to "good government."

The outcome of any referendum depends largely on the local mix of pro and con forces. In Miami and St. Louis referendums were held almost simultaneously; the former passed, and the latter was rejected. Differences in the two communities tell a good part of the story. The Miami area, with few industrial workers, lacked a strong labor movement. St. Louis, by contrast, was a highly industrial city with 35,000 members of the Teamsters alone. Further, St. Louis County had a large number of former city dwellers with strong attitudes toward the city, whereas many Dade County residents were natives of other parts of the country with weaker feelings about the City of Miami. Finally, St. Louis had a relatively larger nonwhite population than Miami.

The effects of still other combinations of influences are illustrated by Nashville's metropolitan proposals, which were defeated in 1958 and accepted in 1962. In the four-year interim there were two major changes. First, the Citizen's Committee for Better Government became better organized and exerted more influence. Second, the mayor changed from an essentially neutral position regarding consolidation in 1958 to a more negative position in 1962. This permitted an influential daily newspaper in the city to advocate consolidation as a way to "beat the machine."

As would be expected, the results of public opinion polls in affected communities show marked differences between respondents according to the influences to which they are most exposed. In Nashville, for example, Booth reports overwhelming pro-metro voting by those in business and professional occupations; generally anti-metro voting is characteristic of those in blue collar occupations. In addition, Booth points to a possible conflict between urban and suburban values as another source of differences. Those suburbanites who valued closeness to big stores, closeness to their place of work, and good municipal services tended to favor metro more than those who were oriented to their neighborhood as a desirable place to raise children and get better property values for their money.

[22] Lee Sloan and Robert French, "Black Rule in the Urban South," *Trans-Action*, 8, 1971.

Although the latter recognized the advantages of city-type living, they apparently felt a conflict between it and the family-oriented suburban style of life they wanted more.

Similarly, in an analysis of all 42 referendums presented nationally between the end of World War II and the late 1960s, Hawkins reports that when suburban family status is higher than in the city (more working wives and fewer children), the suburban area is more likely to favor consolidation.[23] This is surprising in light of the common assumption that greater homogeneity will ordinarily facilitate consolidation. With results to the contrary, however, he suggests that high family-status suburbs may be more concerned with the quality of municipal services and therefore more pro-metro.

The effects of family orientations on suburbanites' attitudes are particularly well illustrated by their attitudes toward school district reorganization. As previously noted, control over schools is frequently a very salient, and emotional, issue in consolidation referendums. Relevant data are provided by Zimmer and Hawley from a survey in six metropolitan areas of varied size.[24] In general, they found central city residents more in favor of creating a single district than their suburban counterparts. Most persons in either the city or suburb would favor a consolidated district if they believed the quality of education would be improved; obviously though, they did not equally agree that consolidation would represent an improvement. Among suburban residents, the greater their involvement with the local schools, the greater their resistance to unification. The investigators present no data on the following point, but it would be consistent with previously discussed studies for us to assume that school involvement correlates positively with familial orientations. This would again indicate that when suburban life styles are more family-oriented, there is greater resistance to metropolitanization in any form. In this regard Zimmer and Hawley do report a very strong relationship between attitudes toward school consolidation and general attitudes toward consolidation.

THE CONSEQUENCES OF UNIFICATION

The outcomes of most referendums have been opposed to metropolitanization, but a number of communities have voted to consolidate into a single political unit, or else to integrate a number of specific services, such as hospitals or police. During the 1960s, affirmative decisions in many sub-

---

[23] Brett Hawkins, "Fringe-City Life-Style Distance and Fringe Support of Political Integration," *American Journal of Sociology,* 74, 1968.
[24] Basil G. Zimmer and Amos H. Hawley, *Metropolitan Area Schools* (Beverly Hills, Calif.: Sage Publications, 1968).

urban communities were stimulated by "crisis" situations in addition to the usual constellation of pressures: rising crime and no local police force, population growth that was outstripping sewerage and sanitation facilities, rising school costs, and so on.

We have previously considered some of the consequences of unification in terms of what advocates and opponents thought would happen: more combined revenue and better services or higher taxes and loss of control. There has generally been at least "professional" agreement that the revenue of consolidated governments would be greater and based less on property taxes than that of city governments.[25] The quality of resulting services is, of course, much more difficult to measure. There are, however, a few studies that have tackled these issues.

Many of the crisis situations described above were faced by metropolitan Jacksonville during the 1960s. There were also the remnants of "old machine" politics in the central city that became the target of reform groups. In 1967 the city and county were merged, with an elected metro-mayor as the chief executive. Over the next five years the consolidated unit's revenue situation changed in the expected ways: total revenue was increased (by almost 70 percent) and the percentage of total revenue raised by taxation declined (from almost 50 percent to about 35 percent). These changes are illustrated in Table 12–2, which compares Jacksonville's revenue during the fiscal year before the merger to revenue five years later.[26]

From the figures it is clear that the consolidated unit had greater fiscal capabilities and was less dependent on taxes, and property taxes in particular. Correspondingly, tax *rates* were lowered to the benefit of many residents. It should also be noted that the new consolidated unit was highly successful in attracting additional funds from both the state and federal government (intergovernmental transfers increased from 30 to 40 percent of total revenue).

[25] Alan K. Campbell and Seymour Sacks, *Metropolitan America* (New York: Free Press, 1967).

[26] Joan Carver, "Responsiveness and Consolidation," *Urban Affairs Quarterly,* 9, 1973.

TABLE 12-2 Annexation and revenue in Jacksonville (in millions).

Source of Revenue	1966-67	1971-72
Taxes (all types)	$ 57	$ 71
Charges: licenses, permits, etc.	7	17
Intergovernmental transfers	33	82
Other and miscellaneous	21	23
Total	$118	$193

Expenditures, especially on human resources, also increased rapidly after acceptance of the consolidation charter. Health and welfare, public safety services, housing and urban development expenditures all more than doubled between 1966 and 1972. In addition, the participation of the black community in local government generally increased as part of the "reform." Prior to consolidation, the city of Jacksonville held elections on a citywide basis. Thus, blacks were not usually able to elect local black representatives, so the consolidation did not produce less minority representation.

In sum, to judge from revenue and expenditures, many human services were improved in Jacksonville following metropolitanization. The physical resources of the community, in contrast, did not gain from the merger. In fact, spending on natural resources, parks, and recreational facilities actually declined. However, the general revenue gains of Jacksonville do not appear to be an unavoidable consequence of metropolitanization, as illustrated by the experiences in Eugene, Oregon, following a 1963 consolidation.

Between 1960 and 1970, Eugene increased its population from just under 50,000 to about 80,000. Annexation was responsible for much of this growth. The community of Bethel, the largest single annexation, had a population of 10,500 in 1963. Although property taxes in the community were very low, services were almost nonexistent. There were, for example, no sewers or local police. By a narrow 52 percent vote, an annexation referendum was passed in 1963. Taxes for Bethel's residents automatically increased right away; some better services followed immediately, others more slowly. In such a situation, a team of investigators proposed, there could be a "taxpayers revolt"; that is, a greater propensity for Bethel's residents to vote against city tax measures in the future, thereby lowering total city revenues.[27]

In order to test this hypothesis, Bethel was subsequently compared to four other city precincts, all of which were matched on residents' income, education, and home values. Between 1964 and 1972 Bethel was found generally to have more negative voting records than three of the four matched communities. On at least three separate tax measures, Bethel's substantial negative votes were sufficient to reject measures that otherwise would have passed. (Bethel voted about 70 percent against. The remainder of the city voted about 51 percent for.) In terms of lost operating revenue for the city, the three Bethel defeats accounted for nearly $2 million.

An overall assessment of revenue indicates that the city's gain in property taxes from Bethel between 1964 and 1972 amounted to about $6 million. On the other hand, expenditures for Bethel—primarily for

[27] Alvin H. Mushkatel et al., "A Model of Citizen Response to Annexation," *Urban Affairs Quarterly*, 9, 1973.

sewerage facilities—cost the city about $6 million. There is an apparent fiscal balance until it is recalled that the consolidated unit lost nearly $2 million from the defeated tax measures. Over a longer period of time, after the initial heavy cost of Bethel's sewers is absorbed, the financial resources of expanded Eugene may yet gain from the consolidation. But, at least in the short run, Eugene's experience indicates that metropolitanization will not necessarily increase revenues and may actually lower them in indirect ways.

Unlike the total consolidations that occurred in Jacksonville and Eugene, more limited and specific arrangements between local governments were established in a number of communities. Most of the agencies and commissions formed in this manner were oriented primarily to specific functional problems, particularly those that inherently seemed to require metropolitan area coordination: transportation, pollution, and so on. In Washington, D.C., for example, a regional metropolitan committee was formed composed of delegates from local governments in the District, Virginia, and Maryland. (The population of the metropolitan area is divided into almost equal thirds in the three.) During the 1960s, coordinated transportation policies for commuters into the congested District area were a major object of the commission's concern. However, their efforts met with very little success because they were unable to integrate highway departments, bus companies, airport authorities, and all local governments

Metropolitan area coordination typically involves only such specific functional problems as transportation. An example is the San Francisco Bay Area Regional Transportation system.

under their jurisdiction. The planning commission was a voluntary organization from its inception, with its activities paid for by voluntary assessments on local participating governments.[28]

Even if jurisdictional boards were not hampered by organizational problems, weak mandates, and limited jurisdiction, it would be unfair to judge their often meager accomplishments too harshly. As we saw in Chapter 10, metropolitan transportation systems are intrinsically impeded by factors such as personal fears, time costs, and commuter patterns.

Police services appear to present a somewhat more manageable problem.[29] Ostrom and Whitaker have questioned the degree to which local community control affects the quality of service received by residents. Viewed in another way, would suburban residents be equally satisfied with the level of police services if they were part of a metro police force? To reflect on this question, the investigators selected three suburban communities adjacent to the city of Indianapolis. The Indianapolis communities and the "independent" ones were carefully matched according to home ownership, length of residence, occupational status, and race.

The sampled residents in each of the communities were asked

[28] Roscoe C. Martin, *Metropolis in Transition* (Washington, D.C.: U.S. Housing and Home Finance Agency, 1964). See also Committee for Economic Development, *Reshaping Government in Metropolitan Areas* (New York: CED, 1970).
[29] At the same time, however, a metro police chief would still face a highly ambiguous situation in setting policies. All top police administrators, Wilson points out, must choose between two conflicting policies. One is to allocate resources so that the total amount of crime in the jurisdictional area is minimized. The second possibility is to allocate resources so that crime rates in all parts of the area are equalized, even though the overall rate may remain high. Either choice would be upsetting to some of the constituency. James Q. Wilson, *Varieties of Police Behavior* (Cambridge, Mass.: Harvard University Press, 1968).

City and metro police forces generally are regarded as less responsive than independent, local police forces (Detroit, Michigan).

TABLE 12-3   Perceived performance of city and local police.

Question	Independent	Indianapolis
% "victimization" reported to police	90	82
% Police responses in less than 5 min.	79	60
% Police responses more than 15 min.	4	16
% rating assistance satisfactory	77	77
% rating police as doing good or outstanding job in general	75	54

whether they or anyone else in their family had been the victims of any crimes. If so, had they reported it to the police? How long did it take the police to respond? Were they satisfied with the nature of the assistance offered by the police? Finally, did they think their police force generally did a good job? The results, by type of community, are presented in Table 12–3.[30] From an examination of these figures it appears that both the Indianapolis and independent police forces were generally perceived as doing pretty good jobs. The residents served by local forces tended to rate overall performance a bit better and that may be related to their somewhat greater likelihood to report crimes. The local police responded faster, but residents reported them both as being equally helpful after arrival. Congruent results were reported from a survey in four metropolitan areas in Missouri in which all city and all suburban residents were differentiated. The suburban residents were more likely to be satisfied with the quality of police protection in their neighborhood, and they perceived their neighbors as being more likely to report a crime in progress to the police.[31]

SUMMARY

We have seen that as the urban population has dispersed and become metropolitan, a proliferation of local governments has resulted. Resistance to political unification has been widespread, with both vested interest and ideological opposition in both cities and suburbs. Where consolidation has occurred it has frequently been stimulated by changing local events that have made the continued separation of governments seem less feasible. Perhaps surprising in light of the intensity generated by metropolitanization issues, examination of consolidated units suggests relatively minor consequences. Total revenue is likely to increase, with corresponding tax relief to city homeowners, but this does not necessarily occur, at least in the short run. Where partial efforts have been made—creating special-function metropolitan agencies—the results have been understandably meager. And there appears to be some empirical support for suburban fears that loss of autonomy means poorer service.

[30] Elinor Ostrom and Gordon Whitaker, "Does Local Community Control of Police Make a Difference?" *American Journal of Political Science,* 17, 1973.
[31] Sarah L. Boggs, "Formal and Informal Crime Control," *The Sociological Quarterly,* 12, 1971.

Appendix

THIS SECTION CONTAINS data on a sample of 33 American cities and SMSAs. The data are both for contemporary characteristics and historical trends, starting as early as 1820. Because the same representative sample of cities is included in every table, it permits comparison of characteristics presented in different tables. For example, city populations in 1940 (from Table A–1) can be assessed against city robbery rates in 1940 (from Table A–3).

The data, from Census publications for the indicated years,[1] cover the range of topics treated in this text: population growth, density, labor force, crime, commuting patterns, etc. For the interested reader these tables provide extensive background information. In addition, many urban courses require research papers, which for students can entail frustrating hours of searching through library stacks. For many possible topics, these tables give sufficient information for student projects. For other research purposes, the tables will provide a convenient source of data from which hypotheses may be assessed in a preliminary way.

[1] Data sources include the *Census of Population* (indicated years), and the *Statistical Abstract of the United States* (indicated years).

appendix

TABLE A-1   Population of cities, 1820 to 1970 (in thousands).

City	1820	1850	1880	1910	1940	1970
Akron	—	3	17	69	245	275
Baltimore	63	169	338	559	859	906
Baton Rouge	—	4	7	15	35	166
Binghamton	—	—	17	48	78	64
Buffalo	2	42	155	425	576	463
Canton	—	3	12	50	108	110
Cincinnati	10	115	255	364	456	453
Columbia	—	6	10	26	62	114
Columbus	—	18	52	182	306	540
Denver	—	—	36	213	322	515
Des Moines	—	—	22	86	160	201
Detroit	1	21	116	466	1,624	1,511
El Paso	—	—	1	39	97	322
Erie	1	6	28	67	117	129
Flint	—	—	8	39	152	193
Jacksonville	—	1	8	58	173	529
Kansas City	—	—	56	248	399	507
Little Rock	—	2	13	46	88	193
Los Angeles	—	2	11	319	1,504	3,175
Louisville	4	43	124	224	319	361
Milwaukee	—	20	116	374	588	717
Nashville	—	10	43	110	167	448
Oklahoma City	—	—	—	64	204	366
Peoria	—	5	29	67	105	127
Philadelphia	64	121	847	1,549	1,931	1,949
Phoenix	—	—	2	5	15	582
Richmond	12	28	64	128	193	250
St. Louis	—	78	351	687	816	622
Salt Lake City	—	—	21	93	150	176
San Diego	—	—	3	40	203	697
Seattle	—	—	4	237	368	584
Syracuse	—	22	52	137	206	197
Tulsa	—	—	—	18	142	332

appendix

TABLE A-2 Historical data on city debts and politics.*

City	Net Public Debt 1910	Net Debt 1940	Total Long-term Debt 1970	Political Affiliation of Mayor† 1910	1940	1970
Akron	na	$ 20.3	$ 39.7	na	D	R
Baltimore	$36.3	142.1	507.6	R	D	D
Baton Rouge	na	2.2	81.7	na	D	D
Binghamton	0.9	5.4	158.2	R	O	R
Buffalo	22.2	98.0	158.2	R	D	D
Canton	na	4.0	2.7	na	na	R
Cincinnati	14.7	38.3	228.7	D	O	O
Columbia	na	na	17.2	na	na	O
Columbus	11.5	27.2	132.5	D	R	D
Denver	0.9	19.1	231.4	R	D	O
Des Moines	1.3	8.2	44.8	D	O	O
Detroit	7.3	328.9	539.7	R	O	O
El Paso	na	5.9	72.0	na	D	O
Erie	0.3	4.6	19.5	R	R	D
Flint	na	5.2	51.1	na	O	O
Jacksonville	1.8	12.1	187.7	R	O	D
Kansas City	4.3	46.5	273.0	D	D	O
Little Rock	0.2	2.4	45.9	R	D	O
Los Angeles	35.9	131.3	1,175.9	D	O	D
Louisville	11.2	33.0	157.7	R	na	D
Milwaukee	9.3	15.9	227.5	O	O	O
Nashville	5.4	10.4	246.3	R	D	O
Oklahoma City	2.4	14.8	260.7	R	D	O
Peoria	0.1	0.1	8.0	D	na	O
Philadelphia	1.5	362.4	859.8	D	R	D
Phoenix	na	9.4	174.6	na	O	O
Richmond	8.8	25.0	112.6	R	D	O
St. Louis	27.8	67.2	161.4	D	R	D
Salt Lake City	4.8	6.4	16.8	O	R	O
San Diego	1.8	1.8	127.1	O	O	O
Seattle	10.0	14.90	266.6	D	O	O
Syracuse	9.3	26.7	35.7	D	R	D
Tulsa	na	9.8	129.3	na	D	R

* Debt figures in millions of dollars.
† R = Republican, D = Democrat, O = other party or city manager.

TABLE A-3   Police and crime in cities, 1940 and 1970.

City	Number of Police Cars		Police Department Expenditures*		Robbery Rate†	
	1940	1970	1940	1970	1940	1970
Akron	40	103	$ 0.6	$ 5.6	66	256
Baltimore	186	726	4.9	50.5	61	1218
Baton Rouge	6	102	0.1	3.3	29	186
Binghamton	12	21	0.3	1.8	1	47
Buffalo	120	na	3.2	15.8	13	325
Canton	12	66	0.2	2.6	91	285
Cincinnati	139	184	1.7	12.6	118	274
Columbia	14	42	0.2	1.7	na	212
Columbus	43	222	0.8	10.5	129	311
Denver	72	88	0.9	13.1	40	396
Des Moines	22	70	0.4	3.6	55	170
Detroit	437	644	11.2	83.1	91	1536
El Paso	12	83	0.2	4.0	83	97
Erie	12	na	0.3	2.0	24	143
Flint	28	125	0.4	6.1	51	292
Jacksonville	39	199	0.6	8.4	117	284
Kansas City	101	271	1.3	13.9	122	596
Little Rock	9	62	0.2	1.8	55	152
Los Angeles	396	1,622	6.7	131.8	150	400
Louisville	40	127	0.9	na	151	370
Milwaukee	73	na	3.1	28.9	12	93
Nashville	30	157	0.5	5.4	133	225
Oklahoma City	37	128	0.5	5.0	79	148
Peoria	16	na	0.3	3.0	55	420
Philadelphia	289	900	11.3	89.1	42	327
Phoenix	32	281	0.3	10.8	143	233
Richmond	35	122	0.6	5.7	114	368
St. Louis	221	436	5.6	27.9	66	854
Salt Lake City	26	na	0.4	2.9	66	199
San Diego	56	107	0.6	14.2	55	120
Seattle	60	225	1.5	15.4	74	342
Syracuse	24	72	0.8	5.7	11	223
Tulsa	24	130	0.3	4.1	179	116

*In ten thousands of dollars.
†Per 100,000 population.

appendix

TABLE A-4   City housing units, 1970.

City	% Lacking Plumbing	% Over One Person per Room	Median Rent per Month	% Owner Occupied	Negro-occupied Households	
					% Lack Plumbing	% Owner Occupied
Akron	3%	5%	$ 86	64%	3%	56%
Baltimore	2	9	90	45	2	30
Baton Rouge	2	10	77	59	7	51
Binghamton	3	4	84	48	4	19
Buffalo	3	5	71	44	2	29
Canton	3	6	73	62	3	51
Cincinnati	5	10	80	39	5	27
Columbia	6	9	62	48	17	28
Columbus	2	6	88	51	2	43
Denver	4	6	94	50	3	47
Des Moines	4	6	95	66	8	55
Detroit	2	8	80	60	2	51
El Paso	8	18	72	60	9	50
Erie	3	6	68	62	2	39
Flint	3	9	106	69	3	59
Jacksonville	5	8	74	68	15	55
Kansas City	4	7	81	58	4	55
Little Rock	3	7	71	61	7	50
Los Angeles	2	8	106	53	2	32
Louisville	4	10	70	44	4	44
Milwaukee	4	7	95	47	3	33
Nashville	4	7	81	60	9	40
Oklahoma City	3	7	74	65	6	55
Peoria	4	6	89	62	5	40
Philadelphia	2	6	76	60	3	47
Phoenix	2	9	103	64	6	53
Richmond	4	8	78	49	6	41
St. Louis	6	13	69	41	8	31
Salt Lake City	3	6	80	51	9	39
San Diego	2	7	113	51	3	44
Seattle	4	4	106	55	4	48
Syracuse	3	5	94	45	2	19
Tulsa	2	5	87	66	5	57

TABLE A-5 Population density.

SMSA/City	In Central Cities* 1950	In Central Cities* 1970	Outside Central Cities* 1950	Outside Central Cities* 1970	SMSA Land Area† 1950	SMSA Land Area† 1970
Akron	5,114	5,167	377	474	413	905
Baltimore	12,067	11,568	377	534	1,106	2,259
Baton Rouge	4,160	5,388	76	278	462	459
Binghamton	7,988	5,883	149	116	710	2,072
Buffalo	14,724	11,178	329	572	1,587	1,591
Canton	8,292	7,696	298	467	573	576
Cincinnati	6,711	5,915	611	450	730	2,150
Columbia	6,790	6,343	76	145	748	1,465
Columbus	9,541	6,217	256	268	538	1,494
Denver	6,224	7,602	52	198	2,918	3,660
Des Moines	3,242	3,179	89	161	594	594
Detroit	13,249	10,953	639	1,482	1,965	1,952
El Paso	5,097	2,954	63	39	1,054	1,058
Erie	6,958	6,911	112	169	812	813
Flint	5,568	6,380	175	239	644	1,300
Jacksonville	6,772	17,688	135	—	770	766
Kansas City	5,665	3,892	229	283	1,643	2,767
Little Rock	4,253	4,356	67	91	781	1,488
Los Angeles	4,370	6,976	545	1,067	4,853	4,069
Louisville	9,251	6,106	239	548	908	908
Milwaukee	12,748	7,986	1,236	502	239	1,456
Nashville	7,923	850	289	84	533	1,629
Oklahoma City	4,793	1,227	124	149	709	2,143
Peoria	8,671	8,696	110	120	1,277	1,803
Philadelphia	16,286	15,164	467	838	3,550	3,553
Phoenix	6,247	3,103	24	43	9,226	9,238
Richmond	6,208	6,621	140	232	734	1,196
St. Louis	4,046	10,167	335	429	2,520	4,118
Salt Lake City	3,379	3,158	131	380	764	1,061
San Diego	3,364	3,579	53	163	4,258	4,262
Seattle	6,604	6,353	129	202	2,134	4,229
Syracuse	8,719	7,795	158	183	792	2,419
Tulsa	6,844	6,824	126	39	572	3,781

* Population per square mile.
† In square miles.

appendix

TABLE A-6 Education patterns by SMSA, 1950-1970.

SMSA	Median School Years Completed, Males 25 and Over		Median School Years Completed, Females 25 and Over		% Males in Labor Force and Enrolled in School	
	1950	1970	1950	1970	1950*	1970†
Akron	10.4	12.2	10.6	12.2	30.2	51.2
Baltimore	8.8	11.1	8.8	11.2	34.6	52.0
Baton Rouge	9.6	12.4	10.0	12.3	na	34.3
Binghamton	9.4	12.2	10.0	12.2	na	44.1
Buffalo	9.5	12.0	9.5	12.0	24.0	48.4
Canton	9.2	12.0	9.9	12.1	27.3	49.7
Cincinnati	9.1	11.8	9.2	11.6	31.5	49.5
Columbia	9.3	12.1	10.2	12.0	na	44.9
Columbus	11.0	12.3	11.5	12.3	34.8	48.8
Denver	11.8	12.6	12.1	12.5	41.6	53.2
Des Moines	11.4	12.5	12.1	12.4	na	59.7
Detroit	10.0	12.0	10.3	12.1	31.4	54.9
El Paso	9.4	12.2	9.1	11.5	na	37.9
Erie	9.9	12.2	10.4	12.2	na	46.8
Flint	9.9	12.0	10.6	12.1	35.7	52.5
Jacksonville	9.5	12.1	9.9	12.0	28.1	44.9
Kansas City	10.4	12.3	11.1	12.3	29.5	53.9
Little Rock	10.0	12.2	10.4	12.2	na	41.5
Los Angeles	12.0	12.5	12.1	12.3	33.1	55.3
Louisville	8.9	11.4	9.0	11.4	29.3	48.2
Milwaukee	9.7	12.2	9.7	12.2	31.2	54.2
Nashville	9.0	11.7	9.7	11.9	22.4	41.6
Oklahoma City	11.1	12.4	11.8	12.3	33.1	54.5
Peoria	9.1	12.1	10.0	12.1	29.5	50.0
Philadelphia	9.4	12.0	9.5	12.0	22.6	45.2
Phoenix	10.1	12.3	10.7	12.3	28.0	58.1
Richmond	9.5	11.5	10.5	11.8	26.1	43.1
St. Louis	8.8	11.8	8.8	11.4	27.6	49.7
Salt Lake City	12.1	12.6	12.1	12.4	40.2	60.8
San Diego	11.7	12.5	12.1	12.4	39.8	59.0
Seattle	11.8	12.5	12.2	12.5	36.7	53.4
Syracuse	10.4	12.2	10.9	12.2	24.6	40.0
Tulsa	11.4	12.3	11.9	12.2	32.6	49.8

*Ages 14-29.
†Ages 16-34.

271

appendix

TABLE A-7 Families in SMSAs.

SMSA	% of Married Couples Without Own Household		% Divorced of Females Ever Married		Median Family Income	
	1950	1970	1950	1970	1950	1970
Akron	6.8%	0.9%	5%	16%	$3,517	$11,047
Baltimore	9.2	1.9	4	14	3,355	10,577
Baton Rouge	6.1	1.4	4	14	3,383	9,627
Binghamton	6.4	1.1	4	9	3,622	10,033
Buffalo	7.3	1.1	2	9	3,494	10,430
Canton	6.5	1.0	4	15	3,354	10,249
Cincinnati	5.3	1.0	5	16	3,313	10,257
Columbia	8.3	1.7	3	11	2,577	8,617
Columbus	7.6	1.0	7	19	3,741	10,460
Denver	6.1	1.0	6	20	3,472	10,777
Des Moines	5.0	0.8	7	17	3,651	10,682
Detroit	9.0	1.5	5	16	3,976	12,117
El Paso	7.3	2.0	5	17	3,048	7,792
Erie	7.1	1.0	3	11	3,401	9,363
Flint	4.9	1.1	4	17	3,897	11,172
Jacksonville	9.5	1.6	5	22	2,827	8,671
Kansas City	6.3	0.9	6	20	3,398	10,568
Little Rock	6.1	1.1	6	20	2,635	8,290
Los Angeles	5.2	1.1	8	24	3,650	10,972
Louisville	7.4	1.3	5	18	3,205	9,814
Milwaukee	7.3	0.7	4	11	3,926	11,338
Nashville	8.6	1.5	5	17	2,887	9,187
Oklahoma City	4.5	0.7	7	22	3,221	9,345
Peoria	5.2	0.7	5	15	3,568	10,641
Philadelphia	9.6	1.8	3	10	3,466	10,783
Phoenix	4.5	1.2	6	21	2,892	9,856
Richmond	1.1	1.9	5	16	3,383	10,034
St. Louis	7.1	1.0	5	16	3,383	10,504
Salt Lake City	4.0	0.8	5	17	3,556	9,952
San Diego	4.0	0.9	7	24	3,456	10,133
Seattle	4.1	0.8	7	23	3,843	11,676
Syracuse	7.8	1.2	2	10	3,459	10,450
Tulsa	4.8	0.8	7	23	3,306	9,286

TABLE A-8   Labor force composition by SMSA, 1950-1970.

SMSA	% of Labor Force Employed in Manufacturing		% of Labor Force Employed as Government Workers		% of Females in Labor Force	
	1950	1970	1950	1970	1950*	1970†
Akron	49%	39%	6%	12%	29%	39%
Baltimore	30	25	10	21	33	44
Baton Rouge	25	17	14	23	30	40
Binghamton	45	38	8	16	34	41
Buffalo	40	33	8	16	28	40
Canton	46	42	6	9	27	38
Cincinnati	33	33	7	12	31	41
Columbia	12	18	18	24	35	46
Columbus	25	23	14	19	34	46
Denver	17	17	12	18	33	46
Des Moines	20	19	11	14	35	48
Detroit	47	37	8	12	29	40
El Paso	12	17	14	23	29	38
Erie	47	41	6	10	30	39
Flint	56	46	6	12	28	39
Jacksonville	13	12	13	17	34	44
Kansas City	24	23	8	15	33	47
Little Rock	15	20	13	19	35	44
Los Angeles	24	27	10	14	32	45
Louisville	31	34	9	13	31	43
Milwaukee	43	35	8	12	34	46
Nashville	23	24	11	15	35	46
Oklahoma City	11	14	17	25	34	46
Peoria	38	34	6	10	29	40
Philadelphia	37	31	8	14	32	42
Phoenix	9	20	13	15	28	42
Richmond	23	21	13	20	39	48
St. Louis	34	29	8	13	32	42
Salt Lake City	14	15	13	21	29	43
San Diego	14	18	18	22	27	39
Seattle	20	24	13	16	33	44
Syracuse	36	28	8	15	33	43
Tulsa	18	21	7	11	32	42

* Over age 14.
† Over age 16.

Table A-9 Work commuting patterns of central city residents, 1970.* Figures in () indicate % using public transportation.

City	Total Labor Force	Work in CBD	Work Elsewhere in Central City	Work Elsewhere in SMSA	Work Outside SMSA of Residence
Akron	99.0 (3.6%)	9.8 (11.9%)	56.2 (2.8%)	18.6 (1.8%)	9.0 (2.8%)
Baltimore	342.6 (27.0)	26.1 (49.0)	203.9 (27.2)	72.5 (17.4)	5.7 (15.2)
Baton Rouge	60.5 (4.4)	4.2 (4.9)	37.9 (4.7)	6.3 (4.1)	5.7 (2.2)
Binghamton	24.3 (6.3)	na	15.9 (6.9)	6.7 (5.2)	0.3 (2.6)
Buffalo	163.9 (21.8)	19.7 (42.8)	92.4 (21.7)	41.1 (11.5)	1.2 (7.4)
Canton	40.2 (6.4)	4.5 (15.7)	21.4 (6.2)	9.2 (2.9)	2.2 (3.0)
Cincinnati	170.7 (15.3)	19.6 (32.8)	95.7 (13.5)	39.1 (8.7)	4.0 (8.4)
Columbia	53.2 (6.6)	na	23.6 (10.0)	24.4 (3.2)	1.5 (3.4)
Columbus	209.9 (11.8)	25.6 (28.3)	126.2 (8.8)	35.9 (8.6)	3.9 (4.2)
Denver	209.5 (8.2)	25.9 (24.6)	137.9 (6.3)	30.3 (2.4)	2.8 (2.5)
Des Moines	84.6 (6.1)	19.2 (13.2)	50.0 (3.9)	7.2 (2.3)	2.3 (3.7)
Detroit	533.0 (18.4)	45.4 (42.7)	272.3 (18.1)	160.6 (11.4)	7.2 (8.4)
El Paso	106.2 (9.5)	11.7 (15.1)	73.9 (8.6)	8.9 (3.9)	4.3 (20.7)
Erie	47.7 (6.0)	6.1 (14.6)	27.6 (4.8)	10.3 (3.6)	0.5 (5.1)
Flint	66.5 (3.1)	6.8 (9.4)	40.8 (2.4)	12.2 (1.4)	1.8 (1.5)
Jacksonville	212.5 (6.7)	15.4 (16.7)	173.5 (5.4)	na	5.5 (4.1)
Kansas City	209.1 (10.4)	16.8 (24.7)	127.2 (9.0)	36.8 (5.2)	3.7 (5.8)
Little Rock	76.7 (5.5)	8.2 (8.0)	55.8 (4.9)	3.5 (5.9)	1.8 (2.8)
Los Angeles	1,260.4 (8.8)	66.5 (27.7)	775.4 (8.4)	295.7 (5.4)	25.2 (4.8)
Louisville	138.0 (12.9)	23.8 (23.9)	74.4 (11.1)	28.6 (7.1)	2.3 (2.7)
Milwaukee	291.5 (19.2)	29.0 (42.7)	173.5 (17.5)	63.0 (11.9)	3.7 (12.8)
Nashville	178.3 (7.6)	24.9 (13.8)	137.3 (6.4)	0.8 (0.9)	4.8 (3.5)
Oklahoma City	150.8 (2.3)	12.4 (6.8)	113.9 (1.7)	12.5 (1.2)	2.6 (2.4)
Peoria	48.2 (5.7)	6.4 (13.7)	25.5 (4.9)	12.5 (3.1)	0.8 (1.8)
Philadelphia	737.3 (37.2)	67.6 (65.4)	489.4 (35.4)	80.1 (20.5)	16.3 (30.9)
Phoenix	225.8 (1.7)	16.5 (4.7)	161.1 (1.4)	29.4 (0.7)	2.8 (2.0)
Richmond	101.5 (24.0)	20.3 (35.2)	56.7 (22.2)	14.7 (15.1)	2.9 (13.6)
St. Louis	223.4 (21.3)	12.0 (44.3)	145.2 (20.6)	42.1 (15.2)	1.4 (11.4)
Salt Lake City	71.2 (4.5)	9.7 (9.6)	44.4 (3.9)	11.4 (2.9)	2.1 (2.5)
San Diego	282.6 (5.5)	15.1 (10.9)	205.8 (5.8)	39.6 (2.9)	3.6 (2.5)
Seattle	239.4 (13.9)	24.3 (40.0)	169.4 (11.6)	28.4 (5.2)	3.8 (6.4)
Syracuse	77.2 (15.7)	11.2 (35.9)	39.0 (13.5)	18.2 (9.0)	0.9 (5.1)
Tulsa	131.7 (3.0)	24.0 (6.2)	89.6 (2.2)	8.9 (0.8)	2.7 (1.4)

*In thousands. Rows do not equal total because approximately 5% of work places are not reported.

appendix

TABLE A-10 Work commuting patterns of suburban residents, 1970.* Figures in ( ) indicate % using public transportation.

SMSA/City	Total Labor Force	Work in CBD	Work Elsewhere in Central City	Work Elsewhere in SMSA	Work Outside SMSA of Residence
Akron	146.9 (1.2%)	5.6 (4.3%)	34.3 (0.6%)	69.3 (0.9%)	29.9 (1.3%)
Baltimore	470.9 (4.3)	19.2 (23.0)	116.7 (5.9)	279.7 (2.4)	29.5 (3.2)
Baton Rouge	39.4 (1.7)	1.6 (1.5)	20.1 (1.8)	9.2 (1.4)	3.9 (0.6)
Binghamton	88.2 (1.6)	na	18.1 (3.2)	57.3 (1.3)	6.4 (0.5)
Buffalo	327.3 (4.8)	17.9 (21.2)	75.1 (6.2)	213.4 (2.9)	5.6 (3.2)
Canton	96.9 (0.9)	4.1 (2.9)	23.0 (0.8)	52.7 (0.9)	13.4 (0.6)
Cincinnati	339.7 (4.7)	26.8 (22.7)	91.8 (4.5)	183.2 (2.4)	23.6 (1.2)
Columbia	81.8 (2.0)	na	35.1 (2.9)	37.0 (1.0)	4.2 (1.1)
Columbus	145.3 (2.7)	13.7 (12.8)	59.6 (2.0)	61.1 (1.4)	4.8 (2.2)
Denver	278.5 (1.6)	16.4 (9.2)	92.5 (1.2)	151.2 (1.0)	5.8 (1.6)
Des Moines	34.4 (1.2)	5.6 (3.8)	15.0 (0.9)	10.9 (0.3)	1.2 (1.1)
Detroit	976.1 (2.7)	33.9 (23.7)	181.9 (4.0)	685.2 (1.3)	28.3 (1.2)
El Paso	16.0 (2.3)	.3 (3.9)	3.3 (3.1)	10.8 (1.9)	.6 (7.8)
Erie	48.5 (1.0)	2.5 (6.9)	13.8 (0.9)	26.8 (0.3)	2.2 (1.8)
Flint	102.4 (0.3)	6.1 (1.4)	42.0 (0.3)	42.0 (0.2)	7.8 (0.1)
Jacksonville	city and SMSA are same				
Kansas City	302.2 (2.1)	15.6 (9.2)	97.1 (2.0)	161.7 (1.2)	8.0 (1.8)
Little Rock	48.2 (1.3)	2.4 (2.6)	26.4 (1.2)	14.4 (0.7)	1.3 (2.0)
Los Angeles	1,479.7 (2.9)	48.6 (12.8)	371.9 (4.0)	910.8 (1.8)	53.5 (2.3)
Louisville	176.4 (1.9)	18.1 (7.3)	60.9 (1.2)	83.9 (1.3)	5.4 (1.5)
Milwaukee	265.6 (4.1)	14.8 (19.7)	74.3 (5.6)	157.8 (1.9)	7.5 (3.7)
Nashville	36.0 (1.4)	1.2 (5.5)	9.8 (1.1)	20.6 (1.2)	1.6 (0.8)
Oklahoma City	109.9 (0.5)	5.2 (2.1)	52.6 (0.3)	44.0 (0.5)	2.9 (1.4)
Peoria	81.5 (0.9)	4.7 (4.5)	17.8 (0.8)	51.8 (0.5)	3.2 (1.0)
Philadelphia	1,112.2 (9.8)	42.4 (60.8)	169.8 (22.8)	736.7 (4.1)	81.3 (6.9)
Phoenix	135.6 (0.5)	3.6 (3.5)	38.1 (0.4)	80.9 (0.3)	2.8 (1.8)
Richmond	114.4 (3.2)	16.5 (8.8)	46.8 (2.7)	38.1 (1.4)	7.3 (2.4)
St. Louis	652.6 (3.6)	18.0 (19.9)	163.5 (5.1)	422.8 (2.2)	10.8 (2.7)
Salt Lake City	131.9 (1.1)	8.5 (4.8)	49.0 (1.1)	61.1 (0.5)	8.0 (0.9)
San Diego	257.1 (3.0)	5.8 (3.6)	75.5 (6.6)	155.6 (1.3)	4.4 (2.4)
Seattle	298.7 (1.7)	12.2 (13.4)	115.4 (1.8)	148.1 (0.5)	9.2 (2.2)
Syracuse	159.3 (2.6)	10.5 (12.7)	34.3 (3.8)	96.0 (1.1)	7.4 (2.2)
Tulsa	51.3 (0.5)	4.0 (0.9)	17.0 (0.3)	25.1 (0.5)	2.9 (0.9)

In thousands. Rows do not equal total because approximately 5% of work places are not reported.

Index

INDEX OF SUBJECTS